MOVING NOTATIO

S0-BRK-428

Performing Arts Studies

A series of books edited by Christopher Bodman, London, UK

MOVING NOTATION

A HANDBOOK OF MUSICAL RHYTHM
AND ELEMENTARY LABANOTATION
FOR THE DANCER

Jill Beck
University of California, Irvine, USA
and
Joseph Reiser

harwood academic publishers
Australia • Canada • China • France • Germany • India
Japan • Luxembourg • Malaysia • The Netherlands • Russia
Singapore • Switzerland • Thailand

Amsteldijk 166
1st Floor
1079 LH Amsterdam
The Netherlands

British Library Cataloguing in Publication Data

Beck, Jill
   Moving notation: a handbook of musical rhythm and
   elementary labanotation for the dancer. – (Performing arts
   studies; v. 6)
   1. Labanotation
   I. Title   II. Reiser, Joseph
   792.8'2

   ISBN 90-5702-179-X (softcover)

This text is jointly dedicated to
Shirley Mordine, Chicago modern dance pioneer
Helen and John Lindberg,
and Robert Beck.

CONTENTS

Chapter Wrap

2   GETTING ORGANIZED

Rhythmic Concepts

Movement Concepts

Notation

Rhythmic Applications

Movement Applications

Chapter Wrap

3   FIRST EXPANSIONS

4   APPROACHING PERFECTION

Movement Concepts

Notation

Rhythmic Applications

Movement Applications

Chapter Wrap

7   CHANGING TIMES

Rhythmic Concepts

Movement Concepts

Chapter Wrap

INTRODUCTION TO THE SERIES

Performing Arts Studies aims to provide stimulating resource books of both a practical and philosophical nature for teachers and students of the performing arts: music, dance, theatre, film, radio, video, oral poetry, performance art, and multi-media forms.

International and multicultural in scope and content, *Performing Arts Studies* seeks to represent the best and most innovative contemporary directions in performing arts education, and will focus particularly on the work of practising artists who are also involved in teaching.

Christopher Bodman

ACKNOWLEDGEMENTS

The creation of this text would not have been possible without the earnest efforts and generous contributions of time, talent and expertise of the following persons.

Ann Hutchinson Guest, for her valuable contributions to the clarity of the text. Julia Sutton and Rachelle Palnick Tsachor, for their research and documentation of the Renaissance dance vocabulary in Caroso's *Nobiltà di Dame* (translated by Julia Sutton, Oxford University Press). Ilene Fox and Virginia Doris at the Dance Notation Bureau, New York City, for their advice and clarifications of Labanotation theory and usage. Nathan Montoya, for his proofreading of *Alta Regina*. Robert Beck, for his excellent advice and encouragement. Velma Cole, for her assistance in the preparation of the manuscript, and Kelly Adams, for her assistance with the index. Deborah Hanan, for her guidance and contributions to the chapter on phrasing and poetic feet. Larry Clark, for his unwavering support, encouragement and movement contributions to the early phases of this text. Richard Cameron-Wolf, for his suggestions and early editorial comments. Robert M. Abramson, for his insightful editing, musical ideas, encouragement and support. Carolyn Soriano, for her wonderful canon. And, last but not least, to Sargon, the Wonder-Mac, for his portability, calmness under fire, and ability to run Microsoft Word, NoteWriter, LabanWriter, SuperPaint, and Ready, Set, Go simultaneously.

Examples, exercises, etudes, and short studies in rhythm were prepared by Joseph Reiser; examples, exercises, etudes, and short studies in Labanotation were prepared by Jill Beck; the canon *Bricks!* was composed by Carolyn Soriano; the dance *Alta Regina* was notated by Rachelle Palnick Tsachor; the dance *Baiduska* was notated by Eleni Ioannou, and the Taiwanese Tribal Dance was notated by Yun-yu Wang.

All illustrations (with apologies) by Joseph Reiser.

Special Acknowledgement: Some of the rhythmic terms and methods presented in this text, especially the code words, "Hand-els", and BOV, were first developed by Asher Zlotnik, music educator, composer, teacher, theorist, and friend, to whom the authors are grateful for his generous permission and support.

INTRODUCTION

Designed specifically for university-level study, *Moving Notation* will benefit students and teachers of both dance and music, offering a complete introduction to the theory and practice of musical rhythm and elementary Labanotation. Traditionally, studies in rhythm and movement notation have been pursued independently, despite the fact that a major difficulty in restaging dance repertory is understanding the rhythm of the choreography and the ways in which the movement interacts with the music. By alternating theory and exercises in rhythm and Labanotation, this book offers help in solving such problems.

For dancers and choreographers, emphasis is placed on the development of sight-reading skills and the quick translation of rhythmic concepts into dance. Lessons explore how variations in rhythm affect the perception and organization of movement, and vice versa. Incorporating movement principles of Emile Jaques-Dalcroze and Rudolf Laban, assignments at the ends of chapters investigate various creative applications of a detailed knowledge of rhythm. Students and teachers of performance and choreography, as they progress through the book, will become increasingly familiar with one essential component of the art of choreography; the myriad ways in which time and movement can interact.

For musicians and composers, the book offers physical as well as conceptual learning experiences, using dance sequences as a means of consolidating and concretizing rhythmic understanding. Musicians who work with dancers will benefit from learning the basics of dance notation, enabling them to contribute more to repertory restagings of choreography while learning the basic steps of some of the most common dance steps and combinations used in both ballet and modern technique.

The rhythmic theory in *Moving Notation* begins with the basic concepts of time, beat and meter, moving towards the reading and composing of modern polymetrics and scoring for percussion ensemble. While the rhythmic information is at the conservatory level, all aspects of musical training that do not pertain to a dancer's use of rhythm have been omitted from the text. These include: tonality (scales, key signatures); harmony (chords, progressions); and form (with the exception of the canon). It is felt by the authors that these areas, however necessary to the overall development of a musically literate dancer, are not integral to rhythmic understanding, and can be added to a curriculum at a later time.

The Labanotation theory in the book covers the entire Elementary syllabus of the Dance Notation Bureau in New York, the organization offering certifying examinations in three levels of dance notation (Elementary, Intermediate and Advanced). In addition, more advanced concepts are included in the text when they are in synchrony with the rhythmic theory being presented. Some simplification of Laban terminology has been undertaken, to bring it in line with parallel musical terms. Whenever possible, links are noted between concepts and techniques in composing and notating rhythm and dance.

How to Use this Book

Designed as a classroom text and reference manual, this text may be used in several ways. Each chapter follows the same format:

1. *Rhythmic Concepts.* Presents rhythmic theory.
2. *Movement Concepts.* Presents Labanotation theory.
3. *Notation.* Clarifies issues concerning the writing of rhythmic and dance notation.
4. *Rhythmic Applications.* Explores movement and/or creative applications of music theory.
5. *Movement Applications.* Demonstrates dance applications of Labanotation theory.
6. *Chapter Wrap.* Includes etudes, exercises, and assignments in reading, writing and composing rhythm and dance.

The text is further divided through the use of Icons and Maxims. The following Icons appear throughout the text and indicate that a particular paragraph/section pertains to either movement, rhythm, or both:

 Pertains mostly to rhythm

 Pertains mostly to movement

 Pertains equally to both

This Icon highlights particularly important points, or Maxims, which appear throughout the text as succinct summaries. A complete list of Maxims (with page numbers) is at the back of the book, to be used as a quick reference guide or quick review mechanism.

As a classroom text, teachers may:

- follow each chapter from sections 1 through 6, which alternates classes in rhythm and movement;
- teach sections 1 and 4 (rhythm), then 2 and 5 (Labanotation), followed by section 3 (calligraphy) and finally 6 (wrap up);
- teach only the Labanotation sections in the classroom, allowing students to reference from the rhythm sections what they do not understand;
- teach only the rhythm sections (assuming a class taught to previous students of Labanotation).

A final note: *Moving Notation* contains sufficient material for a year of study. In order to gain the most benefit from the book's coordination of rhythm and dance study, one of the following approaches is recommended:

- one teacher proceeding through the book sequentially;
- a teaching team of music and dance notation instructors, advised to meet individually with the class once per week, focusing on either rhythm or dance, and together once per week, focusing on the connections and creative interrelationships between rhythm and dance.

In either case, three one-hour class meetings per week would be ideal.

1
GETTING STARTED

RHYTHMIC CONCEPTS

1.1 Time

"Time is nature's way of keeping everything from happening at once."
Woody Allen

As we all know, time is continuous. In traditional music, time's continuity is divided into units called beats. Beats (sometimes referred to as pulses) are nothing more than divisions of time.

Beats are *not always regular* – beats can also change speed. The fascinating thing about beats and speed is that as you listen to them being measured on a metronome, the sound (click) you hear marks only the *beginning* of the beat. It is the length of time *between* the clicks that determines the beat's speed. So, when you use the term "beat", think of the entire "duration" of the beat and not just the click.

 Set a metronome to 120 clicks per minute. Listen for a short time. Now re-set it to 60 beats per minute. It sounds twice as slow because you have added exactly twice the amount of time between the clicks. The effect of adding time slows the beat.

Maxim #1: Speed equals Time. Add more time between beats and you go slower. Reduce the time between beats and you go faster. This is called TEMPO.

1.2 Beat Divisions (Sub-beats)

There are only two subdivisions of beat: a duple division and a triple division. Duple beats are those which are divided into equal halves and are counted **1 &**, and triple beats are divided into equal thirds and are counted **1 a da**:

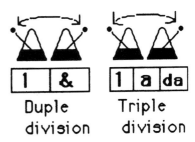

Duple division   Triple division

When you count 1 &, the "and" indicates the duple division of the beat. When you count 1 a da, the "a da" indicates the triple division of the beat.

Notice also that the duple beat looks and feels *square*, while the triple beat feels *round*, the difference between pumping a pump and turning a wheel:

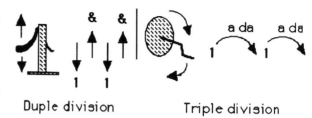

Duple division   Triple division

 Set a metronome to 60 clicks per minute and say "Down up/Down up" while miming the motions of pumping. Then, switch to miming the motions of grinding a wheel while saying "Cir-cu-lar/Cir-cu-lar ". Then try switching between the two divisions, saying: **"Down up/Cir-cu-lar. Down up/Cir-cu-lar."**

Maxim #2: There are two common subdivisions of a beat: duple and triple.

1.3 Rhythm versus Beat

The difference between rhythm and beat is *generally* understood as that which changes and that which does not: rhythm adds a flexible variety of changing sounds against a landscape of regular beats. This definition, while not a "law", does cover a wide range of "rhythmic reality".

Traditionally, beat and rhythm go hand in hand. A beat is selected at a particular tempo and then rhythm is added "to" the beat, "over" the beat, "on top of" the beat. In this manner, beats become the architectural pillars upon which rhythm is supported:

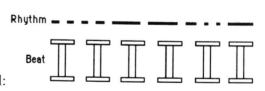

There are only three ways in which rhythmic durations can relate to a beat:

(1) **Thru-beat**. The rhythm's duration is longer than the beat, thereby sustaining *through* the end of one beat into the next. Call this a "thru-beat rhythm".

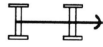

(2) **Full-beat.** The rhythm's duration is the same size as the beat. Call this a "full-beat rhythm".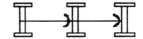

(3) **Sub-beat.** Each rhythmic duration is shorter than the beat. Call this a "sub-beat" rhythm:

The United States National Anthem reveals all three rhythmic activities in the opening musical line:

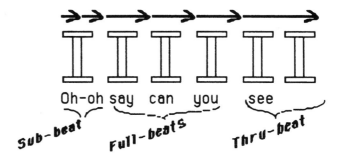

 Set the metronome to 60 and chant one tone, holding the tone longer than one click. Each time you hold through the end of the click into the next, your voice sustains "through the beat". This is thru-beat rhythm. Now chant one note per click to experience full-beat rhythm; more than one note per click for sub-beat rhythm.

In any given musical composition all three categories of rhythmic duration will be present, although composers will from time to time employ one type exclusively for effect. For example, exclusive thru-beats can sound suspenseful, sad, or languid. Exclusive full-beats can sound march-like. Exclusive sub-beats can sound agitated or exciting.

 Cues #1–6 Listen to several examples of each type of rhythmic duration.

Maxim #3: Beats are steady. Rhythm is flexible and comes in three categories: thru, full, and sub-beat.

1.4   Basic Time Values

Note: Notation symbols are brought into play to record the specifics of music and movement. Although rhythmic notation (RN) and Labanotation

(LN) use different symbols to achieve different ends, both address the same problem of *accurately recording the specifics of time*.

Rhythmic notation (RN) uses six basic note and rest values: the whole, half, quarter, eighth, sixteenth, and thirty-second. There are faster and slower values available, but these six are used with the greatest frequency. Each note and rest value represents a specific duration of time. Every notational symbol is a visual representation of how long to **do** something (note value) or **not do** something (rest value):

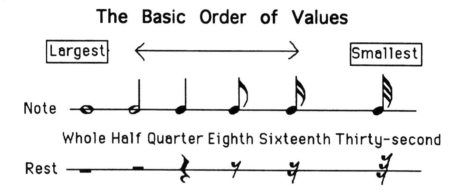

The Basic Order of Values (BOV) is based on the binary numerical progression **1 2 4 8 16 32**. The relationships *between* the notes then become a mathematical hierarchy:

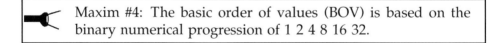

Maxim #4: The basic order of values (BOV) is based on the binary numerical progression of 1 2 4 8 16 32.

1.5   Beat Assignment

So far we have discussed the concepts of time, beat, rhythm, and basic time values. The final link in the creation of a smoothly-working system of notation is the application of the BOV to the concept of a fixed beat. In other words, **the BOV will not function until one of its time values has been assigned *to* the beat.** The question therefore is, "which note value will represent the beat?" And with the answer to this question, you have arrived at one of the principal variables in music: that ANY note value can be assigned to the beat.

Traditionally, the speed of the average musical beat has been considered to be the speed of the average walk, and the quarter note, due to its central position in the BOV, has usually been assigned to that beat.

The expression "the quarter note gets the beat" is quite standard. So what happens to the BOV when the quarter "gets" the beat? All values *larger* than the quarter become *thru-beats* and all values *smaller* than the quarter become *sub-beats*. *The quarter becomes the only full-beat value:*

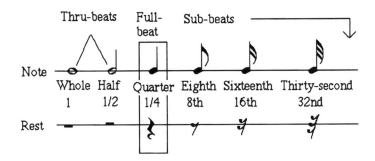

 Set a metronome to 60 clicks per minute. As you listen, stare at the quarter note above: each click represents the passage of one quarter note. Consequently, 2 clicks = a half; 4 = a whole; and, by dividing the time between clicks, you can imagine the 8ths, 16ths and 32nds which are dissecting the beat.

Here is the BOV when the 8th note is assigned as the beat:

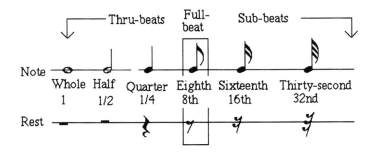

Now set the metronome to a faster 100 clicks per minute and imagine that one 8th-note is passing with each click. The quarter, half and whole are now thru-beats; the 16th and 32nd, sub-beats.

The reason different values are assigned to the beat is mostly due to tempo. For *slower than normal* tempos, use the half or whole note; for *faster than normal* tempos, use the 8th or 16th note. The following tables demonstrate each note when assigned as the beat:

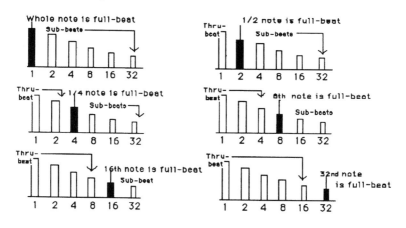

Maxim #5: Tempo (or speed of beat) will in most cases determine the size of the note value assigned to the beat.

The following tree demonstrates the relationships of the BOV when the quarter note is assigned to the beat:

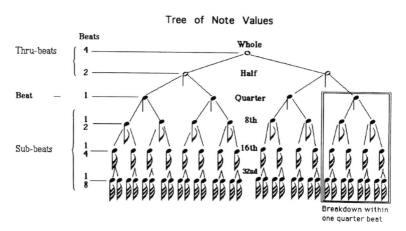

1.6 Tempo

Tempo (*pl.* tempi) is the length of time it takes to get from beat to beat. There are three ranges of musical tempi (slow, medium, and fast), within which a wide range of gradations are possible from extremely slow to extremely fast. There are also three types of tempi: steady; unsteady; and modified. Slowing down and speeding up while performing (a term known as **Rubato**), can add greatly to the expressive qualities of music and movement. This 'plasticity' is the ultimate goal in an expressive 'human' performance.

Note: Although the examples and exercises in this text call mostly for steady (unchanging) tempi, it should be noted that the study of expressive tempo modification is a life-long pursuit of all serious performers: *this text is just the beginning.*

The following table indicates the speed (in clicks per minute on the metronome), and the names of several tempi in both English and Italian, comprising the international language of music. **IMPORTANT**: Tempo markings vary greatly from composer to composer and era to era. The following tables should be considered EXTREMELY general:

Beats per minute	*Range of Speed*	*In Italian*
Approx. 40 to 50	Extremely slow	Larghissimo to Largo
50 to 60	Very slow	Adagio to Lento
60 to 80	Moderately slow	Andante to Andantino
80 to 120	Moderately	Moderato
120 to 160	Fast	Allegro to Vivace
160 to 208	Quite fast	Presto
208+	Extremely fast	Allegrissimo to Prestissimo

Tempo is usually indicated at the beginning of a composition with a small registration showing the assigned full-beat note value followed by a metronome marking. In this example, the quarter is equal to 108 clicks per minute.

Moderato

$\left(\, \downarrow =108 \, \right)$

Tempo can change suddenly or gradually. Sudden changes of tempo are indicated by the implementation of a new tempo or metronome marking where the tempo is to change. Gradual tempo changes, which can progress slowly or rapidly, are most frequently made through the use of the *accelerando* (accel.) and *ritardando* (rit.) markings. Accelerando means to accelerate either gradually or rapidly to a new tempo. Ritardando means to slow down either gradually or rapidly to a new tempo:

 Maxim #6: There are three ranges of tempo: slow, medium and fast. Within these categories lies a wide range of gradations from extremely slow to extremely fast.

MOVEMENT CONCEPTS

1.7 Basic Direction Symbols

Labanotation uses 9 direction symbols to notate most movement. The basic notation symbol is the rectangle, which indicates being "in place". When modified with chimneys or slanting edges, the rectangle transforms to indicate 8 other possible directions in which the body (or its parts) can move.

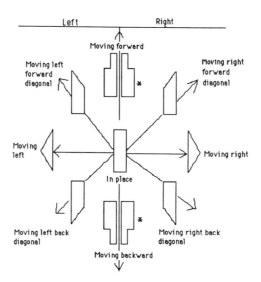

* — There are two forward and two back symbols, one for use on the right and left sides of the staff. This has the effect of keeping all 'chimneys' along the center line.

Note: LN direction symbols relate to the performer, rather than to any fixed directions in the performing area. A forward step is always directly *in front of you*; a backward step is always directly *behind you*; etc., **regardless of where you are facing in the room**.

 Maxim #7: The shape of direction symbols indicates the direction of movement.

 ### 1.8   The Staffs

Beyond the obvious differences between the notation symbols themselves, a major difference between RN and LN is in the use of the staffs: RN reads from left to right while LN reads from bottom to top.

 Rhythmic notation uses a horizontal single-line staff upon which all note heads, rests, and various other symbols are placed. An "X" clef is sometimes placed at the beginning of each staff line which signifies "no tonality". (RN does not involve changes of pitch.)

Read left to right

 Labanotation uses a vertical three-line staff, the center line of which acts like the spine, separating the left from the right side of the body. As in music notation, the primary function of the staff is to provide a framework upon which notational shapes are placed.

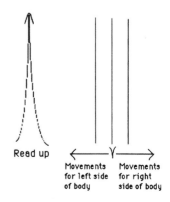

Read up

Movements for left side of body   Movements for right side of body

Movements that take weight are written in the support columns. Although the hands, knees, hips, etc. can take weight as well, it is the feet that are most commonly used in the support columns. You may assume that the feet are the supports unless otherwise stated. Other columns (for other parts of the body) will come later.

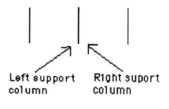

Left support
column

Right suport
column

 Maxim #8:   Always read LN from the bottom to the top. The center line of the LN staff divides left from right. The support columns are found on either side of the center line.

1.9   Level Changes

 The direction symbols can be shaded to indicate whether the body is moving in a Low, Middle, or High level. Therefore, when the level of a movement changes in an upward or downward manner, the directional shapes will change shading to show the new level.

Middle Support or "Place Middle". The body is in a natural standing position with straight but not stiffened legs. (Note that when both feet are in simultaneous contact with the ground, supports must be written in both the left and right support columns.) The notation for standing with feet together is two place symbols with a dot at the center of each rectangle indicating middle level:

Supporting on one foot in middle level

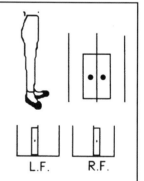

L.F.   R.F.

High Support. The body weight is raised and on the ball of the foot. The notation shows two place symbols which are shaded with diagonal lines running from lower left to upper right, indicating high level:

Supporting on one foot in high level (relevé):

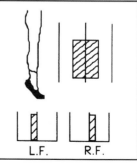

L.F.   R.F.

Low Support. The body weight is lowered by bending the knees with the weight on the whole foot. The notation shows two place symbols which have been colored in solidly, indicating low level:

Supporting on one foot in low level (demi-plié):

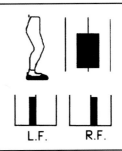

L.F.   R.F.

There are consequently 33 basic direction symbols in three levels:

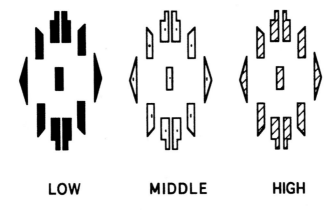

LOW   **MIDDLE**   **HIGH**

 Maxim #9: The shading of a direction symbol will indicate the level of movement: low, middle, or high.

 1.10   Placement of Symbols on the staffs

The primary difference between RN and LN concerning staff placement is that RN generally places its note heads, rests, etc., ON the staff line while LN places its symbols ALONGSIDE its staff lines, in columns.

The placement of each rhythmic symbol on the RN staff indicates when to, or not to, execute a particular rhythmic duration. Note heads and rests are centered on the staff line with stems and flags going up or down depending on the situation. Rules will be given later.

The placement of direction symbols on the LN staff indicates which body part is moving. Symbols placed in the right and left support columns make flush contact with the center line of the staff. For example, a simple walk forward is written this way:

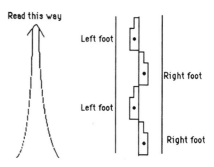

A walk backwards looks like this:

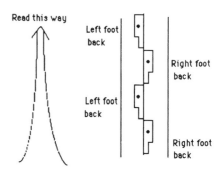

When not moving, the body is considered to be "in place", or, directly over its supports. This position is seen quite frequently in the starting position, which is placed at the beginning of each composition prior to the first movement. The starting position is separated from the first beat by a double line. In the illustration to the right, the dancer is standing on both feet in the starting position. The feet are together but in an (as yet) unspecified turn-out:

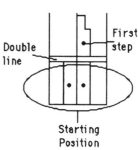

The center line of the staff is visually marked off with "tick marks" to indicate beats, or counts. Symbols are drawn to fill the amount of time a movement takes.

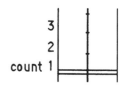

The symbols here indicate a *quick* step *back* on the *right* foot in *relevé*, followed by a *slower* step *forward* on the *left* foot in *plié*:

At the conclusion of both a rhythmic or choreographic statement/section/piece, a double
bar line is written at the top of the LN staff or
the end of the RN staff to indicate "end":

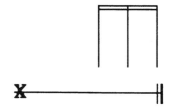

In summary, every direction symbol can indicate up to four separate
pieces of information essential to the performance of any given movement: (1) **direction** of movement by the *shape* of the symbol; (2) **which
body part** is moving by its *placement* on the staff; (3) the **level of
movement** by its *shading*; and (4) the **time** it takes to complete the
movement by its *length*.

 Maxim #10:   For general indication, RN symbols are placed
on the staff line while LN symbols are placed alongside the
staff line, in columns. Different columns "belong" to different
parts of the body.

1.11   Relationship Pins and Hold Signs

Relationship pins can be used to indicate the relative placement of the legs when walking or standing. For example,
when walking sideways
to the right, the notation may specify
whether the left leg steps in front or in
back of the right leg as it crosses the
body. The point of the pin indicates
this relationship:

"in front"

"in back"

left leg will cross   left leg will cross
"in front" of right   "in back" of the
leg   right leg

The pin is also used to indicate the
relationship of movement to the body's
central line. For example, when walking
forward the feet naturally step in front
of the hip joints in a slightly open manner. If it is important to the movement
to place one foot directly in front of the
other (like walking on a tight-rope),

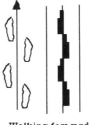

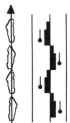

Walking forward   Walking forward
normally from   on a "tightrope".
the hip.

pins are added to the notation. The pins indicate that the feet will step in front or in back of each other along a straight line projecting from the center of the body:

When walking backwards, the pins will face the opposite direction:

Walking backwards normally

Walking backward: "tightrope"

 Maxim #11: Pins indicate the relationship of the feet to each other.

Hold signs (small circles) are used in the support columns to indicate that the weight is to be held on a particular foot or on both feet. Hold signs keep a foot on the floor in the same level it was previously, and are considered to "hold continuously" for any amount of time until (1) cancelled by a new step on either foot, or (2) by leg gestures or actions in the air for the held foot (discussed below).

Holding on 1 foot following a step forward. The L.F. is off the floor, held naturally under the body.

Holding on 2 feet in high level (relevé)

IMPORTANT: When there is no direction symbol or hold sign in a support column, that foot is assumed to be off the floor.

Rules:

1. Hold signs will last continuously until they are cancelled:

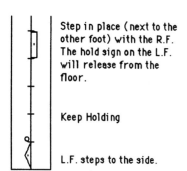

Step in place (next to the other foot) with the R.F. The hold sign on the L.F. will release from the floor.

Keep Holding

L.F. steps to the side.

2. *Any* step immediately cancels a hold sign:

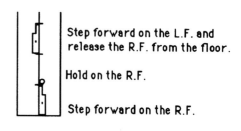

Step forward on the L.F. and release the R.F. from the floor.

Hold on the R.F.

Step forward on the R.F.

3. Hold signs must be repeated if they are not to be cancelled by a new step:

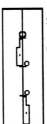

Step forward on the L.F., and continue holding weight on the R.F. (Weight is evenly distributed between both feet with L.F. in front of R.F.)

Hold on R.F.

Step forward on the R.F.

4. Hold signs maintain the *level* of the previous support:

Hold in relevé   Hold in plié

5. If the foot comes to a closed position *after* a hold sign, the hold sign can be repeated *only* if there is no level change:

Compare A and B

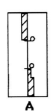   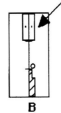

Note that while the steps in A and B are similar, the change in level in example B requires additional notation for the right support. The right foot must adjust to middle level as the left foot closes.

A

Step forward in relevé, hold in relevé, close in relevé.

B

Step forward in relevé, come to mid level as the L.F. closes to place.

Because there is no level change in the example to the right, the hold sign on beat #3 is correct and preferable:

Step side in plié, hold in plié, close in plié.

 Maxim #12: Hold signs must be used to keep one or both feet on the floor. They also maintain the level of the previous support.

1.12   How many Feet?

The simplest way to determine if the weight is on one or two feet is to look at each count of the support column independently. Every count in the support column for which there is notation is a self-sufficient explanation: if weight is on one foot there will be a symbol (direction symbol or hold sign) in one support column; if weight is on two feet, there must be information in both support columns. This can be two direction symbols, a hold sign across the center line, or a combination of a direction symbol on one foot and a hold sign on the other foot.

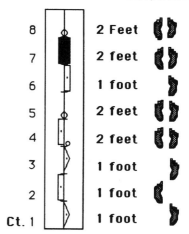

Look at each count independently

8	2 Feet	
7	2 feet	
6	1 foot	
5	2 feet	
4	2 feet	
3	1 foot	
2	1 foot	
Ct. 1	1 foot	

 Maxim #13: To determine the number of feet you are on at any given moment, read each count in the support column INDEPENDENTLY.

1.13   Taking a Step/Moving the Center of Weight

Taking a step involves moving the center of weight to a new place, transferring the weight into the direction specified by the symbol in the support column. This may sound like a simple idea, but it is an important one to grasp fully. In the example to the left, movement is described as side-to-side. The center of weight moves to the right in count 1, then to the left in count 2, then this action repeats. In a correct performance of this sequence, the dancer would feel the weight moving from side to side THROUGH space, and these transferences of weight would be visible to an audience. Only when a step is IN

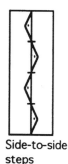

Side-to-side steps

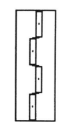

Marking Time: four transferences of weight with no travel through space

PLACE (example at right) is there no visible movement of the center of weight into a new direction.

Steps into the diagonal directions should be performed without turning the body. Moving diagonally means exploring the directions between front and side or between back and side. *Steps in these directions have to be done with the shoulders and hips facing forwards.*

Shoulders and hips face forward

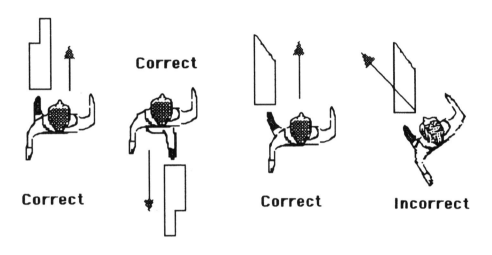

Correct

Correct

Correct

Incorrect

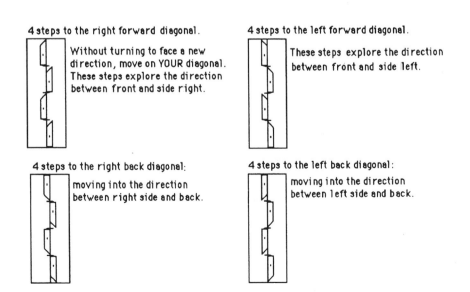

4 steps to the right forward diagonal.

Without turning to face a new direction, move on YOUR diagonal. These steps explore the direction between front and side right.

4 steps to the left forward diagonal.

These steps explore the direction between front and side left.

4 steps to the right back diagonal:

moving into the direction between right side and back.

4 steps to the left back diagonal:

moving into the direction between left side and back.

Relationship pins are not necessary with diagonal steps. It is assumed that the reader will perform what is most natural: forward diagonal steps will cross in front; and back diagonal steps will cross behind. The exception to this rule occurs when an unusual performance is desired; i.e., when forward diagonal steps are to cross behind, or back diagonal steps are to cross in front. In these cases, relationship pins are necessary.

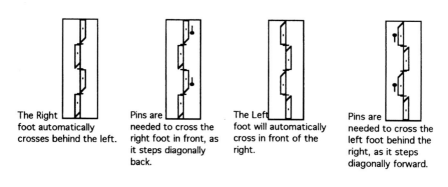

| The Right foot automatically crosses behind the left. | Pins are needed to cross the right foot in front, as it steps diagonally back. | The Left foot will automatically cross in front of the right. | Pins are needed to cross the left foot behind the right, as it steps diagonally forward. |

If the duration of a step is notated as a full beat or a thru-beat (more than one beat), the transference of the center of weight must extend over that amount of time. In the left-hand figure, steps take 1, 2, and 3 counts to perform. In the slower steps, the center of weight must be felt and perceived as moving continuously throughout the time allotted. A common mistake is to take a slow step quickly, and then hold the weight through the rest of the time notated for that action. If stepping and holding were what the choreographer desired, the notation at the right would appear instead:

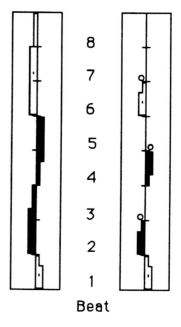

8

7

6

5

4

3

2

1

Beat

Maxim #14:   Taking a step involves moving the center of weight to a new place, transferring the weight into the direction specified by the symbol in the support column. Close attention should be paid to timing.

NOTATION

1.14 Rhythmic Notation

Rhythmic notation is a graphic "code" representing specific musical "motions". Musicians see these symbols and interpret them as either vibration (sound) or silence (rest). There are very few shapes involved in basic music calligraphy: the straight line, the oval, the flag, and a few more complex shapes. Practice all of these until they become familiar to the hand. NOTE: For high quality results, students can use a broad-nibbed fountain or felt tip pen which produces thin and thick lines with a minimum of effort. There are also numerous notation software programs available for computers.

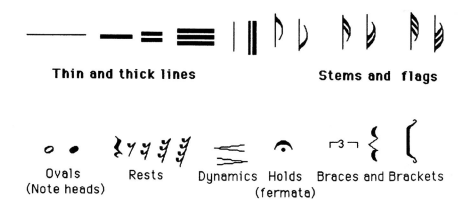

Thin and thick lines   **Stems and flags**

Ovals   Rests   Dynamics Holds   Braces and Brackets
(Note heads)   (fermata)

Note: The above symbols are explained as they appear in the text.

When practicing calligraphy, write each symbol many times to become familiar with the basic shapes required. Make about twenty of each of the above. Notice the number of pen strokes required to make some of the more complex shapes:

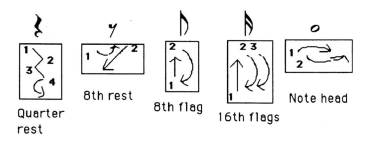

Quarter   8th rest   8th flag   16th flags   Note head
rest

There are a few simple rules governing basic calligraphy:

A. Note heads are ovals which slant from lower left to upper right.

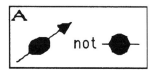

B. Stems can go UP on the right side of a note head, or DOWN on the left.

C. Horizontal "beams" can be substituted for flags – one beam for 8ths; 2 for 16ths; 3 for 32nds.

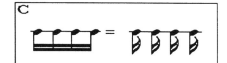

D. Flags should be the same width as the note head, regardless of the position of the stem.

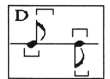

E. Notation symbols are exactly the same size from left to right, no matter how large or small they may appear.

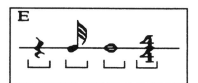

 Maxim #15: Calligraphy is the penmanship of RN. Accurate notation leads to a higher understanding of the components of rhythm.

1.15   Autography/Labanotation

 Autography is the name applied to the actual process of notating movement. Most autography was done by hand prior to 1988, although a Laban font was available for IBM selectric type-writers. In 1988, the process of computerization was begun in England with the excellent IBM compatible software program CALABAN, and it continued at the Department of Dance at The Ohio State University. The OSU program, *LabanWriter*, is software for Macintosh computers. Both CALABAN and *LabanWriter* have profoundly simplified and quickened the process of producing movement notation. It is recommended that students of LN purchase either program. If computer facilities are not available, instructions for notating by hand are included here. Pre-printed Laban score paper is available.

The following covers the basic autographic rules which should be observed during the process of notating movement:

(*A*) *Score paper.* If Laban score paper is not at hand, graph paper is a good substitute, using **(1 square = 1/16th note)** or **(4 squares = 1 quarter).**

There are two staffs in common use:

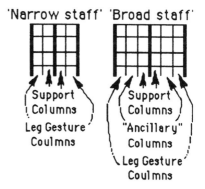

- A 'Broad Staff' adds an "ancillary" column between the support column and the outer column, which (we will see) is used for writing various modifications to symbols in the support and leg gesture columns.
- A 'Narrow staff' (without the ancillary column) is used in older scores and/or when there is no need for the ancillary column.

(*B*) *Basic shapes and 'Chimneys'.* The forward and backward symbols have extensions nicknamed 'chimneys'. The 'chimney' should be approximately 1/3 the length of the forward or backward direction symbol. Also, when placing these symbols on the staff, the 'chimney' always faces the center line, regardless of the side of the staff on which you are writing:

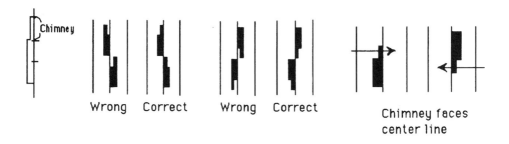

(C) *Diagonal direction symbol 'slants'*. Unlike 'chimneys', the diagonal slant of these symbols will point to the direction of the diagonal movement, regardless of the side of the staff on which you are writing:

Correct

(2 steps to the
left forward diagonal
on the L and R feet)

Correct

(L steps to the
left forward diagonal,
R steps to the
right forward diagonal)

Correct

(2 steps to the
right forward diagonal
on the R and L feet)

(D) *High Level stripes* always slant from lower left to upper right, regardless of direction or position on the staff. Also, do not try to fit too many lines within a symbol:

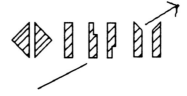

No   Yes

(E) *The Right/Left Side Direction symbol* is the only notation symbol which, as it elongates, also geometrically widens. Since this can cause the symbol to extend beyond the width of a single column, long side symbols may be altered by having their points clipped off. This is to keep the side symbol within the confines of the staff/column arrangement. However, it is always preferable to draw points on side symbols, *especially* when side movements are of a short duration:

Correct:

Correct:
A slow sideways
action with the
point clipped off.

Too wide

Quick sideways actions:

(F) *Hold Signs* are placed at the beginning of the beat where the hold is to take place, directly over both feet, or directly over the single holding foot:

Hold on
1 foot

Hold on
2 feet

(G) *Pins* are placed in the ancillary column on the same side of the staff as the symbol they modify. The pin is drawn at the center of the symbol and not too high or low:

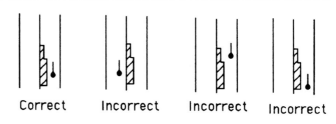

Correct   Incorrect   Incorrect   Incorrect

 Maxim #16: Autography is the penmanship of LN. Accurate notation leads to a better understanding of the components of movement notation.

RHYTHMIC APPLICATIONS

 ### 1.16   The Code Words

In RN, the first goal is to learn what each beat looks like and how each beat sounds. Increasingly, as you recognize the "look" of the beat, the sound should become immediately associated with it. Below are six different combinations of full and sub-beat rhythms (rests included) each equalling exactly one quarter note beat. Each rhythm has been assigned a **Code Word**. The code word has the same syllabic rhythm as the notes themselves: speak the word and the rhythm of the word corresponds to the rhythm of the notes and rests. The purpose of the code words is to lend verbal association to rhythmic pattern.

Procedure:
Look at the chart below and say each code word aloud. Gradually move into speaking in a slow, steady tempo. Look at the notes. Listen to the rhythm of the word. Count the number of syllables; each word's syllabic construction corresponds to the number of notes/rests in the matching rhythm. When rests appear, say nothing. THINK the word instead, or pronounce it silently.

Value	1 Beat	Code Word	How to Count
Quarter		One	1
Quarter rest		((One)) Silent	1
2 8th notes		Num-ber	1 &
1 8th note / 1 8th rest		Num - ((ber)) Silent	1 &
1 8th rest/ 1 8th note		((Num))- ber Silent	1 &
4 16th notes		Di-a-ton-ic	1 e & a

Notice how each box is a visual beat. If rests are present, at first practice saying the syllable in parantheses softly, then silently.

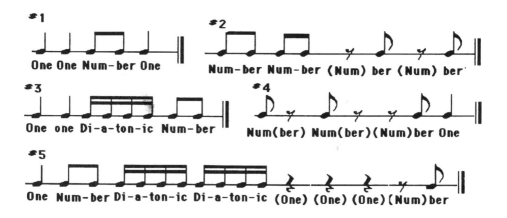

#1

One One Num-ber One

#2

Num-ber Num-ber (Num) ber (Num) ber

#3

One one Di-a-ton-ic Num-ber

#4

Num(ber) Num(ber)(Num)ber One

#5

One Num-ber Di-a-ton-ic Di-a-ton-ic (One) (One) (One)(Num)ber

Flash cards

Make four flash cards for each of the six code words. Use a 3 × 5 index card which has been cut in half. Duplicate the notational symbol on the front of the card, and on the back write the associated word:

Flash Card Examples

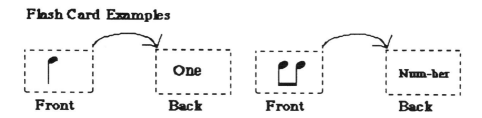

Front   Back   Front   Back

Step 1 – Mix and shuffle any 16 of the 24 cards and lay them out in four rows of four in front of you, with the word-side up. Set the metronome to 40 and read each card from left to right, one card per beat. If you have a tape recorder handy, record yourself as you complete the following steps. Make sure:

• to sustain the sound of your voice *through* the duration of the beat.
• to be silent when you encounter a rest.
• to keep the same pace as the metronome.
• to *keep reading* if you make an error – DON'T STOP!

Step 2 – Without changing the order, flip each card note-side-up and repeat the same process. Only this time you'll be looking at the notes while saying the code words. Don't stop for errors!

Step 3 – Now, read the cards one more time in the same order but instead of saying the code word, try chanting the syllable "DAWH" for each rhythm. Don't stop for errors! Record your chant, then play back the tape and see how accurate you were. Do you sound "musical?" Did you sustain through all the note values or did you "chop" off the ends? Did you rush the beat or maintain a steady tempo?

A Word on Duration
Duration implies length of action – continuity – the full length of time it takes to sustain a note or movement. When one beat moves to the next beat with no rests, sound (or motion) should be continuous. The beats should "flow together" without perceptible breaks. *Rests* imply articulation through the interruption of sound or motion.

 Maxim #17: All rhythms are assumed to be connected, continuous, and flowing, unless the insertion of a rest (or some other instruction) is introduced.

1.17   Sub-division and "Hand-els"

"Slow down! You're rushing the beat."

 The most common misconception the beginning student has about beats is that of a bowling ball rolling down stairs – BOOM! BOOM! BOOM! The problem with this image is that the full length of the beat is not being experienced, just the attack. This frequently leads to "rushing" (getting ahead of) the beat. For example, dancers will naturally shave off the ends of previous beats to be "up" on the next. A steady stream of clipped beats almost guarantees that the dancer/musician will "race" ahead. The breaking down of the time between beats is a process known as "sub-division", which fills up the time between beats and helps the performer measure more accurately the distance between beats.

When rhythm is comprised mostly of sub-beats (8ths, 16ths, 32nds), the sub-division is automatic – you can hear the beat's internal components and therefore are not tempted to rush. However, when the rhythm is comprised mostly of full-beats and thru-beats (quarters, halves, and wholes), there is very little audible sub-beat rhythm available. In cases like this, you must internally sub-divide the beat.

The general rule of thumb for internal sub-division is to "feel" a note value at least twice the speed of the note value you are performing: feel two 8th notes for each quarter; feel two 16th notes for each 8th; etc.

 Try this. Set a moderate tempo **without** a metronome and clap the written rhythm below. Simultaneously say the code words written beneath the notes. Remember the code words represent the internal subdivisions.

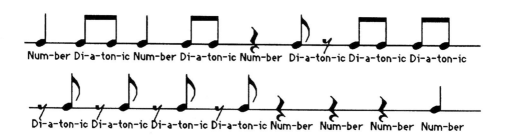

Note: If this seems too difficult at first, have a partner say the words while you chant the rhythm, or record the spoken sub-divisions on a cassette and play them back as you clap (or chant).

 Maxim #18: Sub-division is a highly effective internal process in the battle against "rushing the beat." It is especially helpful when working with slow, lyrical passages.

An effective method for "physicalizing" sub-division is the use of "hand-els", or, using your hands to sub-divide as you read and analyze rhythm. Each time you sight-read the Code Word cards, use one of the two hand-els suggested below. Once you've developed a little facility with the hand-els, switch back and forth between 8th and 16th as the rhythm changes. There are two hand-els:

8th 'Hand-els' – Each time you are about to read a rhythm in which the fastest value is the eighth, use this 'hand-el' in a steady, rocking motion: rock your right hand back and forth over the left a few times. The right thumb represents "Num" and the right pinkie, "ber".

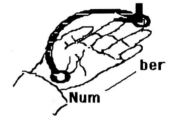

16th 'Hand-els' – Each time you are about to read a rhythm in which the fastest value is the 16th or faster, use this 'hand-el': "walk" your right hand out your left palm, each touch representing one syllable of the code word Di-a-ton-ic.

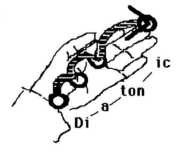

 ### 1.18 Synchronizing LN to RN

The length of time it takes to perform a movement (its duration) is determined by the length of the movement symbol itself. Therefore, a step which is to take 10 seconds will be drawn twice as long as a step that takes 5 seconds.

IMPORTANT: Note that this is a completely different method of notation than that used in music. Musical notes NEVER change size. The timing of musical notes is determined by the color of the note head and/or the presence of a stem, flag, or beam. LN movement symbols change *length* to determine rhythmic duration and change *shading* to indicate level changes.

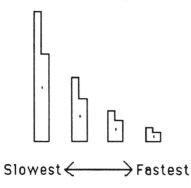

Slowest ⟵⟶ Fastest

Depending upon how long you decide to make your slowest movement, all faster movements must stay graphically in proportion. Since movement is not always choreographed using rhythmic time values based upon beats, the notation must therefore rely upon the *visual* relationship between the symbols:

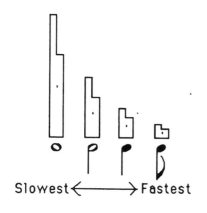

Slowest ⟵⟶ Fastest

When linking LN to RN, you simply state which length movement symbol will be equivalent to which rhythmic value:

At the start of Laban scores you will see this equivalent stated in the following registration:

Tempo indications may also include a metronome marking:

On a sheet of graph paper, if you decide that the quarter will take four squares, then the 8th will take two:

When applying specific rhythms, the staff must be marked off at regular intervals with **beat strokes** (also called 'tick marks').

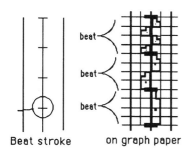

Beat stroke   on graph paper

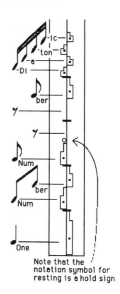

On graph paper, using the formula one square = one 16th, you will get one quarter every four squares:

Note that the notation symbol for resting is a hold sign.

How to count. Rhythm is counted sequentially from beat to beat under the following hierarchy:

(1) for Thru-beats, count each beat, stressing those which correspond with the start of each new duration;

(2) for full-beats, simply count sequentially in a flowing, each continuous manner;

(3) for Sub-beats, count sequentially and include the fastest sub-divisions present within each beat;

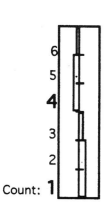

Count: 1

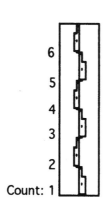

Count: 1

Count: 1

The previous example can
therefore be counted in 5
beats as follows:

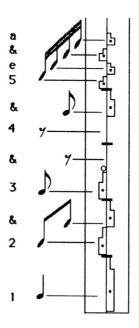

 Maxim #19: The timing of Laban movement symbols is determined by the size (length) of the symbol itself. Musical notes
NEVER change size. The timing of musical notes is determined by the color of the note head and/or the presence of a
stem, flag, or beam.

MOVEMENT APPLICATIONS

1.19   The 5 Positions of the Feet (Western Dance)

The five positions are divided into Closed and Open categories based on
the relationship of the supports to the center of weight. Closed positions
are those with the supports directly below the center of weight (1st, 3rd &
5th). Open positions are those with the center of weight between the
supports and not over them, due to the feet being separated (2nd & 4th).

Note: Nothing is stated in the following notations about turn-out, so the
reader should use the most natural stance. Turn-out of the legs will be
discussed in Chapter 5. Also, recall that pins say nothing about turn-out.
For a closed position, they tell the reader whether the feet in are in a

side-by-side, diagonal, or front-to-back relationship. Thus their name: Relationship Pins.

CLOSED POSITIONS

First Position

Normal standing position with heels together. Supports are directly beneath the center of weight. No need to use pins; side-to-side relationship is understood.

First Position Pins

Usually, pins are not necessary in 1st position. Notation for both feet together, "in place", suffices. The exception is when the dancer has been previ-

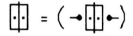

ously standing in another position, and then one foot changes the position by stepping (closing) into 1st. When this occurs, a 1st position pin may be used to clarify which foot moved. The pin points directly sideways, since the relationship of the feet in 1st position is side-by-side.

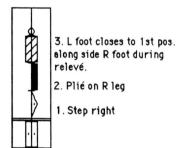

3. L foot closes to 1st pos. along side R foot during relevé.

2. Plié on R leg

1. Step right

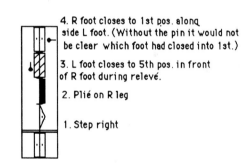

4. R foot closes to 1st pos. along side L foot. (Without the pin it would not be clear which foot had closed into 1st.)

3. L foot closes to 5th pos. in front of R foot during relevé.

2. Plié on R leg

1. Step right

No Pins necessary
It is clear which foot
closes into 1st.

Pins necessary

When changing level in a closed position of the feet, pins must be repeated. A closed position without any pins will always be read as first position (feet together).

Third Position

The pins indicate that the supports in 3rd position are in a diagonal relationship to each other. Although both supports are directly beneath the center of weight, the feet are placed as if on a diagonal line, here shown with the R.F. front.

Fifth Position

As with 3rd position, the pins in 5th position indicate the relationship of the feet to each other: here they are in a direct front/back relationship. Both supports are beneath the center of weight, but the left foot is placed directly behind the right.

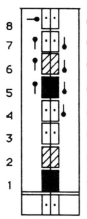

8	Ct. 8: L.F. steps (closes) into 1st pos.
7	Ct. 7: Return to middle level, 5th pos.
6	Ct. 6: Releve'(rise) into 5th pos.
5	Ct. 5: Plie'(bend) in 5th pos.
4	Ct. 4: R.F. steps (closes) into 5th pos.
3	Ct. 3: Return to middle level, 1st pos
2	Ct. 2: Releve'(rise) in 1st pos.
1	Ct. 1: Plie'(bend) in 1st pos.
	S.P.: 1st pos.

One pin is used in counts 4 and 8 to show that one foot is actively closing into a new position. Two pins are used in counts 5, 6 and 7 to show that both feet maintain their relationship in 5th position. (There is no single active foot.)

 Maxim #20: Two pins are used when (1) notating starting positions, and (2) when the same position of the feet is repeated with a change of level. One pin is used to show an active foot closing into a new position.

OPEN POSITIONS

Second Position

Each support is to one side of the center of weight, which is centered between the feet.

Fourth Position. Depending on preference or training, there are four variations on fourth position:

4th opposite
1st position
(feet forward and
back of the hips).

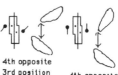

4th opposite
3rd position

4th opposite
5th position

Open diagonal
position (also
called 6th pos.).

Maxim #21: Closed positions of the feet are those with the supports directly below the center of weight; open positions are those with the center of weight *between* the supports.

1.20 Stepping into the Open Positions

Stepping into 2nd or 4th position is written differently than standing in those positions. The notation shows which foot remains in place with either a hold sign or a place symbol, plus the direction in which the other foot steps to make the new position:

Stepping into 2nd position:

From standing on the L.F. step out with the R.F. to 2nd pos., holding on the left. All actions are in the same level, so a hold sign can be used.

From standing on the L.F., step out with the R.F. to 2nd pos. plié. The L.F. stays in place, but changes level. So "place" is used rather than a hold sign, to show the new level.

Standing in 2nd position:

In both these examples, after stepping into 2nd position, remain standing in that position. The notation for counts 3 and 4 shows rise and a return to middle level while standing in 2nd, keeping one foot to each side of the center of weight. Again, notice the difference in notation due to the change of level: the hold sign can not be used on beat #2 in the right example.

Stepping into 4th position:

From standing on the R.F., step forward with the L.F. into 4th pos., holding on the right. All actions are in the same level, so a hold sign can be used.

From standing on the R.F., step back with the L.F. into 4th pos. plié. The R.F. stays in place, but changes level. So "place" is used rather than a hold sign, to show the new level.

Standing in 4th position:

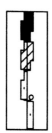 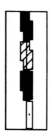

In both these examples, after stepping into 4th position, remain in that position, but change level. The notation for counts 3 & 4 shows relevé and plié in 4th, keeping 1 foot forward and one foot behind the center of weight.

Maxim #22: *Stepping into* open positions involves one active foot and one foot staying in place, holding or changing level.

Staying in an open position involves keeping the feet where they were in their relation to the center of weight.

1.21   Basic Movement Clusters

Basic movement clusters (patterns of LN symbols) are very much the same as the Code Word rhythms for notes, rests, and beats. Once you learn what different steps look like on paper, you will begin to recognize the patterns of their notation more quickly, and will not have to continue to read each individual step-component. As with RN, the eye will scan the step pattern and recognize the "cluster". Once you have read the following clusters, practice *recognizing* them rather than *reading* them. Train your eye to scan these patterns, identifying them with greater and greater speed.

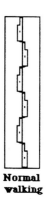 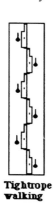 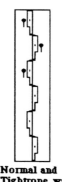 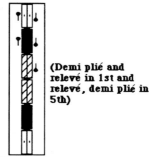

(Demi plié and relevé in 1st and relevé, demi plié in 5th)

Normal walking   Tightrope walking   Normal and Tightrope walking backwards   Changing levels in the same position:

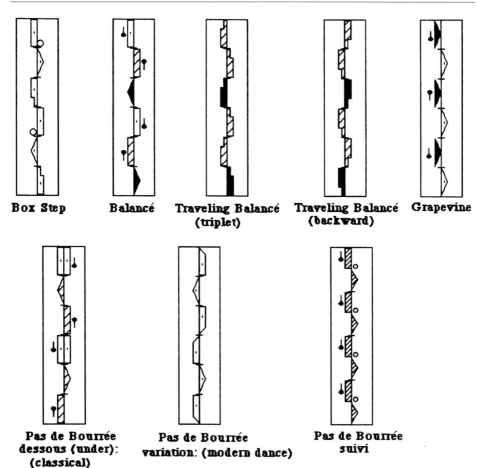

Box Step   Balancé   Traveling Balancé   Traveling Balancé   Grapevine
(triplet)   (backward)

Pas de Bourrée   Pas de Bourrée   Pas de Bourrée
dessous (under):   variation: (modern dance)   suivi
(classical)

CHAPTER WRAP

1.22   RN Etudes

Using 8th 'Hand-els', sight-read the following two-part etudes, each line separately at first, then together (note that the brackets indicate "2-lines-at-a-time"). In pencil, write in the abbreviations of the code words under the beats: use **1** for One, **N-b** for Number, and **D-a-t-n** for Diatonic. Chant the top part and clap or walk the bottom. Continue reading each etude until you reach the double bar line (II).

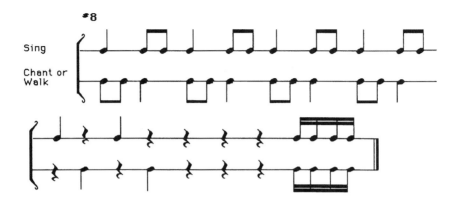

1.23 Tricky Rhythms

The following exercises contain simple movement and complex rhythm patterns. How quickly can you read and perfect the movement **and** the rhythmic complexities? Try them in different tempi, starting slowly and then gradually accelerating to fast and very fast.

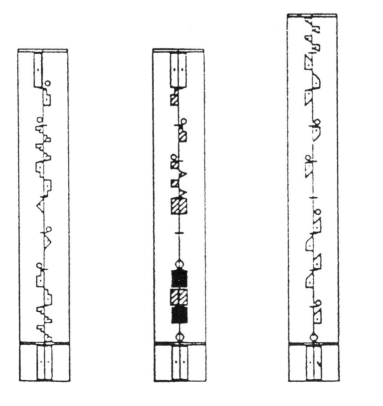

1.24   Suggested Assignments

 Make the 24 code-word flash cards. (See 1.16.)
Be sure each card is an exact duplicate of the example on the code word table. Drill the flash cards relentlessly; the more you read the faster you will develop your "eye". Deal them out in rows of four; set the metronome at a relatively slow pace (m.m 50–60). Don't stop for errors. Increase the speed of the metronome only when you are beginning to recognize the beats. Try to wean yourself from speaking the code words to chanting the tone DAWH as soon as possible.

Write the rhythmic notation that would correspond to each of these movement combinations. In B, which counts show movement of the center of weight?

• Practice moving these combinations. Try to sustain the thru-beat movements accurately.

A   B

• Write the RN rhythms that would correspond to the Tricky Rhythms in 1.23.

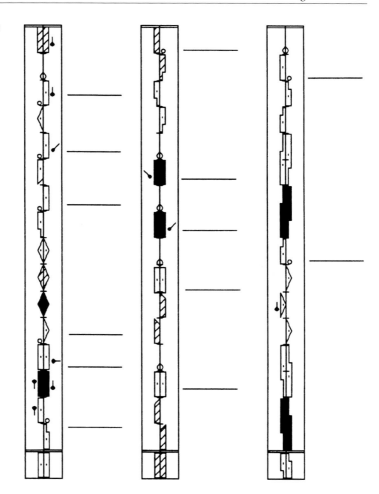

Write the name of the positions you have stepped into in each count where there is a blank line.

Write out a few lines of Code Word rhythms (8 beats each). Then:

(a) re-write the exercises in LN;
(b) memorize the steps;
(c) have someone chant the RN against the LN while you move.
Check to see if all durations and rests are the same.

OR

Combine step clusters to form a movement combination of moderate length. Introduce some pauses in the sequence, and change the duration of some of the steps (making them slower or faster).

Then:

(a) re-write the exercises in RN;
(b) memorize the combinations;
(c) have someone chant the RN against the LN while you move. Check to
    see if all durations and rests are the same.

   Write a walking combination demonstrating thru, full, and sub-
beat rhythms and changes for the center of weight.

• Take one of the 2-part etudes from 1.22 and choreograph a walking duet,
  using the top rhythm for one dancer and the bottom rhythm for a second
  dancer. Score out the duet in LN on graph paper.

To develop a basic sense of tempo for "slow" and "fast", memorize
the speed of 60 and 120 beats per minute.

• Bring in scores, recordings, etc. of pieces which demonstrate thru, full
  and sub-beat rhythm. For example, the first 2 measures of the Bach air
  in C is a glorious example of a thru-beat in the treble melody.

• Bring in 10 life examples each of thru, full and sub-beat rhythms. For
  example: Running = sub-beat; soldiers marching = full-beat; gliding on a
  bicycle without pumping = thru-beat.

2
GETTING ORGANIZED

RHYTHMIC CONCEPTS

2.1 Meter

Meter is a generic term referring to the organization of numbers of beats or pulses into "measures" of time. In short, meter measures musical time, and displays each measure with the insertion of 'bar' lines:

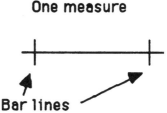

One measure

Bar lines

Visually scan example A. Without counting each individual quarter note (a time-consuming process), it is difficult to tell how many notes there are in the line:

A ♩♩♩♩ ♩♩♩♩ ♩♩♩♩♩♩ ♩♩♩♩♩♩ ♩♩

By dividing them into groups of fours, separated by thin, vertical bar lines, your eye instantly sees "six measures of four beats". A little quick multiplication and presto: 24. This is one of the primary functions of barlines, the visual organization of beats into measures of time:

B |♩♩♩♩|♩♩♩♩|♩♩♩♩|♩♩♩♩|♩♩♩♩|♩♩♩♩|

 Maxim #23: Meter is the organization of numbers of beats into "measures" of time. In short, *meter measures musical time*.

2.2 Time Signatures

Depending upon the *type of beat* in use (duple or triple), and the *number of beats* in each measure, meter requires the use of a **Time signature** – two numbers, one on top of the other – which is placed at the very beginning of a composition, prior to the first note.

Upper = Metric Pattern: the upper numeral indicates the number of beats that must occur in each and every measure.

Lower = Beat Assignment: the lower numeral indicates which member of the BOV has been assigned to the full-beat, known throughout the musical world as "the beating note".

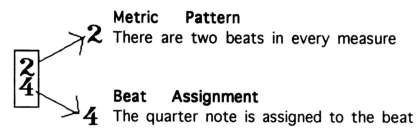

Metric   Pattern
There are two beats in every measure

Beat   Assignment
The quarter note is assigned to the beat

A more modern approach to writing time signatures is to show the assigned note value rather than its numerical equivalent. When this method is used, the time signature is placed either above the staff line or between the parts of a score:

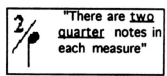

"There are <u>two</u> <u>quarter</u> notes in each measure"

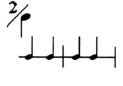 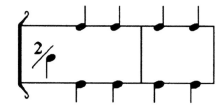

 Maxim #24: The note assigned to the beat and the number of beats that are to occur in each measure will determine which time signature is in use.

2.3   Simple Time

Each note/rest value within the BOV is referred to as **Simple** since each can be evenly divided by 2 without a fraction. Simple Time is therefore a category of meter referring to *any time signature in which a simple note value has been assigned to the beat, or, where the beating note is divisible by 2 without a fraction.*

Simple time signatures are therefore based exclusively on the duple beat subdivision. (See Chapter 4 for time signatures based on the triple beat.)

Since we have established that the quarter note is a common beat assignment, the most common time signatures based on the quarter note in Simple Time are:

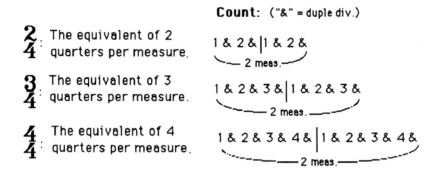

Count: ("&" = duple div.)

$\frac{2}{4}$: The equivalent of 2 quarters per measure.

1 & 2 & | 1 & 2 &
— 2 meas. —

$\frac{3}{4}$: The equivalent of 3 quarters per measure.

1 & 2 & 3 & | 1 & 2 & 3 &
— 2 meas. —

$\frac{4}{4}$: The equivalent of 4 quarters per measure.

1 & 2 & 3 & 4 & | 1 & 2 & 3 & 4 &
— 2 meas. —

 Maxim #25: Simple Time refers to any time signature where the beating note is divisible by two without a fraction.

2.4   Metric Characteristics

How does one go about choosing a time signature? Will the meter you pick suit your choreography, or will you pick a time signature that is contrary to the needs of your movement?

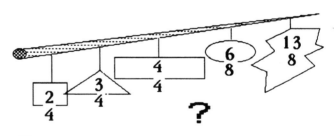

Each time signature has a metric "character" that makes it unique from all others, and these characteristics are based upon an energy cycle of release, sustain, and preparation *within each measure*. Therefore, each new measure "renews" itself in the same way in which we inhale and exhale.

There are three qualities of beat energy within each measure:

(1) **Crusis:** the release of energy which occurs on the 1st beat in every measure, called the **Downbeat (Db).**
(2) **Anacrusis:** the preparation of energy which occurs on the last beat of each measure, called the **upbeat (Ub).**
(3) **Metacrusis:** the neutral beats which fall *between* the Db and Ub.

Every measure beings with a Db and ends with an Ub, *regardless of the time signature in use*; and, because it is the nature of meter to apply different qualities to the beats within each measure, it will soon become apparent that IDENTICAL NOTE VALUES IN THE SAME MEASURE ARE NOT ALWAYS FELT IN THE SAME WAY. Like the differences between identical twins, a quarter note falling on the crucis (Db) of a measure will have a drastically different 'personality' than one that falls on the anacrusis (Ub).

Note on Terminology:
To avoid confusion as we proceed, use the following as a guide. Say:

* Measure or Bar to describe each complete METRIC cycle.
* Downbeat (Db) to describe the Crusis.
* Upbeat to describe the Anacrusis.
* "2nd beat, 3rd beat, etc.", to describe each Metacrusic beat.
* **On**-beat to describe the beginning of any single beat in the measure.
* **Off**-beat to describe the sub-division(s) within any single beat.

 Maxim #26: Meter applies different qualities (energies) to beats depending upon their position within a measure. These energies are referred to as Crusic, Metacrusic, and Anacrusic.

Let's look at 2/4:

You now know that in 2/4 there are two beats per measure and the quarter note is assigned to the beat. Every measure is therefore constructed on an alternation of a single downbeat followed by a single upbeat. Consequently, a decision to select 2/4 would be based on the need to "feel" a downbeat *every other beat*, which implies an *equal amount* of crusic and anacrusic energies: Db/Ub Db/Ub. Since the anacrusis is the preparation (inhale) for the *next* Db, it can be said that it "belongs" to the next measure: it literally falls over the bar line from a metrically higher position.

The characteristic "feel" of 2/4 can therefore be established as DOWN/OVER:

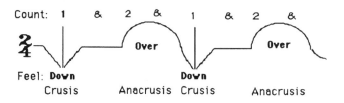

3/4 You now know that there are 3 beats per measure and the quarter note is assigned to the beat. Every measure is therefore constructed on an alternation of a single downbeat followed by **one** metacrusic beat and **one** anacrusic upbeat. Consequently, a decision to select 3/4 would be based on the need to "feel" a downbeat *every third beat*, which implies an *unequal amount* of crusic and non-crusic energy. In effect, the last beat in each measure should feel as if it were about to "fall across" the bar line and land on "1". The "feel" of 3/4 then is **Down/Release/Over**:

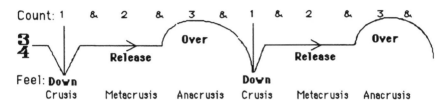

Note that the quality of the 2nd metacrusic beat is to be horizontal without implying any motion towards the next measure. It is in the horizontal position between the more active 1st and 3rd beats.

4/4 You now know that there are 4 beats per measure and the quarter note is assigned to the beat. Every measure therefore is constructed of a single downbeat followed by **two** metacrusic and **one** anacrusic beats. *However, the two metacrusic beats are NOT the same*: the first is a release from the crusic energy of the Db while the second has a more growing quality as it approaches the rising lift of the anacrusis. The "feel" of 4/4 can be expressed as **Down/Release/Increase/Over**:

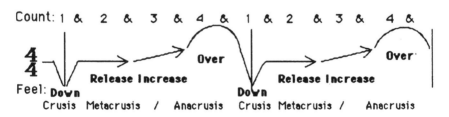

In summary, *meter adds DIRECTIONALITY to rhythm: Downward; Horizontal; and Rising or Lifting.*

Historical note: The metric qualities described above for 2/4, 3/4 and 4/4 are to be considered 'normative' in the performance of music of the 17th, 18th and 19th centuries. There are many instances when, for effect, composers such as Beethoven will change these normative qualities with diacritical marks such as accents, crescendos, sudden changes of volume etc. However, this does explain why composers of the Baroque period (Bach especially) *use very few markings at all*: it was assumed that as the notes were played, the *performer* would supply the missing 'metric motion'.

 Maxim #27: The characteristics of each time signature are based upon a specific pattern of crusic and non-crusic qualities.

2.5   Applying Rhythm to Meter

When rhythm is applied to meter, two events take place: the *meter influences the rhythm* with its crusic, metacrusic and anacrusic qualities, **and,** the *rhythm influences the meter* with its varying durations of sounds and silences.

The four rules below should be thought of as nuances to the rules of meter presented above in 2.4. They add weight, lift, and plasticity to rhythmic patterns and phrases.

Rule #1   Longer note values receive more weight in performance than shorter note values, REGARDLESS OF THEIR POSITION IN A MEASURE.

Rule #2   Multiple sub-beat rhythms (sub-divisions) within **any** given beat will create more "lift" in that beat due to the increased physical activity.

Rule #3   Rests (silences) also create lift: the longer the rest (silence), the greater the lifting quality, REGARDLESS OF THE POSITION IN A MEASURE.

Rule #4   *All* notes preceded by faster rhythms (**OR** rests) will receive more weight (accent) than they would normally, REGARDLESS OF THEIR POSITION WITHIN THE MEASURE.

IMPORTANT: The above rules apply **UNLESS** the composer/choreographer stipulates otherwise.

Concerning Rule #1   (Length = weight)
In physics, the longer an object, the greater its weight. In music, a whole note is four times longer than a quarter note, thus requiring four times the effort to sustain it.

Try this: In moderate tempo, take four normal steps (quarters) followed by one giant step (whole note) during which you slowly shift your weight over four counts. Repeat this several times. Can you feel the weightiness of the whole vs. the lighter quarters?

For example, in the code word pattern ONE/NUMBER, the quarter note receives more weight than the 8th notes due to its full-beat length. The sub-beat 8th notes receive added lift derived from the additional rhythmic activity within the beat (see Rule #2 below). Thus, ONE/NUMBER matches perfectly the Crusic and Anacrusic metric pattern of the time signature 2/4.

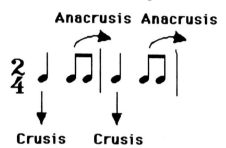

However, when we turn the rhythm around to NUMBER/ONE, the rhythmic pattern is now saying something quite different than the metric pattern: the 8th notes lift on the crusis while the quarter note's weight pulls DOWN on the anacrusis. This sets up a *double pull* on each beat, making a lighter Db and heavier Ub, adding a very subtle dialogue between the rhythm and the meter:

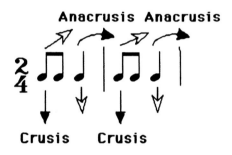

Meter: "Down." Rhythm: "No, up."
Meter: "UP." Rhythm: "No, down."

Try this: Stand up, repetitively chant ONE NUMBER, and move around the room with a **WALK** JOG-JOG/**WALK** JOG-JOG. Feel the weight as you settle into ONE on the crusis, which gives the walk a weighted quality. Feel the lift as the 8th notes rise on the anacrusis. The movement flows easily from measure to measure.

Now, turn the pattern around and do Jog-Jog Walk/Jog-Jog Walk. Do you feel the difference? This is now a very interesting rhythm – do you feel the quarter note pulling down against the rise of the anacrusis?

This is one way that rhythm modifies the normative qualities of meter, making subtle changes to the metric flow with the placement of heavier notes on beats which are 'normally' lifted.

Concerning Rule #2   **Activity** (Increased activity (sub-division) = lift)
The law of physics also states that when you go faster your energy must increase while your physical motions become smaller. And the opposite is also true: going slower usually requires larger movements. This constant adjustment of time, space, and energy is at the root of what we call technique. [For a quick proof, briefly try clapping rapidly using your full arm space: not only is this a poor physical adjustment to the speed, it is awkward and potentially injurious.] Consequently, the faster we play or dance, the more energy we must use, and rapid physical activity creates *lift*.

When violinists play fast, continuous 16th notes, they must use a very small amount of bow and a great amount of energy with small finger action – this creates lift and forward motion with as little effort as possible.

The code word pattern ONE/ NUMBER/DIATONIC demonstrates this as beats 2 and 3 demand progressively more and more energy. This rhythmic pattern is therefore a perfect match for the time signature 3/4.

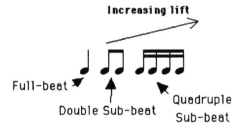

Try this: Stand up, repetitively chant ONE NUMBER DIATONIC in a moderate tempo, and move around the room with a **WALK/JOG-JOG/ RUN-RUN-RUN-RUN**. Watch as the feet take a naturally smaller step on the 16th notes while the entire body **lifts** away from gravity to keep the weight off the feet. This is why faster notes create lift: the body instinctively understands that to go faster it must free itself from gravity.

Concerning Rule #3   (Rests create lift)
Just as sub-divisions create lift through increased activity, rests create lift through "breathing". The longer the rest, the greater the lift (and breath in the lungs).

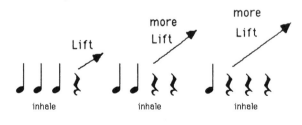

Concerning Rule #4   (THE AGOGIC ACCENT: Extra weight after lift)
Any note, regardless of its position within a measure, will take more weight than it would normally when immediately preceded by a rest or

a faster rhythm. This rule will modify slightly the natural metric flow qualities by weighting them a little more than normal.

At left, the measure rises through its sub-beats, making the downbeat of the 2nd measure heavier than that in the 1st measure.

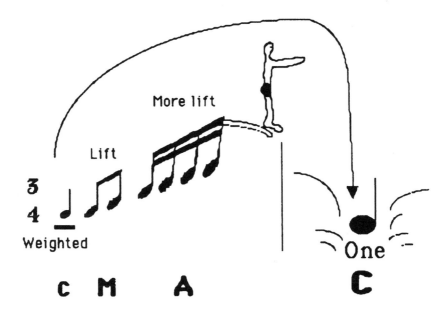

Here, in a measure comprised of only quarters, the lift is inhibited: the subsequent Db therefore receives less than normal crusic energy.

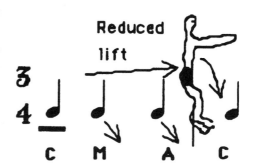

Examples of rhythm when applied to 2/4, 3/4, and 4/4

2/4 Below are 4 measures of rhythm in 2/4. Practice chanting them a few times until memorized:

The same rhythm in LN might look as follows. Try moving this while chanting the rhythm:

3/4   Below are 2 measures of rhythm in 3/4. Practice chanting them a few times until memorized:

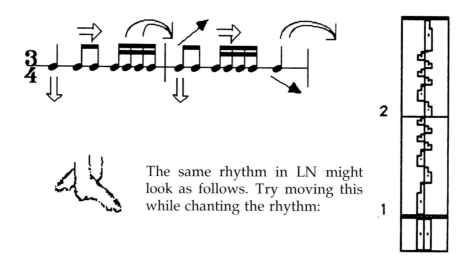

The same rhythm in LN might look as follows. Try moving this while chanting the rhythm:

4/4   Below are 2 measures of rhythm in 4/4. Practice chanting a few times until memorized:

 The same rhythm in LN might look as follows. Try moving this while chanting the rhythm:

Maxim #28: When rhythm is applied to meter, it will tend to modify the basic metric characteristics (crusic, metacrusic, anacrusic), depending upon which rhythmic patterns occur on which beats.

2.6 Preparation and Release

Certain actions in life organically require a preparation followed by a release: the wind-up before the pitcher's fast ball; the back-swing before the batter's swing; the sneeze ...

The Aaaaa is the preparation required to fill the lungs (anacrusis) before the explosive Chooo (crusis).

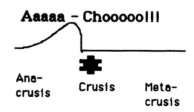

Preparation and release occur in dance at the start of movements that require a preparation in the body: the step before the skip; the plié before the jump; the relevé before the triplet. In music, it occurs when there is a need to add more 'lift' or 'amplification' to a particular beat or word. For example, melodies do not always begin on a downbeat; many times a song begins before the downbeat, before the actual 1st measure has begun. These preparations are called **pickups**.

Basic principles:

(1) Preparations usually occur on the anacrucis.
(2) Releases usually occur a downbeats, which are the strongest part of the measure.
(3) Preparations *can* be placed on other beats as well.

There are literally thousands of popular songs that begin with a pickup. [Note: teachers, please choose any other more appropriate examples.]

• In *Happy Birthday*, the pickup "Happy" prepares "Birthday."
• In *I Left My Heart In San Francisco*, the pickup "I left my" prepares "Heart."
• In *Hey Jude*, the "Hey" prepares "Jude."
• In *76 Trombones*, the "Seventy" prepares "Six".

Terminology.   Pickups take their names from the number of beats they occupy, "a 4-beat, 3-beat, 2-beat, or 1-beat pickup". If shorter than one beat they are referred to as "an 8th pickup, a 16th pickup," etc.

 Maxim #29: Pickups are used when a preparation is required. They amplify the downbeat since they occupy a weaker division of a previous measure.

2.7   Pickups: external ("& One")

There are two types of pickups: External and Internal. External pickups are those which occur before the first measure of a composition: the "&" which precedes the "1". (Internal pickups will be covered in the next chapter.) Observe the following pickups:

In an external pickup, the time signature is written normally, the quarter note is placed in the position of the last beat of a preceding imaginary measure, and finally, the bar line is drawn and the 1st complete measure begins:

Here, the pickup is a single 8th note (half beat). The time signature is placed normally, then the 8th note is placed before the bar line:

Note: In the above examples, the word "4" represents a full-beat pickup. The 8th pick-up takes half the time of the quarter and the word "&" is used instead.

The song *Happy Birthday* is an excellent example of an external pickup: "Happy" is not a full measure in 3/4. It requires only one beat. The song therefore begins with a '1-beat pickup'. The syllable 'birth' occurs on the downbeat of the first measure. The pickup 'Happy' is positioned on what would be the anacrusis in a preceding imaginary measure.

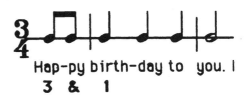

Clarification: External pickups amplify the arrival of the downbeat by "falling" onto it from a metrically higher position: the anacrusis. In a song with a similar rhythmic structure to Happy Birthday, the US National Anthem employs the same preparation:

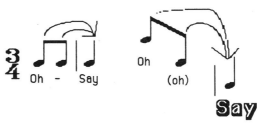

General principle: Anacrusis amplifies crusis, and the more subdivisions within the anacrusis, the heavier the downbeat. Therefore, a preparation involving 16th notes will have more energy than a preparation involving only 8ths or a quarter:

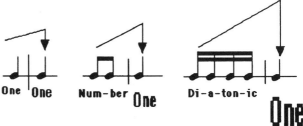

In compositions of short to moderate length, external pickups are thought to be "borrowed" from the final measure. For example, if a composition has a 1-beat pickup, there will be one beat missing from the final measure. In effect, the composition is "displaced" one beat to the left:

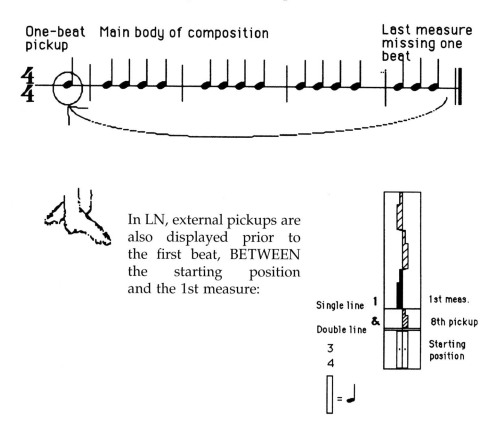

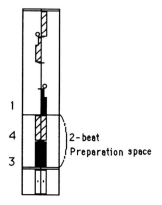

In LN, external pickups are also displayed prior to the first beat, BETWEEN the starting position and the 1st measure:

The Preparation Space. External pickups are usually referred to by dancers as "preparations". The space within which the external pickups or preparation is written in the movement score is called the "preparation space".

Note that the double line that indicates when movement is to begin is placed, as always, *after the starting position*. The line separating the preparation from the 1st measure is a single line (a bar line).

Maxim #30: External pickups occur prior to the first beat of a composition, adding weight and amplification to the crusis.

 ## 2.8 "One &" versus "& One"

While dance preparations will generally occur on the anacrusis (before the Db), some movement combinations can shift their preparatory actions to occur **on** the downbeat. This "phrase shifting" can drastically effect the energy of a movement combination.

In example A, a preparation appears prior to ct. #1. In rhythmic terms, this is counted:

The 3rd ct. of each measure is sub-divided, creating an "&" on ct. #3 prior to each downbeat:

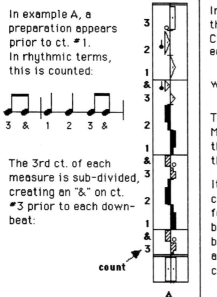

In example B, the 2 quick actions that lead into slower steps occupy Ct. 1 of each meas. The rhythm in each meas. is

which is counted 1 & 2 3

The 1st beat of these meas.'s MUST be counted "1 &", with the counts' name said first (1) then sub-divided with "&".

It would never be correct to count example B "& 1". In order for a movement sequence to be counted "& 1", there must be a preparatory action which precedes count #1.

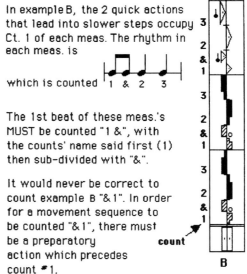

Notice the difference in quality between these 2 combinations. In A, the quick steps occur on the anacrusis, providing a sense of preparatory lift before the slower steps. In B, the quick steps fall on the Db, making them heavier while the slower steps become metrically lighter.

 Maxim #31: Movement that begins on the first count of a measure is always called "1". Movement occurring in a preparation space is called "&, & a, e & a", etc.

MOVEMENT CONCEPTS

2.9   Step Size and Levels

The level in which a step is taken determines, to a certain extent, the size of the step. That is, moving in high, middle, or low level will affect how far a step will naturally travel, without any special notation. The following formula applies unless otherwise indicated:

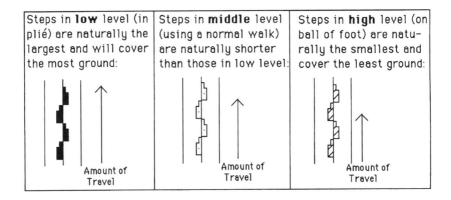

Steps in **low** level (in plié) are naturally the largest and will cover the most ground:	Steps in **middle** level (using a normal walk) are naturally shorter than those in low level:	Steps in **high** level (on ball of foot) are naturally the smallest and cover the least ground:
Amount of Travel	Amount of Travel	Amount of Travel

2.10   Lengthening and Shortening: steps and positions

Beyond normal differences in step sizes due to level, the size of a step (and all other movements) can be altered to suit the demands of a dance. There are two symbols that are used in conjunction with standard notation symbols that will either lengthen or shorten a specific movement: the backward **N** means that the movement is to be lengthened*; the **X** means that the movement is to be shortened. Called '**pre-signs**', **X** and backwards **N** are placed prior to direction symbols. These pre-signs *must be repeated each and every time a lengthening or shortening modification is to continue*. Also note that the pre-sign is incorporated into the symbol's original size so that if a step takes one count (4 squares), the X or backward N will occupy the first of the 4 squares, and will become part of the timing of the movement:

****Note:** Be aware that lengthen here refers to *spatial* and not *temporal* lengthening.

longer step   shorter step   wide step to side   short step backwards

By using these two modifiers, you can alter the natural size of steps as described in 2.10 above. The example on the left shows shorter than normal steps to the side in plié; the example on the right shows a mixture of backward steps in relevé:

 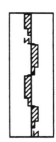

X and backward N can also be used with open positions to shorten or lengthen the distance between the supports. Notice that one modifier is placed across the center line of the staff when shortening or lengthening the stance in an open position.

Small 2nd pos.   **Wide 2nd pos.**   **Small 4th pos. in plié**   **Wide 4th pos. in relevé**

 Maxim #32: The pre-signs X and backward N can be used to modify the sizes of steps and open positions of the feet.

Extreme lengthening and shortening

When *very* small or narrow, or *very* long or wide steps or positions are desired, X and backwards N can be altered. The "doubled" symbols look as follows:

 The center slash is doubled

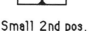 Both lines are doubled

        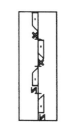

A very small 2nd pos.   **A very wide 4th pos. in plié**   **2 very long then 2 very short diagonal steps**

 Maxim #33: Double X and double backward N can be used in the support columns to indicate a more extreme change of scale for steps and open positions.

2.11   Stepping versus Shifting Weight: moving from 2 feet to 1 foot

The examples at right show a starting position on 2 feet, followed by a step onto 1 foot in count #1:

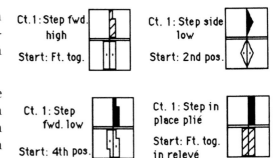

Ct. 1: Step fwd. high

Start: Ft. tog.

Ct. 1: Step side low

Start: 2nd pos.

In each of these examples, the R.F. is understood to lift from the ground in order to step in the direction indicated in count 1.

Ct. 1: Step fwd. low

Start: 4th pos.

Ct. 1: Step in place plié

Start: Ft. tog. in relevé

Carets

There is another possible way of moving from 2 feet to 1 foot: by shifting the weight onto 1 foot *without picking it up*. In a dance score, this action is indicated by adding a **caret,** which is a linking symbol, to the notation. Simply stated, a caret in the support column means "the same", the same support, thus it results in a shift (do not step). The caret links two symbols in the support column, indicating that a transference of weight is occurring, but that it will happen without a release of the foot from the floor. *From standing on 2 feet, the dancer will move to standing on 1 foot by simply shifting the weight.*

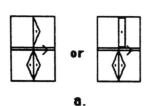

or

a.

Start in 4th position. On count 1, shift the weight onto the right foot without picking it up. Two support symbols for the right foot are linked to indicate that there is no step (no separate action) on count 1. Notice that there are 2 possible ways of describing the action in this example:

(1) as a *shift of the weight* to the side to get onto the right foot; or
(2) as a *shift to a new place* (with the weight now centered over the right foot). BOTH ARE CORRECT.

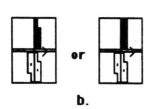

or

b.

Start in 2nd position, middle level. On count 1, shift the weight onto the right foot and lower to plié. The caret ensures that the weight will transfer without stepping. Notice again the two ways of describing this action: as a weight shift "forward" onto the front foot, or as a shift to a new "place". BOTH ARE CORRECT.

c.

From 1st position relevé, the dancer lowers to plié on the right foot without stepping. Since this action occurs in place, with no movement of the center of weight into a new direction, there is no alternative way of describing this movement. The shift occurs in place, with a change of level as the weight move onto 1 foot.

Without a change of level, a shift in place from 2 feet to 1 would look like this:

 Maxim #34: The presence of a caret in the ancillary column means a shift of weight from 2 feet to 1 WITHOUT taking a step.

2.12 Changing Level within Steps

Changes of level can take place within one step. When changing to a new level within a single step, the notation will change shading within a single symbol. Regardless of whether the step takes less than a beat, one single beat, or longer, the shading will reflect the level change when it occurs within the total duration of the movement. Any of the basic direction symbols can be made to change level:

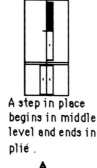

A step in place begins in middle level and ends in plié .

A

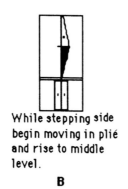

While stepping side begin moving in plié and rise to middle level.

B

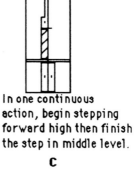

In one continuous action, begin stepping forward high then finish the step in middle level.

C

Note: Example B produces an "undercurve," as the dancer's weight moves in an arc like this:

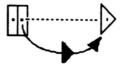

Example C produces an "overcurve," with the dancer's weight carving the following shape:

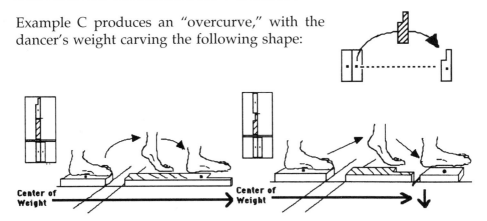

Here, the centre of weight (CW) will move fluidly through this step, constantly moving forward as it rises and then returns to middle level.

In the example below, each step (transference of weight) takes two beats to complete:

Here is a different action in which the CW moves directly to forward high, and after completing the step, lowers to middle level:

In the example below, each step is completed in one half beat:

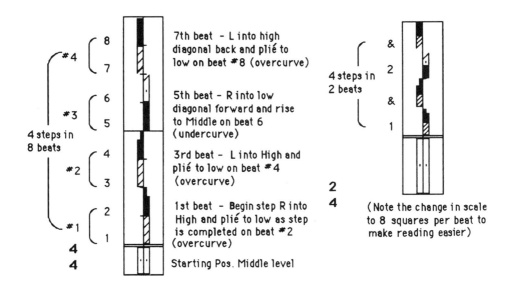

4 steps in 8 beats

7th beat – L into high diagonal back and plié to low on beat #8 (overcurve)

5th beat – R into low diagonal forward and rise to Middle on beat 6 (undercurve)

3rd beat – L into High and plié to low on beat #4 (overcurve)

1st beat – Begin step R into High and plié to low as step is completed on beat #2 (overcurve)

Starting Pos. Middle level

4 steps in 2 beats

(Note the change in scale to 8 squares per beat to make reading easier)

Maxim #35: When reading steps within which there are changes of level, emphasize fluidity in the transition between levels and keep the center of weight moving in the direction indicated. These steps will produce *undercurves* and *overcurves*.

NOTATION

2.13   Setting up LN Measures

Time signatures are placed to the left of the starting position of the first staff of a score (or to the left of the left-hand staff of a duet). This may be accompanied by a registration indicating the size of the movement symbol in relation to the beat:

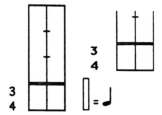

Beats are marked with short lines called "tick marks" or beat strokes:

Beats are usually drawn 4 squares in length:

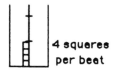

Measures are indicated by drawing a bar line which horizontally connects all three staff lines:

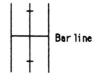

Measures are numbered along the left-hand side of the staff:

Individual beats, often of the first measure only, are placed between the measure numbers and the staff:

Note: The practice of numbering measures makes it easier to "tie in" to musical scores and the floor plans of choreographers. These are covered later.

2.14   RN: beaming

Beams serve many purposes in RN, two of which are: (1) the reduction of time it takes to write out individual flags; and (2) the visual grouping of complex rhythms. When beams are used as substitutes for flags, use one beam (primary) for 8th notes; two beams (secondary) for 16th notes; three beams (tertiary) for 32nd notes:

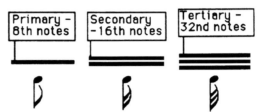

Beams make the reading of complex rhythms much easier since they are frequently used to enclose all rhythmic activity visually within a single beat. If we look at the code word Di-a-ton-ic, we can appreciate how the four 16th notes (enclosed within the beams) are easier to read than those written with separate flags:

In fact, note heads are really unnecessary when it comes to non-tonal, purely rhythmic notation; the eye tends to read only the beams and stems:

Rules:
A. Always beam all 8ths, 16ths, 32nds, etc. together *whenever* they occur within the same beat:

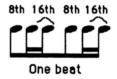

B. Secondary and tertiary beams must be broken when rests are involved within the same beat:

C. Regardless of whether the stems are up or down, secondary (and tertiary) beams are always placed on the inside of the beat, between the note head and the primary beam:

 Maxim #36: Beams serve many purposes in RN, two of which are: (1) the reduction of time it takes to write out individual flags; and (2) the visual grouping of complex rhythms.

2.15 Alignment

Alignment is a notational process that graphically permits the writing of more than one part at the same time. In a conductor's full score there can be as many as 60 separate instrument parts per page, and each part is vertically aligned beat by beat so the conductor can "see" which notes are to occur simultaneously. When more than one dancer is moving at the same time, their parts must be aligned as well so that is clear which actions are happening simultaneously. The process is quite similar in RN and LN.

The simplest form of "multi-part" writing is the duet. Below are two separate parts, each with the same number of beats:

As written above, a percussionist would read the parts separately, **A** followed by **B**. To indicate that the parts should be played together, the proper aligning of the parts "to each other" is required. This is called **scoring**.

Below we will score parts A and B, along with a dance duet consisting of movement that follows the rhythms precisely.

Step 1 – Make a score by drawing two single staff lines and connect them with a bracket on the left side. The bracket tells the performer to read both parts simultaneously. Without the bracket, the parts would be read separately:

Two staves are drawn side-by-side and connected by a single line at the starting position to show that the choreography is to be shared by two dancers. Note that the connecting line is an extension of the top of the doubleline:

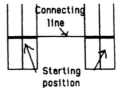

Step 2 – Sequentially number each beat in both parts. Lightly write a #1 between the staff lines to the right of the bracket – this will be the position of the first beat. The quarter note of part A is placed directly over the #1 on the top line with stem up. The 8th rest of part B is placed directly under the quarter:

Dancer **A** takes a full-beat step at the start of beat #1. Dancer **B** can't move until an 8th later (ber) so a hold sign on both feet IS MANDATORY at the start of beat #1:

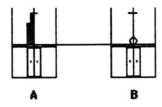

Step 3 – In part B, the 8th note (ber) must now be placed *to the right* of the quarter in part A since it occurs one half beat *after* the quarter note. Stems are uniformly placed up on the top part and down on the bottom. Since the quarter note lasts the entire length of the first beat, nothing will be written above the new 8th note:

Dancer **B's** step may now be notated on the "&" of beat #1. This step will cancel the hold sign as the weight transfers to the left foot and the right foot releases from the floor:

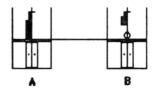

Step 4 – Beat 2 is exactly the same as beat one in both parts so the alignment should look identical for both beats:

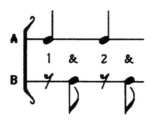

A transfers weight while **B** again waits for "ber". A hold sign must be used on the left foot until cancelled by the step onto the right:

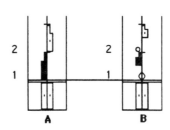

Step 5 – Beat 3 becomes more complicated as the four 16th notes in part B must align with the two 8ths in part A. Imagine a grid, each column equalling one 16th: the notes are evenly placed to the right:

Following the rhythmic scheme, the steps for B will be twice as fast as those for A:

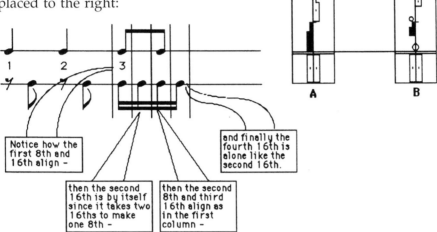

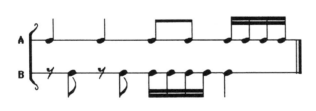

Step 6 – Finally, the 4th beat places the four 16ths from part A against the quarter from part B. Note that the double bar line signifies completion:

A hold sign is used on the left foot of dancer A as the right closes to "place middle" alongside the left on the last 16th. As written, dancer B ends standing on the left foot only:

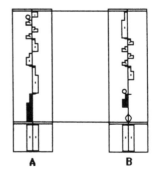

Notice that in your final copy, the beat numbers (between the staff lines) are removed.

Note that the RN double bar line signifies completion, and that LN uses another connecting line at the end of the score to join the two staves. This line is drawn out from the bottom of the double bar which closes the score:

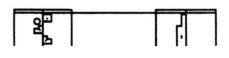

Finally, LN uses symbols to denote the gender of the performer. Any of these may be written at the bottom of a staff to indicate which dancer is to perform which part:

Maxim #37: Alignment is the notational process that graphically permits the writing of more than one part at a time.

   2.16   RN: small repeats

Repetition is a powerful force in music, whether the simple repeating of a single one-beat rhythm or the repeating of a 60-measure section of a symphony. Notationally, there are just a few symbols which act as musical 'ditto' marks, used both as time-savers (when writing) and visual aids (when performing). In the following example, a professional musician would prefer to read the **lower** rather than the **upper** notation since once the 1st measure has been played, the constant re-printing of the same measure makes it possible to get lost. The numbered repeat symbols allow the players' attention to focus on the "number" of repetitions which are to be played:

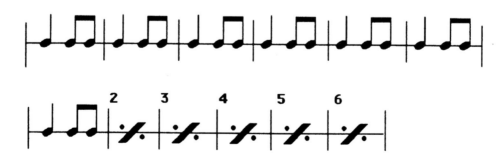

Below is a demonstration of the most commonly used repetitional devices, divided into small, medium and large groupings under the following guidelines:

1. The single note repeat symbol (slanted bars) may be used beat by beat for an entire measure. If that measure were to be repeated, the one-measure repeat symbol would be used instead. Note: the number of slashes corresponds to the number of beams in the notes to be repeated.

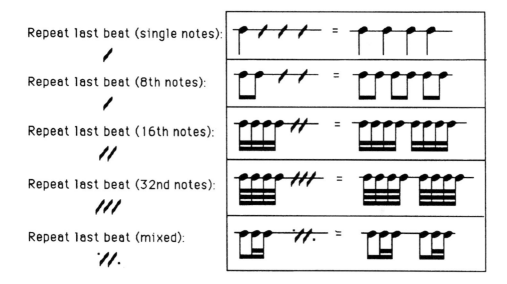

2. The single measure repeat symbol (slanted bar with dots) may be used measure by measure until the repetition is interrupted by a new rhythm.

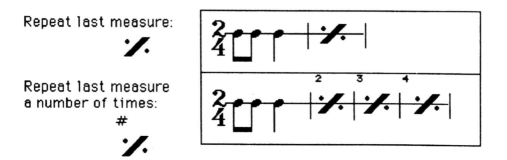

3. The 2-measure repeat symbol (slanted bar with dots across bar line) may be used every two measures until the 2-bar repetition is interrupted by a new rhythm.

4. The multi-measure repeat symbol (book-ended double bars with dots) may enclose from 4 to 8 measures at a time.

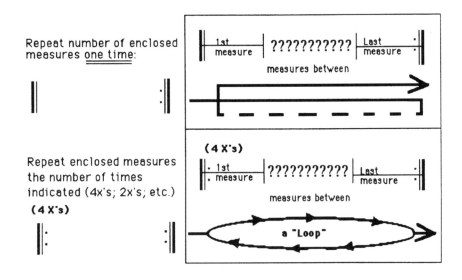

2.17   LN: small repeats

As with RN, repeat signs can be used in LN when repetition is present in the movement. However, since movement can be repeated on both sides of the body, there are two versions of the standard repeat sign:

The two signs are used inside the staff in three ways: (1) to repeat individual beats within a measure; (2) to repeat whole measures; and (3) to repeat a series of measures. These are referred to as beat repeats and bar repeats.

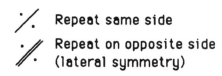

Repeat same side

Repeat on opposite side (lateral symmetry)

Maxim #38: Regardless of the repeat sign and its instructions, all repeat signs in RN and LN refer back *to the last written notation* and NEVER to a previous repeat sign.

Beat repeats are written on the center line of the staff and are used when one or more beats within a measure are to be repeated. For example, if a complicated running pattern occurs on beat one in 4/4, the notation would be easier to write AND READ using repeat signs on beats 2, 3, and 4:

This notation is easier to write and read . . . .

than this notation which is visually too complex.

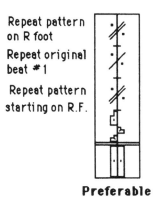

Preferable   **Less preferable**

If a pattern were one which alternated feet from beat to beat, the *opposite side repeats* would be used as shown here.

Repeat pattern on R foot

Repeat original beat #1

Repeat pattern starting on R.F.

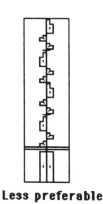

Preferable   **Less preferable**

By positioning the repeat sign mid-way between two beats, a **"2-beat repeat"** will occur:

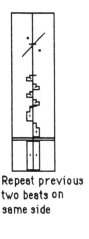
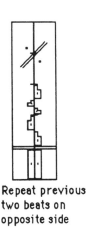

Repeat previous two beats on same side

Repeat previous two beats on opposite side

When entire measures are to be repeated on the same or opposite side, the repeat sign is placed directly in the center of the number of measure(s) to be repeated:

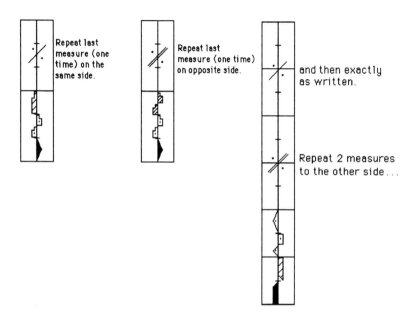

▬◖ Maxim #39: Repeat signs inside the staff are always centered in the amount of material (beats or measures) to be repeated.

To repeat an entire measure a number of times in succession:

(1) Two repeat signs are placed in positions *outside* of the staff, *lower left* and *upper right*. (Note that they are drawn horizontally and do not slant.)

(2) Extension lines are drawn on the inside of the top and bottom of the measure as shown, which "bracket" the measure to be repeated.

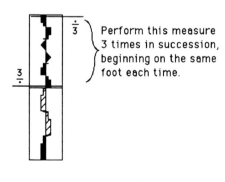

(3) The inside dots of the repeat signs are replaced by a number indicating *the total number of times the bracketed measure will be performed.*

When repeating measures as shown above, the measure numbers of each repeat are shown to the left in parentheses to aid the reader in keeping track of how many repeats there are in the overall composition.

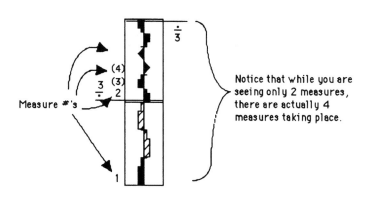

Notice that while you are seeing only 2 measures, there are actually 4 measures taking place.

 The ad lib. sign can be used in place of a number in repeat signs. It literally means repeat *ad libitum* (with liberty). An ad lib. repeat means the number of repetitions is left open to the performer.

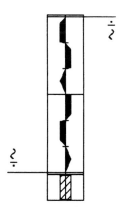

Perform as many of these circular patterns as you wish.

More information on repeat signs (the use of measure numbers in repeats inside the staff, large sectional repeats, and variations in repeated material) is presented in chapter 8.12.

RHYTHMIC APPLICATIONS

 ### 2.18 Code Words: derived "Diatonic"

When permutated, the code word rhythm "Di-a-ton-ic" yields the beginnings of more complex sub-beat rhythms. Notice how each rhythm "looks and sounds" different from the others.

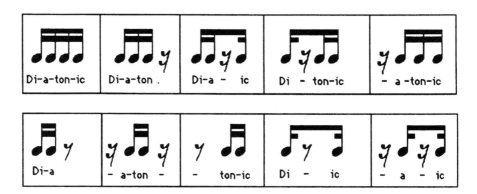

Use 16th Hand-els and slowly tap out the syllables of each beat. With practice, it will not be necessary to read each note individually: rather, *the eye will see the composition of the whole beat at once and the **sound** of each rhythm will be immediately associated with the **look** of each beat.*

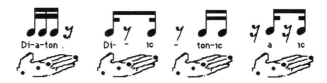

Make 4 flash cards for each code word below, but DO NOT mix them with the cards from Chapter 1. PRACTICE THEM SLOWLY at first, and gradually increase speed.

2.19   Metric Re-grouping

During the choreographic process, it is sometimes necessary to take a movement phrase which is in a 2-beat meter and try it in a 3 or 4-beat meter to see how a new metric pattern might influence the character of the movement. Re-grouping is a similar process which allows for the placement of an original rhythmic phrase (whether metered or non-metered) into a new time signature. During the procedure, the rhythm is not to be changed from its original composition. Rather, the original rhythm is maintained in the new time signature. Below is a non-metered, eight-beat rhythmic phrase, which we will call "the original".

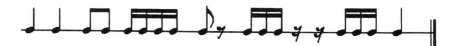

Without meter, the beats in the original are performed with *equal value.*
To change the character of the original, we'll put it in a "2":

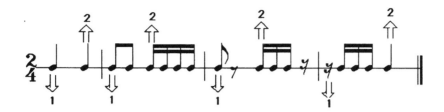

The 1st, 3rd, 5th, and 7th beats of the original have now become
downbeats while the 2nd, 4th, 6th and 8th are now anacrusic. Fall/
Recover; Down/Over.

In 4-beat time, there will be half the number of downbeats present:

Compare the 2/4 and the 4/4 examples above: the 3rd and 7th beats
(which were downbeats in 2/4) have become metacrusic in 4/4. The 2/4
feels 'weightier' than the 4/4, or more grounded. The 4/4 example feels
"longer" or more sustained as there is a greater distance *between* downbeats.

Now the original in 3/4:

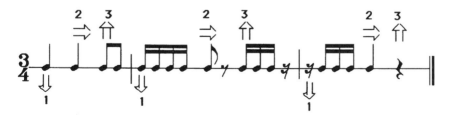

There are now more downbeats than the 4/4, but fewer than the 2/4. The
four 16th notes on beat #4 now fall on a downbeat. Notice also that a
quarter rest has been added at the end to complete the last measure.

Set a metronome to 60 and try walking the following LN scores which match the rhythms of the above re-groupings. Move in a circle. Do each example repeatedly at first, then do all three examples together in a non-stop chain from 2/4 through 4/4 and start again. Chant the rhythm out loud as you move, or have a partner chant it for you. Make sure the sound of the rhythm and the movement are synchronized. The "feel" of each re-grouping should be different. Allow yourself to sense the characteristic of each meter, with its own sequence of crusic, metacrusic and anacrusic beats. Also, which of these beats has been modified by the rhythmic activity (see 2.5).

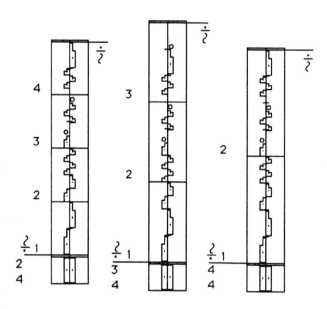

Cue #7

 MOVEMENT APPLICATIONS

2.20   Movement Clusters in 2/4, 3/4 and 4/4

The following clusters show movement patterns which require the characteristics of a particular meter in order to be performed correctly. As in Chapter 1, allow the eye to "scan" each cluster, identifying them through visual recognition.

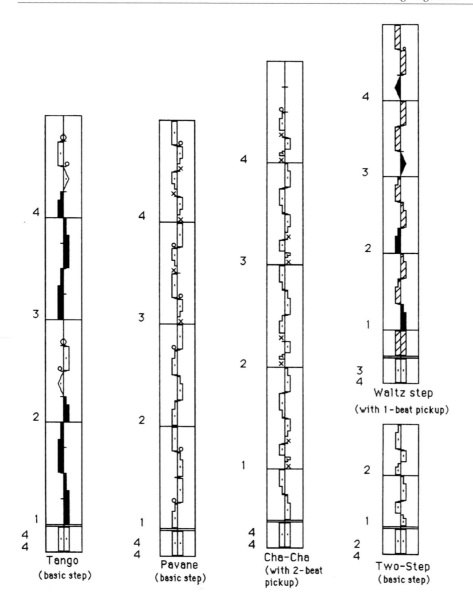

Tango
(basic step)

Pavane
(basic step)

Cha-Cha
(with 2-beat
pickup)

Waltz step
(with 1-beat pickup)

Two-Step
(basic step)

2.21   Conducting Patterns

The conductor is the dancer of the orchestra. While the other musicians harness their movements into the motions necessary to produce sound on their instruments, the conductor does not make sound per se but rather **encourages** it through the visual medium of **expressive movement**.

The conductor conveys tempo, meter, expression and dynamics to the orchestra and does so *visually*. The right or "beating" arm rhythmically describes visual metric patterns and tempo changes while the left or "expression" arm demonstrates those non-rhythmic properties such as expression and dynamics. Regardless of the number of players in the orchestra and their distance to the podium, they can play together because they can "see" the conductor's beat.

The Preparatory Stroke. The conductor must give a preparatory stroke that is one beat long, which must convey *tempo* (by its speed), *dynamics* (by its size), and *expression* (by its energy). The preparatory stroke is a visual anacrusis, a curving line which pulls up through space, alerting the players to focus and BREATHE together. This 'breath' is done by all players, regardless of whether they play flute or piano – it is a psychological action of unification. It is the conductor's way of saying: "Ready?".

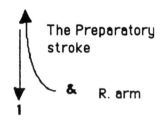

The conductor's arm then follows a visually metric pattern that repeats itself at the start of each new measure. *Within* each measure, the individual beats are clearly displayed by the directional changes of the moving arm. This is an important concept to grasp, that *a change of direction in a moving path will visually articulate a new beat or rhythm*. That is why the members of an orchestra can follow a conductor: they watch for each new change of direction.

Below are displayed the basic patterns for beating in 2, 3, and 4. Practice them for a while right now. Count to 2 slowly over and over in a moderate tempo and trace the pattern in the air in front of you. Then try it in 3 and the 4, counting out loud as you do. Pretend that your arm and

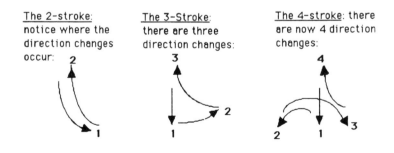

wrist are moving through water – feel the resistance as you trace the curves.

Notice as you practice that the directions of the strokes correspond exactly to the crusic, metacrusic, and anacrusic beat qualities. Beat #1 goes down; beat #2 moves horizontally "inward"; beat #3 moves outward horizontally to the opposite side; and beat #4 moves in a rising, lifting motion. **THIS IS NO ACCIDENT:** With each new measure, the conductor reminds the players to perform with "directionality" in their metric flow.

CHAPTER WRAP

2.22 RN Etudes

Chant the top line and clap or walk the bottom.

#5

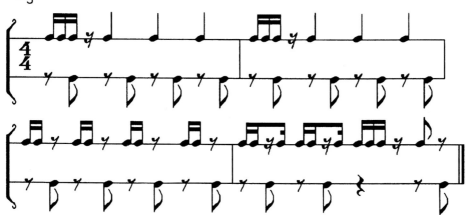

2.23 LN Etudes

Phrase-shifting

Learn the non-metered original phrase below, then perform it in the different time signatures at the right. Be careful to observe the different crusic and non-crusic beats, which will change the dynamics of the movement in each time signature.

Cue #8

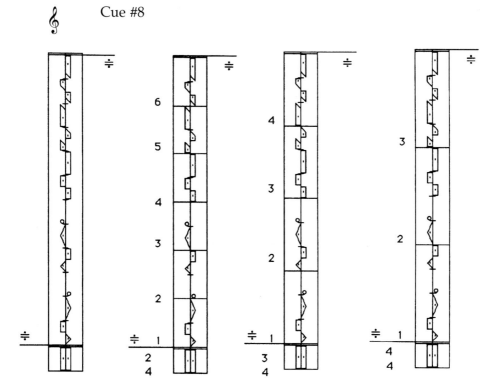

2.24   More Tricky Rhythms

Be aware of the preparations and watch the metric characteristics. Should you wish to repeat, omit the preparation space and start at the beginning of the 1st measure.

Remember: read these "for the rhythm".

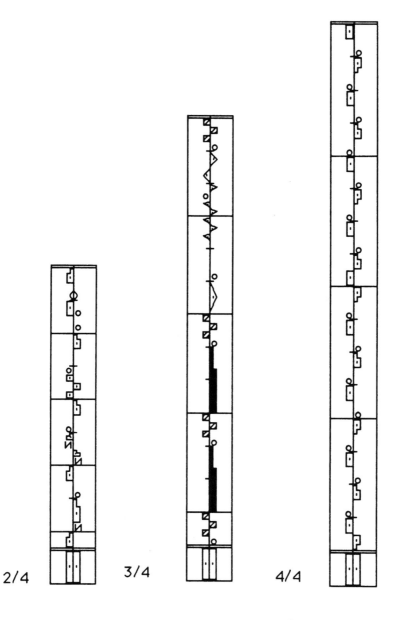

2/4   3/4   4/4

2.25   Suggested Assignments

Make 24 new code word flash cards for each derived diatonic rhythm (two cards for each). Practice them separately from the original cards, using 16th 'Hand-els' exclusively. Start at a slow tempo and progress steadily. Remember, speed is not as important as accuracy.

- Re-group the following "original" into 2/4, 3/4, and 4/4, adding rests at the ends **only** if the original runs out of rhythm before the last measure ends. There are 14 beats in the "original": circle each complete beat before writing the assignment. Use a single-line staff for each solution.

- Align parts A & B into a duet in 2/4. Make your own score paper. Number the beats before starting. Place the time signature *between* the two parts and write all stems up in the top part and all stems down in the bottom.

 Take the above alignment exercise (parts A and B) and choreograph a walking duet. Experiment with complementary or opposing directions in space.

- Prepare the Phrase-shifting etude (2.23) as a trio, each person taking a different meter. Have a 4th person clap a metrically neutral 12 beats. Be certain that each dancer's phrase captures its particular metric characteristics.

- Rewrite the following "2-Step" using repeat signs. There is more than one possible solution.

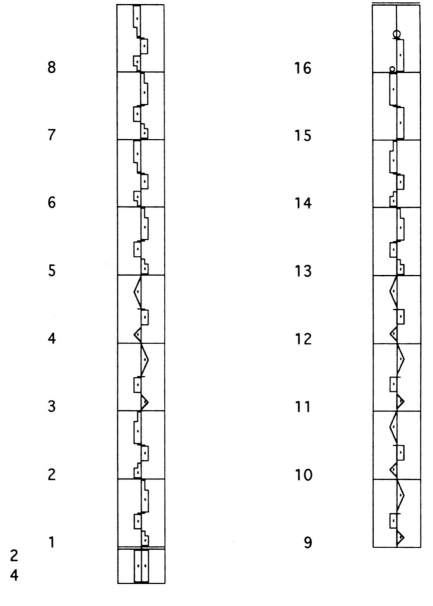

- Bring in a list of 20 life examples of actions which require a preparation (pick-up). For example, the twist of a door knob before the push to open the door; the forward lean prior to standing up from a chair; etc.

3

FIRST EXPANSIONS

RHYTHMIC CONCEPTS

3.1 Dotted Values

In Chapter 1, you were introduced to the notes and rests of the Basic Orders of Values (BOV): the whole, half, quarter, 8th, 16th, and 32nd. To find the values that lie *between* these binary values, the original notes/rests are "dotted". When a dot is placed to the right and slightly higher than the center of a note or rest, it indicates the **addition** of the *next smaller value* in the BOV **to** the dotted symbol. Or, a note or rest when dotted will equal **3** of the **next smallest value** of the BOV:

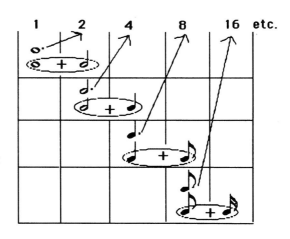

Therefore, a dot:
 adds a half to a whole:

 adds a quarter to a half:

 adds an 8th to a quarter:

 adds a 16th to an 8th:

Unlike the binary values that are divided evenly by 2, dotted (ternary) values, whether notes or rests, are divided evenly by 3 without a fraction:

The following table displays all dotted values through the 16th *as they relate to a quarter note beat assignment*:

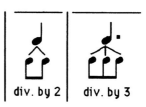

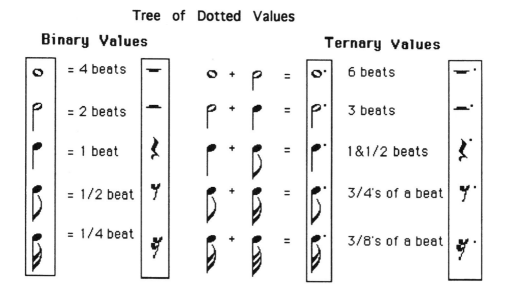

Tree of Dotted Values

The Ternary Series. To calculate the relationship between dotted notes and the BOV, the Ternary Numerical Progression (TNP) is extremely helpful.

1 3 6 12 24 48 96   96 48 24 12 6 3 1

The principle: Any single dotted value equals 3 of the next plain shorter value in the BOV, and then 6 of the second next plain shorter value, then 12 of the third next plain shorter value, etc. So one dotted whole note/rest equals the following number of plain smaller values:

Maxim #40: Dots are added to notes and rests to create ternary values (divisible by 3 without a fraction). A dot indicates the addition of the next smaller value in the BOV to the dotted symbol.

3.2 Phrases and Cadences

Dance and music, as human creations, must breathe on a regular basis. Performers need to breathe. Audiences require time to reflect (the brain needs time to convert patterns of motion and sound into perceived designs). Music and dance both breathe through *phrases*, and reflect or stop at *cadences*. Phrases in traditional Western music are normally four measures in length and end in cadences which either (1) reflect and continue (mid or semi-cadence), or (2) terminate (closing or final cadence). In the simple round "Row, Row, Row your Boat", the phrasing and cadences are clearly evident. On examination, the lyric reveals two phrases which, when combined, create a "verse" representing a complete musical statement. Each phrase contains 8 beats and is therefore "metrically" in balance. This balance is reinforced by the rhyme "stream/ dream":

1st phrase					mid-cadence

Row   row   row your boat   gently down the stream;
1   2   3   4   5   6   7   8

2nd phrase					closing cadence

Merrily, merrily, merrily, merrily, life is but   a   dream.
9   10   11   12   13   14   15   16

The function of any phrase is to gather together into larger thoughts the individual elements of rhythm, beat and meter. Therefore, the primary goal when reading RN and LN is to transcend the individual elements and perceive the "gestalt", the over-view, the larger statement as quickly as possible. In other words, *beat, rhythm and meter exist only as tools for the creation of phrases*. Creative score reading entails discovering the meaning and length of music and dance phrases and ways of moving **through** them. We can see a parallel to this in poetry. A poet would 'scan' the above song lyric in an attempt to understand the "poetic feet" and where the real grammatical emphasis lies. In the Greek poetic "feet" described below, note that long syllables receive greater stress than short syllables:

Greek Name	Stresses	Sounds like:
Iambic	● ━━	Va-VOOM
Anapestic	● ● ━━	Inter-ACT
Trochaic	━━ ●	ROOST-er
Dactylic	━━ ● ●	WHEEL-barrow
Spondaic	━━ ━━	MOON-BEAM
Phyric	● ●	Mom-my
Amphibrachic	● ━━ ●	Um-BREL-la
Bacchic	● ━━ ━━	Re-MEM-BRANCE
Cretic	━━ ● ━━	ROW your BOAT
Choriambic	━━ ● ● ━━	HOW could I KNOW?
Mollossus	━━ ━━ ━━	TREE-LINED STREET
Tribrachic	● ● ●	Motorboat

The children's song above can now be analyzed for its poetic feet:

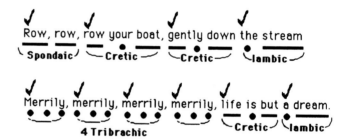

The syntax is now clearer. For example, the oft-sung "lifeisbutadream", is actually "life is but – a *dream*". The emphasis isn't on life but on DREAM. The delineation between the last two feet makes all the difference. But we still need to find the longer line in the phrase and we do this by asking what the "meaning" of the line is.

Most people sing the song by pounding out the beat and slugging the words: **ROW ROW ROW** your <u>**Boat**</u> **GENTLY Down** the **STREAM**. In this version, phrasing is lacking. The root phrase is actually "Row your boat *gently* down the stream". So, to phrase the song **musically**, pound less on the beats, and refrain from breathing between boat and gently. The difference is subtle:

Row, row, row your boat gently down the stream

The phrase then runs from Row to Stream with a longer, more lyrical line. This example also illustrates how phrasing adds subtlety to raw meter. The amount of crusic energy in downbeats is not always the same, due to the meaning and length of phrases.

It is also important to recognize when there is repetition in a phrase. The "Row-rows" at the start of the song should not be sung identically. The function of repetition in art is to create increasing **OR** decreasing emphasis. In this case, each repeat should become progressively more emphatic – not necessarily louder – just more emphatic: Row, **row, row.**

Finding the phrases in poetry, music, and dance begins with an examination of the components, the goal being an understanding of the greater meaning. Subtle modifications between the notation and its performance usually occur in the attainment of that goal. In this, the discovery of phrasing and fresh interpretation go hand-in-hand.

 Maxim #41: Phrases gather together into larger thoughts the individual elements of rhythm, beat and meter. Cadences help phrases "breathe" by introducing pauses (mid-cadences) or conclusions (closing cadences).

3.3 Pickups: internal

Internal pickups are usually "echoes" of an external pickup, which add a sense of familiarity to a phrase through the creation of a rhythmic "motif" (the pickup itself). In the U.S. National Anthem, we can see internal pickups at work:

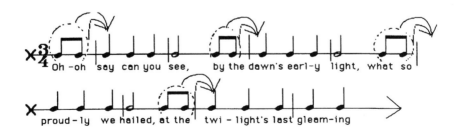

There are two phrases in the opening:

"Oh say can you see by the dawn's early light"; and
"What so proudly we hailed at the twilight's last gleaming".

Measures 3, 5, and 7 are each preceded by echoes of the original external pickup, lending emphasis to these downbeats AND a rhythmic familiarity:

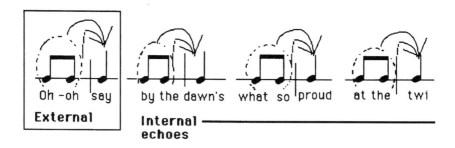

Measures 2, 4, 6, and 8 are **not** preceded by internal pickups and do not therefore receive additional emphasis. This alternating pattern of a *stressed measure* followed by a *non-stressed measure* gives the song its **pacing.**

- Without meter the 1st phrase would smoothly rise to its cadence:

Oh say can you see by the dawn's early light

- Set in a "3", the meter tends to defeat the natural rise of the phrase by constantly dragging it down to "1". At baseball games, the song is often sung in this way, with too much pounding. This is considered extremely *un-musical*:

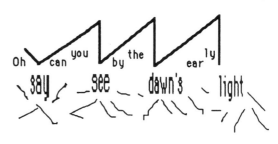

- Downbeats which are not preceded by pickups will tend to be lighter in quality, receiving less crusic energy.

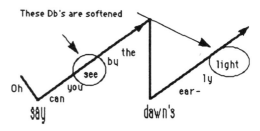

These Db's are softened

- To stretch the phrase further, the downbeat of the 3rd measure should not receive as much emphasis as the opening as it lies along the path between opening and cadence:

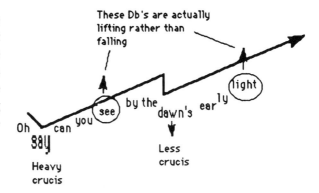

Finally, consider the melody and how its shape supports the *phrasing* of the lyrics through combinations of low and high notes, to support phrasing through aural shape. This is also true of movement and its rises and falls throughout a dance.

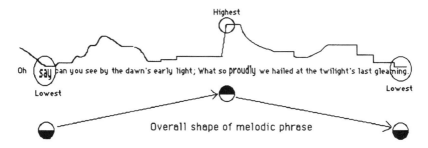

 Maxim #42:   Internal pickups can occur as echoes of an external pickup. They help to shape phrasing and create a rhythmic 'familiarity'.

3.4   Articulations and Accents

Every sound involves Attack (beginning), Sustain (duration), and Release (finish). Saying the word "Help" gives us the sense of this: the attack is formed in the consonant "H", which is followed by the sustaining vowel group "el", the release being formed by the consonant "p". By altering the length of the sustain and intensity of the attack and release, the word can take on different meanings: you're lost in New York and just need a little "**help**", or you're being chased by angry bees and need some

Heeeeeeeeeellllllllp!

Articulation is the musical term that refers to the way in which the elements of attack, sustain, and release are combined. Any given sound can be articulated in many different ways. Below are three common articulations:

- **Staccato.** A single note is shortened or "clipped" by roughly 50% depending on tempo. The placement of a dot over or under the note head (opposite the stem) creates a noticeable "gap" between this note and the next, *as if a rest were present.* Staccato performance therefore adds *lift* to any note.

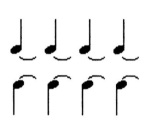

- **Legato.** There is no special symbol for legato articulation, as it is considered standard for all non-modified note values. It entails smooth and connected performance, with *no break in the sound or movement between notes.* Sometimes, to stress the legato effect, a shortened tie is used to encourage performance with extra connectedness.

- **Tenuto.** Notes become "pressed" by adding a dash over or under the note head (opposite the stem). The effect resembles speaking emphatically, the difference between saying "I hate you" and *"I HATE YOU"*.

Cue #9

 In movement, similar articulations may be achieved. Lightly staccato movement is indicated by separations between actions. In the support columns, this will will involve hold signs. (See 3.5 & 3.7 for staccato actions for the arms and legs.)

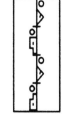

Clipped movement, with gaps between actions.

Staccato

As with RN, *Legato* is considered the normal articulation for all movements which appear continuously one after the other on the staff.

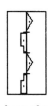

Connected actions, following one another without interruption.

Legato

The equivalent of *Tenuto* in movement terms may be "press", the quality of performing an action with more strength and sustainment than normal. To experience "press", move your arm as if you were encountering some steady resistance. "Press" may be applied to movement by any part of the body; its symbol is

Lengthened walks forward with a sense of extra strength and sustainment.

Tenuto

Accents (moveable crusis). Accents deal with the element of attack, and affect the degree of crusic energy focussed in a note.

Light Strong Forceful

There are three types of accent: light, strong, and forceful. Accents affect both the attack of a given note and its volume relative to the other notes around it. (Rests are never accented.) An accented note will generally be performed with greater volume than the current dynamic marking indicates, giving it added force, sharpness, and crusic energy. Any note in any position within a measure can be accented, in effect becoming crusic. The accent symbol affects the attack of one specified note value **only** and does not "carry over" to an adjacent note. By combining articulations and accents, we arrive at a wide variety of single note productions:

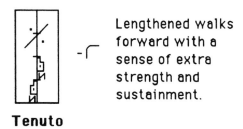

Note: To indicate a phrase of continuous accents, the term *Simili* is placed after the first accent in the phrase and all subsequent notes will be accented.

TABLE OF ARTICULATIONS AND ACCENTS

Type of Articulation

Type of Accent	Staccato - Short and sharp	Legato - Smooth and connected	Tenuto - Sustained, with pressure
Normal	𝅘𝅥	𝅘𝅥	𝅘𝅥
Strong	> 𝅘𝅥	> 𝅘𝅥	> 𝅘𝅥
Forceful	∧ 𝅘𝅥 ∨ 𝅘𝅥	∧ 𝅘𝅥 ∨ 𝅘𝅥	∧ 𝅘𝅥 ∨ 𝅘𝅥

Note: The above table indicates only a small selection of accents and articulations available: professional musicians need at least 20 accents at their disposal for every possible note.

Other highly dramatic types of attack combine accent with dynamics: the Sforzando (*Sfz*), Sforzando-piano (*Sfp*), and Forte-piano (*fp*). (See 6.5 for more information on dynamics.) All three are meant to surprise and startle, with an extremely loud and forceful attack. Sfp and fp will immediately (as fast as possible) drop to piano (soft).

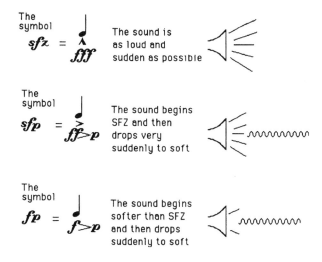

The symbol *sfz* = 𝅘𝅥 ∧ *fff*   The sound is as loud and sudden as possible

The symbol *sfp* = 𝅘𝅥 > *ff>p*   The sound begins SFZ and then drops very suddenly to soft

The symbol *fp* = 𝅘𝅥 *f>p*   The sound begins softer than SFZ and then drops suddenly to soft

Maxim #43: Articulation and accent alter the way in which a sound is attacked, and how long and with how much energy it is sustained.

MOVEMENT CONCEPTS

3.5 Accents

Just as accents can be used in RN to add crusic energy or emphasis, accents are used in LN to add extra attack to any single movement, or series of actions. The LN accent is crescent-shaped, and its point is directed at the action that is to be emphasized. As with relationship pins, accent marks are placed in the ancillary column for steps.

In the following three examples, crusic energy is located in the modern dance triplet in different places and to different degrees.

a.

Example (a) shows a standard traveling balancé (triplet), with the crusic energy being slightly enhanced due to the drop of weight on the Db.

b.

In example (b), the amount of crusic energy in the step on the Db is *increased* due to the presence of the accent. The dancer will show a stronger sense of giving in to gravity, of moving into the floor on this step. The accent renders "1" by far the strongest count in the measure. It serves to *heighten the attributes* of the first action, which is the lowering of the center of weight.

c.

Example (c) is both similar to and different from (b). It is similar in that the accent serves to heighten the attributes of one action. However, since the action on count 3 involves rising, it is the raising of the center of weight that is highlighted here. In performance, this might give a feeling of "suspension" to count 3, as it heightens the anacrusic feeling.

Accents of extraordinary strength are indicated in an LN score with shading. Unlike RN, which demands one accent symbol per note (or the use of the term *simili* for contiguous accents), LN may use a bracket to indicate that several actions are accented, and to clarify where the ac-
cented sequence begins and ends. In
these examples, each arm gesture
in the series will be performed with
additional crusic energy. In example (b) only the 2nd action would
be accented without the bracket.

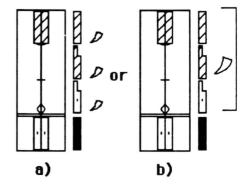

a)   **b)**

Note: Arm gestures are written outside the staff and are covered in 3.8.

When contact with the floor (or other object or body part) occurs, a shaded accent produces sound, and may be referred to as an *audible accent*. The step in count #3 to the right therefore becomes a stamp.

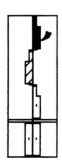

   Maxim #44:   Accents heighten the attributes of specific actions, stressing them and rendering them of special importance in a movement sequence. Strong accents are shaded.

3.6   Leg Gestures

Rudolf Laban, the creator of the dance notation that has come to be known as Labanotation in North America, UK, and Australasia (and known as Kinetography Laban in continental Europe), also worked to im-
prove the quality of verbal communication between dancers. Part of his enormous contribution to the field is a lexicon of words that provides dancers with a vocabulary of shared meanings. Using Laban's terms, people can discuss and describe dance in clearer and more specific ways, and understand more precisely what is meant by the communications of others.

One of Laban's basic distinctions is between supports and gestures. In contrast to a support, a gesture is any movement that *does not bear weight*. Supports and gestures, separate kinds of actions, are placed in separate columns on the LN staff.

The columns for supports and gestures of the legs are labelled below:

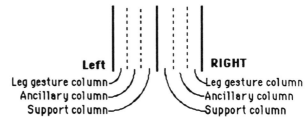

Left

Leg gesture column
Ancillary column
Support column

RIGHT

Leg gesture column
Ancillary column
Support column

> **Maxim #45:** A gesture is an action that does not bear weight.

For the moment, we will concentrate on leg gestures that are straight, with no bend in the knee. Kicks in different directions and the ballet position *arabesque* are common examples of straight leg gestures. The *direction* of leg gestures is judged by comparing where the foot (the free end of the leg) is in relationship to the hip (the fixed end of the leg). The free end (the foot) can also be called "the extremity," and the fixed end (the hip) can be called the "point of attachment." If a leg gesture brings the foot in front of the hip, that leg gestures is "forward." If the foot is brought behind the hip (as in arabesque), the leg gesture is "back".

The *level* of the gesture is judged by using the same foot-to-hip analysis. In a leg gesture where the foot remains lower than the hip, the gesture is in low level. A mid-level leg gesture brings the foot to the same level as the hip. For a leg gesture in high level, the foot must rise to a level higher than the hip.

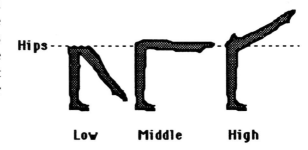

Hips

Low   **Middle**   **High**

> **Maxim #46:** The direction and level of leg gestures are determined by the relationship of the foot to the hip. The terms "free end" and "extremity" apply to the foot; "fixed end" and "point of attachment" apply to the hip.

Below are some examples of leg gestures in different directions and levels:

Walks forward followed by low forward gestures:

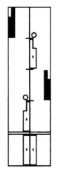

Plié in starting position. Two forward walks in relevé followed by a slow gesture of the right leg back (arabesque). The right foot should rise to the level of the hip:

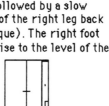

Battements (kicks) to side high, close. Make sure you understand the hold signs:

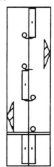

In the starting pos., the R. leg is lifted fwd. low. Cts. 1-4 are a slow circle of the leg (rond de jambe)

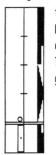

to the side and back. These are examples of legato leg gestures:

Slow lift of the left leg to fwd. middle (as in an adage):

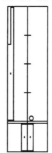

Low kicks to the fwd. diagonals, on relevé:

IMPORTANT: *Hold signs do not need to be used with leg gestures* since gestures do not involve the body's weight. A leg in the air will stay where it is until new notation describes its next action.

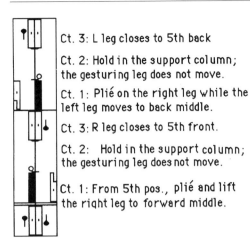

Ct. 3: L leg closes to 5th back

Ct. 2: Hold in the support column; the gesturing leg does not move.

Ct. 1: Plié on the right leg while the left leg moves to back middle.

Ct. 3: R leg closes to 5th front.

Ct. 2: Hold in the support column; the gesturing leg does not move.

Ct. 1: From 5th pos., plié and lift the right leg to forward middle.

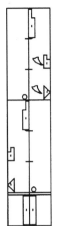

Quick gestures of the leg to the side and forward, with "held time" between the actions: the gesture occurs on 'Num' and the hold occurs on 'ber'.

These are examples of lightly staccato leg gestures. In measure 2, the accents sharpen the staccato effect.

 Maxim #47: Hold signs are not necessary for leg gestures because they do not take weight.

3.7 The Step–Gesture Rule

One of the advantages of Labanotation is that it is based on a system of *movement analysis*. This means that the rules that guide Labanotation are dictated by the needs and requirements of the body in action. While other systems of dance notation concentrate on picturing the different shapes the body achieves as it dances, Labanotation reveals the mechanics of what actually occurs as the body moves.

One example of the movement analysis inherent in the system is the *step–gesture rule*, concerning the timing of steps followed by leg gestures. The rule reflects the mechanics of what actually happens as a person takes a step. All their body weight is not transferred immediately; taking a step is a process. A step begins when a foot makes contact with the floor, and weight starts to move onto the new support. The step will not be completed until the entire weight of the body comes to rest on the new support. This takes time to accomplish, even when fast.

The step–gesture rule simply states that a step and a leg gesture may not happen at the same time. *Leg gestures can begin half-way through the process of taking a step,* by which time the weight will have transferred suffi-ciently onto the new support to allow the other leg to perform an action in the air.

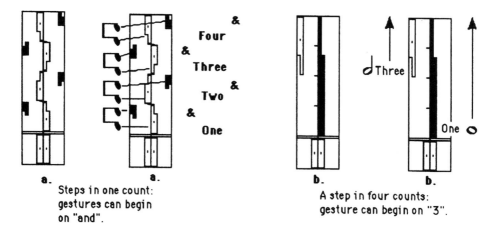

a.   a.
Steps in one count:
gestures can begin
on "and".

b.   b.
A step in four counts:
gesture can begin on "3".

Note here in example (c) that the leg gesture is drawn to fill the entire starting
position space. Since the starting position is
a "static" position involving no transference of weight, the step-gesture rule does
not apply.

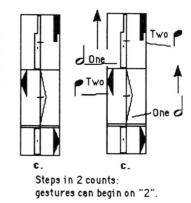

c.   c.
Steps in 2 counts:
gestures can begin on "2".

Here is an example of an
action that is physically impossible: none of these steps
with gestures can be per-
formed, since they ask that
a weight transfer onto one
leg begin at exactly the same
time as an action in the air
with the other.

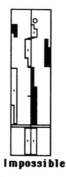

Impossible

The correct notation
would be:

Maxim #48: Steps and leg gestures can not happen at the
same time. Leg gestures can begin halfway through a step.

3.8 Arm Gestures

Gestures of the arms are written in the arm gesture columns which lie **outside** the staff. Since previously we have dealt with the use of columns **within** the three staff lines, the eye must now be "stretched" to read beyond the staff as well.

One column is left blank on either side of the staff, between the staff and the arm gesture columns. Actions of the torso and its parts can be written in these blank columns. For now, the blank spaces between the staff and the arm columns will make reading easier, separating movements of the arms from those of supports and leg gestures.

 Maxim #49: Arm gestures are written outside the staff, with one column left blank between the staff and arm gestures.

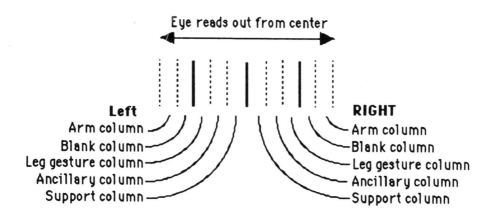

Arm gestures are movements of the arms that do not support weight. Like leg gestures, the direction and level of a movement for the arm is determined by comparing the **free end** (the hand) to the **fixed end** (the shoulder joint). When the hand is forward of and **higher** than the shoulder, the arm is gesturing FORWARD HIGH:

When the hand is at the side of and *at the same level as the shoulder*, the arm gesture is SIDE MIDDLE:

When the hand is behind and lower than the shoulder, the direction and level of the arm gesture is BACK LOW:

Maxim #50:   Judge the direction and level of arm gestures by comparing the free end (hand) to the fixed end (shoulder).

When not in use, the arm hangs naturally beneath the shoulder, which is **PLACE LOW**. When the arms are stretched directly over the shoulders, the arms are PLACE HIGH:

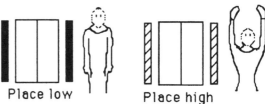

Place low   Place high

The 'place' direction for the arms, then, is along the line of the body when the dancer is standing vertically. Gestures in place do not extend the arms out into any direction in space, but they do reach to high and low levels. Place high reaches toward the ceiling; place low is toward the floor. Place middle for the arms brings the hands to the same level as the shoulders (the free end to the same place as the fixed end).

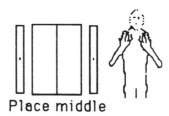

Place middle

Gestures for the arms are notated in much the same way as are leg gestures:

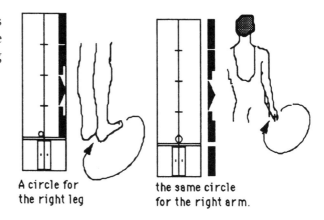

A circle for
the right leg

the same circle
for the right arm.

The Timing of Arm Gestures. Symbols in the arm column that follow one after the other represent actions that are fluid and continuous. When there is no time between symbols in the arm column (i.e., empty spaces that represent counts or parts of counts), the arm should move without interruption, passing from one destination to the next. Recall that this continuous dynamic is called "legato".

Note: The 'hair-line' gap between symbols is needed for visual separation; the gaps do not indicate any break in the movement flow.

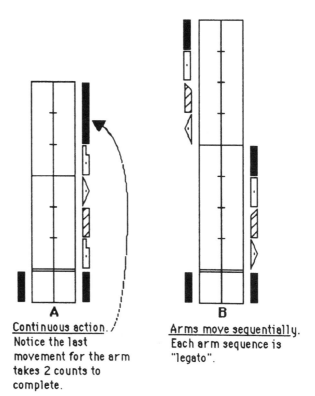

A

Continuous action.
Notice the last
movement for the arm
takes 2 counts to
complete.

B

Arms move sequentially.
Each arm sequence is
"legato".

Maxim #51:   Movements for the arms are smooth and continuous (legato) when there is no separation (i.e., time) between
direction symbols.

As with leg gestures, when there are no new symbols in the arm column,
for however many counts, the arm is understood to stay in the position
it was in previously. In the arm column, **no symbols** means **no movement**. Hold signs are therefore *not* necessary to keep the arm still.

In example B above, one arm will remain in place low while the other
moves.

 Maxim #52:   Hold signs are not needed in the arm columns.
No new symbols mean *no new movement*.

Symbols in the arm column that are separated by spaces (representing the
passage of counts or parts of counts) are distinct actions, often with a
more clipped dynamic (staccato). In the example below, the movements
of the arms are interrupted, separated into well-defined, individual
actions. Accents in counts 3 and 4 sharpen the staccato articulation.

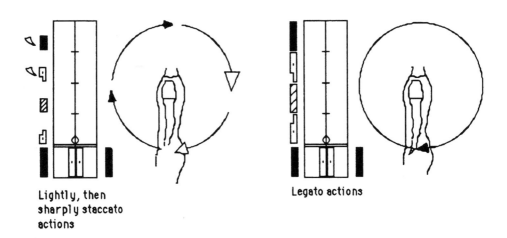

Lightly, then
sharply staccato
actions

Legato actions

 Maxim #53: Movements for the arms are separate and distinct
when there is empty space (i.e., time) between direction symbols.

Palm Facings. Palms are assumed to face in on all sagittal arm gestures.

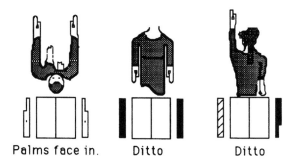

Palms face in.   Ditto   Ditto

The exception to this general rule are side arm gestures, where the palms are assumed to turn to face front as the arms rise to middle level.

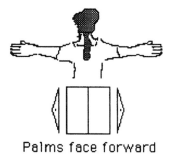

Palms face forward

Note: A wider range of palm facings will be discussed in Chapter 8.

3.9   Relationship Pins on Arm Gestures

Relationship pins can be used to indicate the placement of arm gestures vis-a-vis the body. In each example to the right, when the L. arm moves to the right, it crosses either in front of or behind the body.

L. arm is assumed to cross in front of the body as it reaches to the right side low

L. arm crosses behind the body. A pin is necessary to show this.

Pins can also clarify how the arms relate to each other.

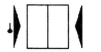

The L. arm crosses in front of the R. arm, as both arms cross in front of the body.

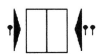

The R. arm crosses behind the left arm, as both arms cross behind the body.

Pins can modify forward, back, and place arm gestures, aligning the free end (the hand) with the center line of the body, rather than with the shoulder.

The arms reach fwd. middle of the center line of the body. Without the pins, the arms would be fwd. of the shoulders.

The R. arm reaches overhead, the hand aligned with the center of the body. Without the pin, the hand would be directly over the shoulder.

 Maxim #54:   Relationship pins can add detail as to how the arms relate to each other or to the body.

NOTATION

 3.10   RN: ties

Ties elongate rhythmic durations by *connecting* one note value to the next. Recall that dots **enlarge** one single value; ties connect two separate values.

The combined values of two tied notes are added together to create one larger, continuous duration. The new duration is a combination of the two tied notes; an action is begun on the first note and is "held through" the second. In effect, the second value loses its attack. Any two note values can be tied together, smaller to larger or larger to smaller.

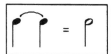   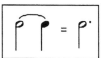   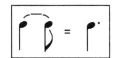

Ties are placed from note-head to note-head, opposite the direction of the stem. They should be oval-shaped and not a high, looping half-circle:

A tie may never connect more than one note to another note. If several notes are to be tied in a row, tie each one separately to the previous note:

Because ties and dots both elongate time values, they tend to be used interchangeably. As a general rule of thumb, *dots are preferred to ties* since one notational symbol is almost always easier to read than two or more. (Specific instances of this will be covered in later chapters.)

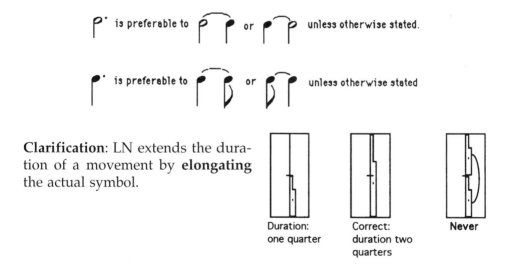

Clarification: LN extends the duration of a movement by **elongating** the actual symbol.

LN symbols can therefore transcend bar lines, being "stretched" across many measures. RN symbols CAN NOT do this. RN symbols can only extend across measures through the use of ties.

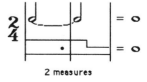

> Maxim #55:   In RN, ties combine any two notes into one new longer duration. Similar to dots, ties *connect* two note values while dots *enlarge* a single note.

3.11   Bows: ties, slurs, and phrases

Ties, slurs, and phrases all use essentially the same notation symbol: an arcing bow, written either vertically or horizontally.

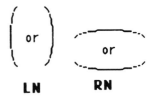

LN   RN

• In RN, **ties** involve combined timing, or "2 becomes 1". Two notes and only two are rhythmically combined resulting in the 2nd note losing its attack. (See 3.9 above.)

The most common use of a tie in LN occurs when a step and a turn are combined into one smooth action. (For a full discussion, see chapter 5.)

• **Slurring** is the act of blurring together the separate articulations of notes or movements. The timing of the actions within the slur is not affected.

Slurs occur in music notation when notes change pitch, moving up and down the 5-line tonal staff. Since the nature of musical slurring is tonal, slurs never occur in pure RN and are therefore not covered in depth in this book.

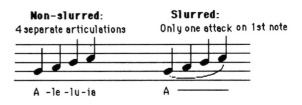

Non-slurred:
4 separate articulations   A –le –lu –ia

Slurred:
Only one attack on 1st note   A

Slurs occur in LN linking movements between different columns of the staff. Unlike music notation where many notes may be slurred together, LN permits the linking of only two actions at a time. The symbol for slurring in LN is the Zed Caret.

Zed Caret

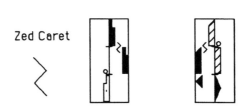

In these examples the leg gestures link (blur) into the subsequent steps, with as little articulation as possible.

• **Phrasing Bows** are frequently used as a visual indication of the length of a phrase. Although not always necessary, phrasing bows can serve as reminders to readers to be especially careful of the phrasing of a particular series of notes or movements. Bows place a special emphasis on the connectedness of notes/actions, and encourage the performer to move *through* the bow toward the end of the phrase.

In RN, phrase bows are drawn from note-head to note-head, but may be drawn higher to avoid contact with stems, beams, ties etc. Should ties be present within a phrase, they are included within the phrasing bow:

Finally, phrase bows in RN are sometimes written as dotted lines so as not to be confused with slurs:

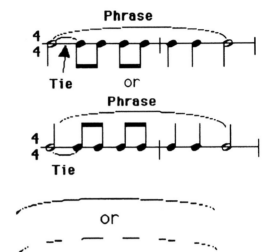

Generally used with arm and leg gestures, the LN vertical phrasing bow is placed in an adjacent, unoccupied column.

Correct

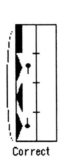
Correct

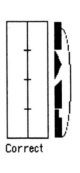
Correct

Two phrases
(complete ideas)
within one legato
series

Unlike ties and zed carets, phrasing bows may link any number of actions, even across measures.

 Maxim #56: Bows are linking tools that connect notes or actions in time or intent.

3.12   Rules: writing and beaming "by the beat"

The following rules cover "traditional" notational practices when working in Simple Time. They stress the importance of visually separating each beat whenever possible. There are exceptions described later.

(A) One time signature is placed at the start of a composition and another is not needed.

(B) Always beam beat by beat, one beat at a time. Never beam two beats together and NEVER beam across the center of a measure of 4/4 between beats 2 and 3.

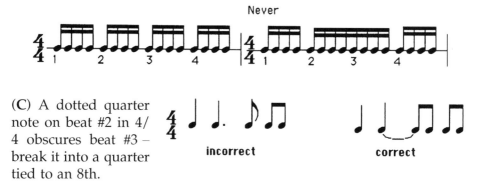

(C) A dotted quarter note on beat #2 in 4/4 obscures beat #3 – break it into a quarter tied to an 8th.

(D) Dotted quarter notes may be placed on upbeats ("bers") but dotted quarter rests must be broken down into an 8th rest/quarter rest to show the division of the beats:

(E) Never use two dotted quarter notes in a measure of 3/4: break the second into an 8th tied to a quarter to allow the eye to see beat #3 clearly:

(F) Dotted quarter notes and rests are equal to one and a half beats. Consequently, when they fall **on** a beat, they should be immediately followed by an 8th (or equivalent value) to visually "round off" a two-beat grouping:

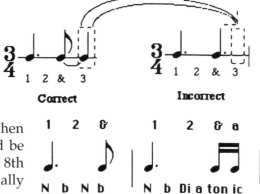

(G) When you approach the right margin of a page, NEVER "break" a measure in two pieces. Plan ahead so each measure is fully reproduced on the same line it began:

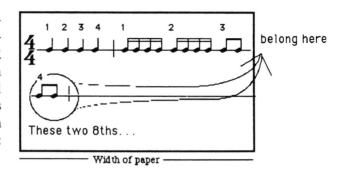

Note: The same holds true for LN scores when the top of the page is reached: never break a measure into 2 pieces.

3.13 RN: common errors

The following is a list of common errors made during the process of RN notation.

1. Barlines and stems should be exactly vertical and never slant:

2. Flags are always placed to the right of the notehead regardless of whether the stems are up or down:

3. Keep all notational symbols within proportion – none too small or too large.

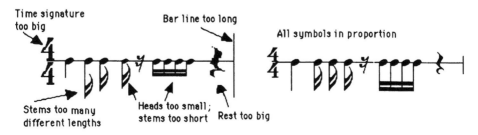

4. Once you have decided on a direction for stems (up or down), be consistent throughout the length of the part. Do not change stem direction whenever you feel like it.

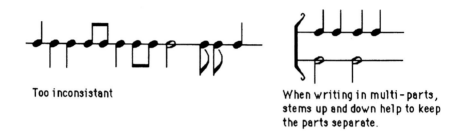

Too inconsistant

When writing in multi-parts, stems up and down help to keep the parts separate.

5. Don't cram notation symbols together – space them evenly across the page.

6. Make sure the alignment of multiple parts is EXACTLY vertical. (See 2.15.)

 3.14   LN: common errors

A. Forward and back direction symbols in the leg and arm gesture columns are drawn the same as those for the support columns: the 'chimneys' are always placed closer to the center line of the staff for visual ease.

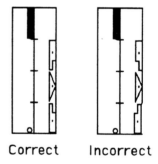

Correct   Incorrect

B. Direction symbols should not run one into the next, making their timing, or in some cases the directions themselves, difficult to decipher. A hair-line gap is needed for visual definition.

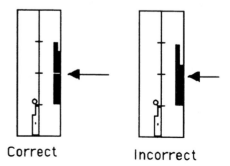

Correct   Incorrect

C. Symbols for the arms shouldn't creep toward the staff, but should remain one column removed, in the arm gesture column.

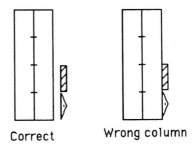

Correct   Wrong column

D. Accents should point toward the symbols they modify and be placed according to their timing, with the narrow tip of the accent mark aiming directly at the moment in the movement to be accented:

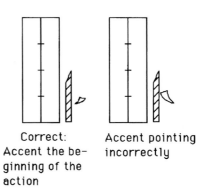

Correct: Accent pointing
Accent the be-   incorrectly
ginning of the
action

E. When an entire count is accented, including every action of every body part, the accent mark should be drawn on a larger scale, outside the staff to the right:

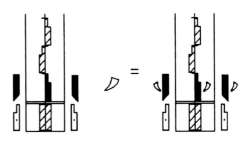

F. When an entire movement sequence is accented, one accent mark within an enclosing bracket may be used rather than writing one accent per symbol. This is placed outside the staff for visual clarity, and applies to every action within the bracketed time. In cases where some body parts are accented and some are not, individual accents must be written.

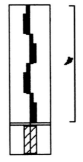

G. Carets for shifts of weight are drawn in the ancillary column and overlap 2 symbols. They are flipped to be written either < or >, depending on their placement on the staff. The open side of the caret does the overlapping:

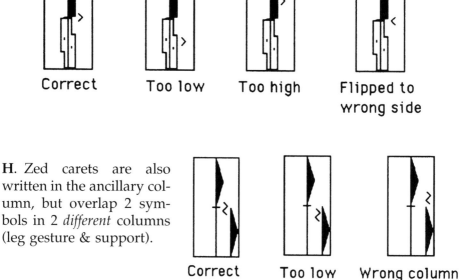

| Correct | Too low | Too high | Flipped to wrong side |

H. Zed carets are also written in the ancillary column, but overlap 2 symbols in 2 *different* columns (leg gesture & support).

| Correct | Too low | Wrong column |

RHYTHMIC APPLICATIONS

3.15   Code Words: 8th and 16th combinations

As we have seen, the code word Diatonic can be modified to demonstrate different combinations of 8ths and 16ths within one beat. Because 8th notes have a duration twice that of 16ths, be sure you *hold through* any non-articulated 16th note which is "inside" a notated 8th. For example, in the code word Di Ton-ic,

the 2nd 16th note "a" is not pronounced because it is "inside" the 8th note which falls on Di. Space is left in the notation as if "a" were there:

Di (a) ton-ic

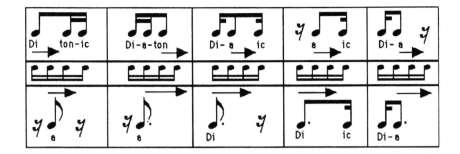

Read each one of the above using 16th Hand-els. Start slowly, gradually increasing speed. Make 4 flash cards for each.

Notice the similarity of some of the above rhythms to the derived diatonic cards from Chapter 2. Although the rhythms are the same, the "sound" is different due to the rest vs. 8th note articulations:

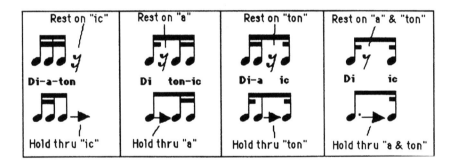

CODE WORD UPDATE: You should now have three separate decks of code word cards from Chapters 1, 2 & 3. Practice separately: when all three decks can be read in the same tempo, shuffle them together into one deck and read slowly at first, gradually increasing tempo.

3.16   Re-grouping: thru-beats

Due to their longer duration, dotted whole, whole and dotted half notes tend to overlap into adjacent measures. When this occurs, the original values are broken into smaller values, and ties are used to re-connect them across bar lines. Below are displayed all of the possible thru-beat combinations in 2/4, 3/4, and 4/4. Please note that *each box below represents only one note value,* even though some values have been broken into as many as four separate pieces. Numerical counts are included to show how the note in question relates to the beats of the measure.

1. *The dotted whole note* is 6-beats in duration, which is longer than any time signature yet discussed in this text. It must therefore always be split **between** measures. Say the numbers out loud as you look at each example, stressing all "1's":

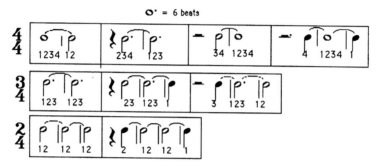

2. *The whole note* is a 4-beat duration which is exactly the same size as one measure of 4/4, but too long to fit in 3/4 or 2/4. Say the numbers out loud as you look at each example below, stressing all "1's":

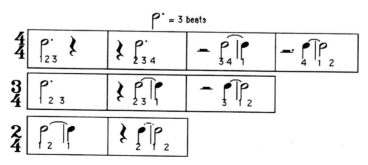

3. *The dotted half note* is a 3-beat duration, which is perfect in 3/4 and too long to fit in 2/4. Say the numbers out loud as you look at each example below, stressing all "1's":

Re-grouping procedure: The re-grouping of thru-beat rhythms is based on the transferring of a particular rhythm from one time signature (or non-metered rhythm) to a new time signature WITHOUT CHANGING THE RHYTHMIC CONSTRUCTION OF THE ORIGINAL. When working with values larger than one beat you must take into consideration the **size** of the new measure, the **size and order** of the note/rest values coming from the Original, and on **which beat** of the new measure each value is to occur. During the process, ALWAYS FINISH ONE MEASURE BEFORE GOING ON TO THE NEXT, and be very careful not to skip over certain values in the Original.

For example, a whole note is twice too large for a measure in 2/4 time, and in 3/4 it is one beat too large. In both cases, the *largest single value possible* is taken from the whole note and placed in the 1st measure: the remainder of the whole note is then placed on the 1st beat of the next measure and both notes are tied together. This procedure is called **borrowing**. You borrow **from** the note what the current **measure** requires, placing the remainder of the original note's value in the next measure.

In the 2/4 example, a half note is **borrowed** from the whole note which completely fills the first measure *in one notational symbol*. The remainder of the whole note (a half note) is placed in the second measure. Both are tied together so that in performance we will "hear" a whole note and not two separate halves.

 In the 3/4 example a dotted half note (three beats) is **borrowed** from the whole note to completely fill the 1st measure *in one notational symbol*. The remainder of the whole note (a quarter note) becomes the first note in the next measure which is then tied to the dotted half.

General Rules for re-grouping:

- If the note is **larger** than the measure, borrow from the note the measure's full value *in one notational symbol* and place the remainder of the note's value in the next measure. Tie these together across the bar line.

- If the note is **exactly the same size** as the measure and falls on beat #1, use it without alteration.

- If the note is **smaller than the measure**, use it without alteration. THEN, calculate how many more beats there are in the measure. Once you have determined this, look back to the original to continue. If the next note is bigger than you need to complete the measure, you'll have to borrow.

Below is a non-metered rhythm which we will call "the original". The task is to re-group the note values to conform to the time signature's specifications. The original must be used note-by-note from left to right in the order in which it comes: DO NOT select notes from the original at random. Let's try it in 4/4:

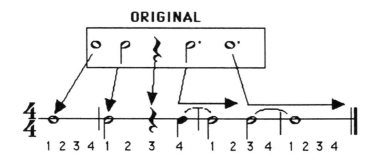

ORIGINAL

Explanation:

In Measure #1, the whole note fits perfectly: the measure is complete.

In Measure #2, the half note occupies beats 1 & 2, and the quarter rest falls on beat 3. But, we now must **borrow**, from the dotted half of the Original, the quarter note required to complete this measure.

In Measure #3, the remainder of the borrowed dotted half note (a half note) is placed on beat #1 and tied to the quarter in measure #2. This takes care of beats 1 & 2. We must now **borrow** beats 3 & 4 from the dotted whole note in the Original since it is too large for the remainder of the measure. A half note is borrowed.

In Measure #4, the remainder of the borrowed dotted whole note (a whole note) fills the entire measure. It is tied to the half in measure #3.

Here's the same Original re-grouped in 3/4.

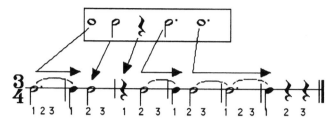

Notice how, in the 1st measure, the whole note becomes a dotted half tied to a quarter. And notice what becomes of the dotted whole: a half tied to a dotted half tied to a quarter. Since the Original ended early when re-grouped in 3/4, quarter rests were added to complete the 6th measure.

 Maxim #57: Always write rhythm in one notational symbol whenever possible. If this is not possible, use the fewest number of symbols. Dotted notes are always preferable to ties under this rule.

3.17   Code Words: displacing the quarter in 2 beats

Two of the most common 2-beat rhythmic combinations in both poetry and music is **One/Number** and **Number/One**, which can be heard over and over again in compositions throughout the world. The rhythms are in effect the Dactyl and Anapest.

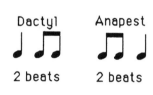

Another extremely common rhythmic figure occurs when, in the same 2-beat time frame, the quarter is displaced one 8th to the right **between** the two 8ths, creating in effect an Amphibrach.

In this pattern, the quarter must begin on the offbeat and hold through the start of the next beat. (The quarter starts on **ber**.)

Consequently, the code word for a quarter note is not always "one": it is "ber" when a quarter note begins on "ber" and holds through "Num".

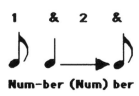

The Code Word "Di-a-(ton)-ic" has exactly the same rhythm as Num-ber-(Num)-ber, only transposed to 8ths and 16ths from quarters and 8ths:

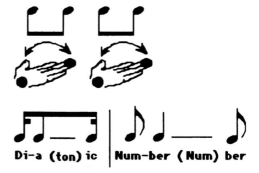

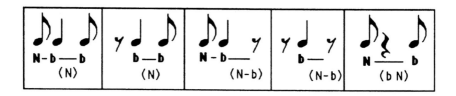

Di-a (ton) ic | Num-ber (Num) ber

The following Code Words represent several of the possible permutations of the displacement of the quarter in 2 beats:

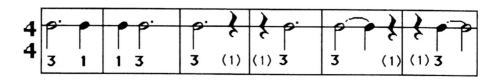

3.18   Code Words: dotted quarters and larger

With the advent of the tie and dot, the student of rhythm can now become facile at reading rhythms that are both longer and more complicated. The code words for values of 2 beats and larger take their names from their durations:

For the dotted whole note/rest say "6". For the note/rest say "4".

For the dotted half note/rest say "3". For the half note/rest say "2".

For example, the code word for the dotted half note in Simple time is "3" EVEN WHEN INVOLVING HALVES AND QUARTERS TIED TOGETHER:

The dotted quarter equals one-and-one-half beats in Simple time, and is therefore only one 8th short of 2 beats. Consequently, the dotted quarter is thought of as being *either the beginning or end of a 2-beat grouping* and will therefore ALWAYS be accompanied by an 8th equivalent:

In Counts   1 & 2 &   1 & 2 &   1 & 2 &   1 & 2 &

In
Code Words   N———b   N b———   b   N   N
             (b N)   (N b)   (N b N)   (b N b)
                                                                or

Looking at the above example, you can see that a dotted quarter can begin on either **Num** or **ber**. When it begins on the 1st 8th of a beat, *call it Num and hold through ber and the following Num.* When it begins on the 2nd 8th of a beat, *call it ber and hold through the following Num-ber.*

When reading dotted quarter/8th combinations, use 8th Hand-els as shown here:

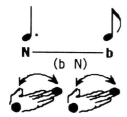

- Say **Num** and hold as you tap out **ber** and **Num** on your hand, finally saying **ber** at the end of the 2nd beat.

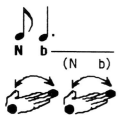

- Say **Num-ber**, then hold through Num-ber again as you tap out the 2nd full beat.

N(bN) b	N b (Nb)	N (bNb)	(N) b (Nb)	N (b N b)	(N) b (NB)

Make 4 flash cards for each of the above and practice them separately from the other cards you now have.

The 2-beat configurations (shown above) present no problems in 2/4 and 4/4 since a dotted quarter and 8th combination occupy 2 beats. In 3/4, however, there will always be one extra beat, equivalent to a quarter. The following represent just a few of the possible combinations in 3/4: Train your eye to see that when a dotted quarter is present, IT WILL ALWAYS

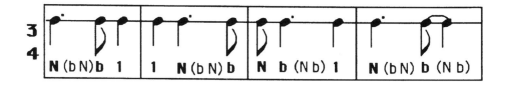

BE PART OF A 2-BEAT GROUPING. All you must determine is whether it begins on Num or Ber of a beat, and the 8th equivalent to which it belongs will be easy to find:

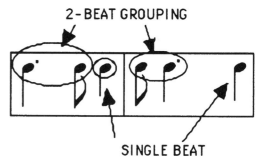

Maxim #58: Dotted quarter notes will always belong to a 2-beat grouping in Simple Time, and can begin on either the Db or the Ub.

 MOVEMENT APPLICATIONS

3.19 Clusters: leg gestures

The following clusters include leg gestures and meter.

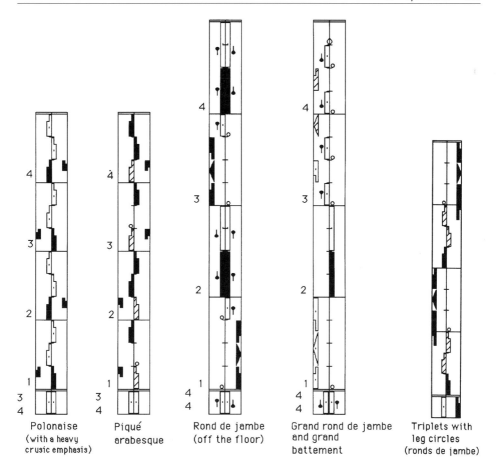

| Polonaise | Piqué | Rond de jambe | Grand rond de jambe | Triplets with |
| (with a heavy crusic emphasis) | arabesque | (off the floor) | and grand battement | leg circles (ronds de jambe) |

3.20 Reading Arm Gestures

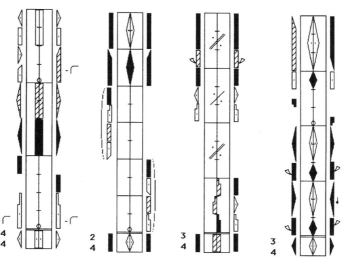

CHAPTER WRAP

3.21   RN Etudes

Chant the top and clap or walk the bottom.

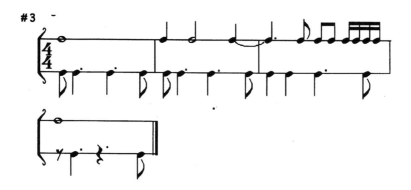

3.22   LN Etudes

1.   Arm and leg gestures

 Cues #10A and B

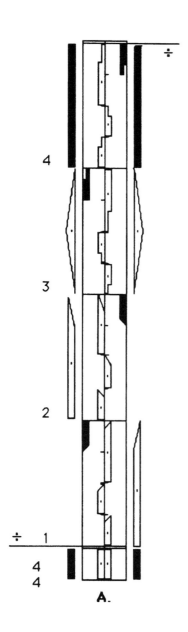

A.

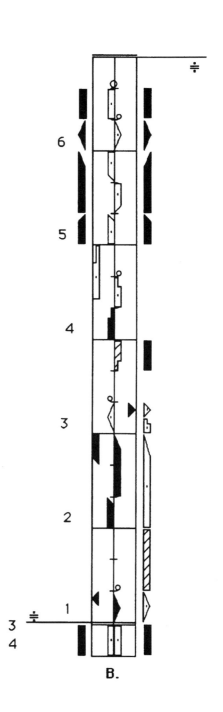

B.

2. Phrase-shifting

Practice the non-metered original below, then dance it in the time signatures to the right. Allow the meter to influence the original phrase.

Cue #11

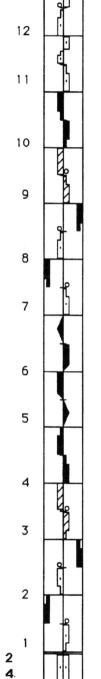

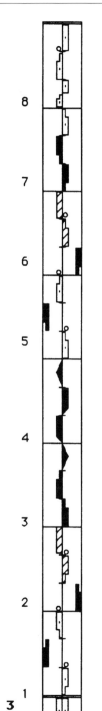

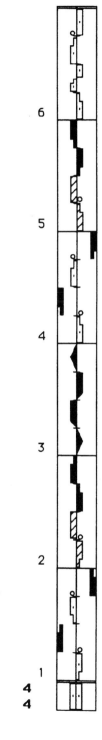

3. Accents

Cue #12

Bend the
arms as
needed to
achieve a
full swing.

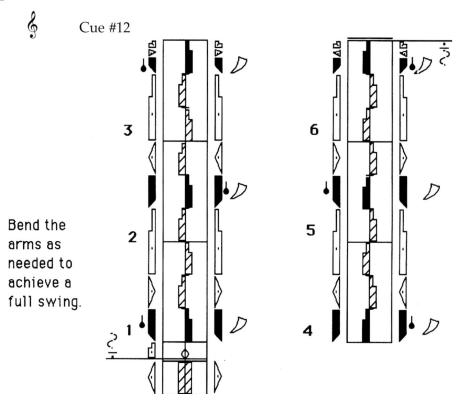

3.23   More Tricky Rhythms

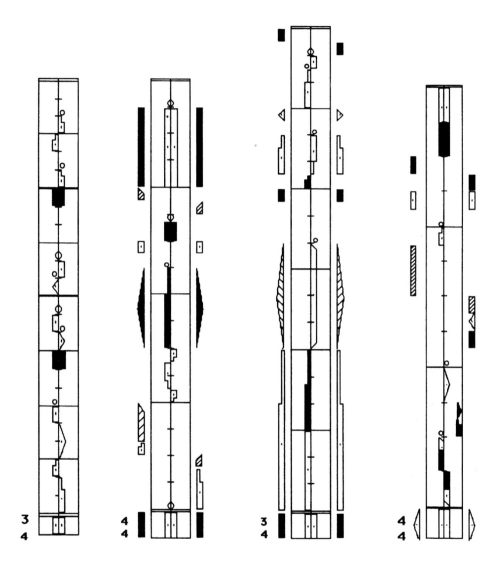

3.24   Suggested Assignments

Make four cards for each new code word rhythm. Keep them in a separate deck and practice separately from the others. Use 16th Hand-els throughout. Be aware of the longer durations that the 8ths and dotted 8ths demand.

- Re-group the following original into 2/4, 3/4, then 4/4 time. Stems should go up or down consistently throughout:

- Align the following three parts together in 2/4. Keep the stems up for the top two parts and down for the lowest part. Make your own score paper with three staff lines enclosed within a bracket:

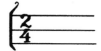

Also, bar lines should run from the top to the bottom staff lines and not beyond:

Part A

Part B

Part C

Phrasing assignment

The information you will need for this assignment has appeared throughout this chapter. The questions that follow deal with interpreting an adaptation of a well-known choreographic phrase. Over 8 measures, the use of accents, repetition, and level changes combine to create a single phrase and cadence. Exactly how this is achieved will be revealed as you move through the following questions.

Cue #13

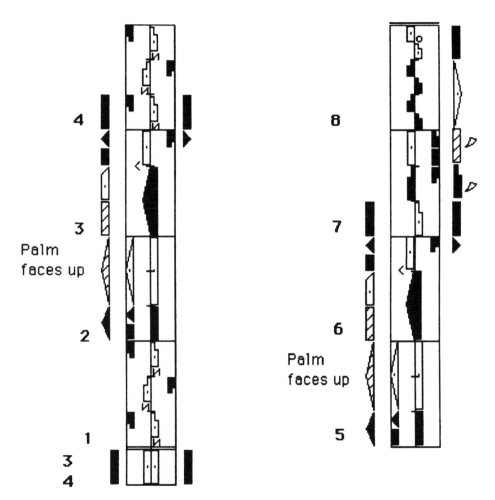

Find the unified statements (short phrases) within the 8 measure phrase above, which is based on a theme from Doris Humphrey's *Passacaglia & Fugue in C Minor* (1938), to music by J. S. Bach.

(a) Which measures group together to make the first complete statement?
(b) Is this statement repeated?
(c) How, then, are the 8 measures divided and grouped by the choreographic material?
(d) Listen to the music for this sequence (audio tape). Is the musical phrase divided in the same way?
(e) Look at the 1st movement statement more closely. In measure #1, what is the basic movement?
(f) In measure #2, what rises?
(g) Measure #3 is not about rising. Describe the supports in counts 1–2.
(h) A part of the body resists this lowering. What is it?
(i) Describe the last count of measure #3.
(j) Is this a transitional movement, or one of major significance in and of itself?
(k) Which of the following shapes best pictures the choreographic statement of the first 3 measures (its dynamics and uses of level)?

1.   2.   3.

(l) When the statement repeats, should overall energy rise slightly or remain the same?
(m) Measure #7 is noteworthy. Why?
(n) The actions in measure #7 produce the high point (climax) of the phrase. What happens in measure #8?
(o) Draw the overall shape of the 8-measure phrase.

Practice performing this phrase, experiencing and showing the rises and falls in the choreographic structure.

(p) Identify some of the aspects of movement that can produce rises and falls of phrasing, not just in *Passacaglia*, but in general.
(q) Choreograph phrases with the following shapes, remembering that they describe gradations of energy, level, use of space, and repetition, rather than direction of travel.

PASSACAGLIA ANSWER SHEET
(a) meas. 1-3
(b) yes
(c) 3-3-2
(d) No
(e) Walking
(f) Left arm and leg, and the center of weight.
(g) Plié in 2nd position
(h) Left arm
(i) Shift of weight onto the left foot, in preparation for the repeat of the phrase.
(j) Transitional
(k) 2: the long walks have a forward momentum that produces a slight building effect.

Rising begins immediately in measure #2 in the left arm, spreading to include nearly the whole body.

Measure #3 represents a gentle diminution, the left arm slowing the descent of the body. The last count is a neutral transition into a repeat of the phrase.

(l) Rise slightly. The most usual function of repetition is to create increasing or decreasing emphasis. (See Ch. 3.2.) The shape of the repeating phrase would therefore be:

(m) There are 2 accented movements in quick succession.
(n) A descent from the climax.

(o)

(p) Energy level (and accents), repetition (increasing or decreasing emphasis), changing spatial levels, amount of travel, and parts of the body that are moving are some elements that can give shape to choreography.

4
APPROACHING PERFECTION

RHYTHMIC CONCEPTS

4.1 Compound Time

Recall that there are only two types of beat subdivision (the **duple** and **triple**), and there are two types of note values, **simple** (duple) and **compound** (triple). Consequently, there are two categories of meter: **Simple Time** and **Compound Time**. Since simple time refers to any time signature where the beating note is divisible by 2 without a fraction, compound time refers to *any time signature where the beating note is divisible by 3 without a fraction*.

VERY IMPORTANT: Both simple and compound time concern themselves ONLY with the type of note assigned to the beat (the bottom number of the time signature) and NOT the number of beats per measure.

Remembering that triple beats are divided evenly into three equal parts, all compound time signatures are felt "1 a da 2 a da" etc. Since the standard beat assignment in Simple Time is usually the quarter note, the standard beat assignment in Compound Time is the dotted quarter note. By comparing these beating notes, we see that the quarter note beat is comprised of two 8th notes while the dotted quarter note beat is comprised of three – the compound beat is *larger* by one 8th note:

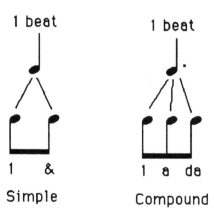

 Maxim #59: Compound Time refers to any time signature where the beating note is divisible by 3 without a fraction.

4.2   Compound Time Signatures

As in simple time, the most common time signatures in compound time are also based on 2, 3, and 4 beats per measure. However, unlike simple time, there is a problem relating to the manner in which these compound time signatures are written (and understood).

2 Beats per measure is called 6/8?!   Following the rules set down in chapter 2, one would deduce that in 6/8, there are 6 beats per measure and the 8th note "gets the beat." But this is not the case. Except in very slow tempi, the beat in compound time is **not** felt as six individual 8ths per measure: it is based on the triply-divided beat. Therefore, each beat in Compound time is *"felt"* in groupings of three 8ths. In effect, each beat is the equivalent of a dotted quarter note. 6/8 is therefore misleading:

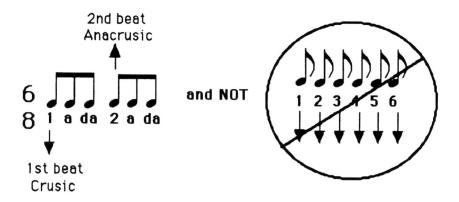

Today, by mixing graphics and numbers, compound time signatures can be re-written to arrive at a more exact visual representation of how they work:

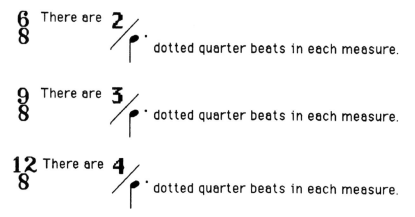

When using the more graphic signatures, place them above the staff and not directly on it:

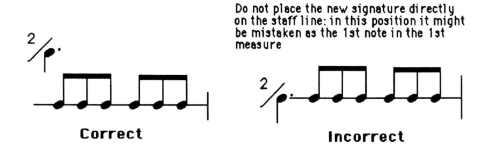

Do not place the new signature directly on the staff line: in this position it might be mistaken as the 1st note in the 1st measure

Correct   **Incorrect**

Maxim #60 : Compound time signatures are misleading: the triple division of the compound beat indicates that the dotted quarter and not the 8th note is the assigned full-beat in each measure.

The following is an examination of the three most common Compound time signatures, how they are constructed and how they are 'felt':

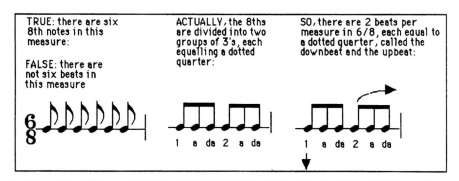

TRUE: there are six 8th notes in this measure:

FALSE: there are not six beats in this measure

ACTUALLY, the 8ths are divided into two groups of 3's, each equalling a dotted quarter:

SO, there are 2 beats per measure in 6/8, each equal to a dotted quarter, called the downbeat and the upbeat:

1 a da 2 a da

1 a da 2 a da

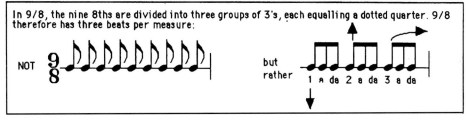

In 9/8, the nine 8ths are divided into three groups of 3's, each equalling a dotted quarter. 9/8 therefore has three beats per measure:

NOT

but rather

1 a da 2 a da 3 a da

It is now possible to count to 2, 3, and 4 in two different ways:

Count:	In Simple Time	In Compound Time
2	1 & 2 &	1 a da 2 a da
3	1 & 2 & 3 &	1 a da 2 a da 3 a da
4	1 & 2 & 3 & 4 &	1 a da 2 a da 3 a da 4 a da

4.3   Perfect Meter

With the introduction of meter based on the triple division of the beat we can now combine simple and compound time under a larger metric "umbrella" called Perfect Meter.

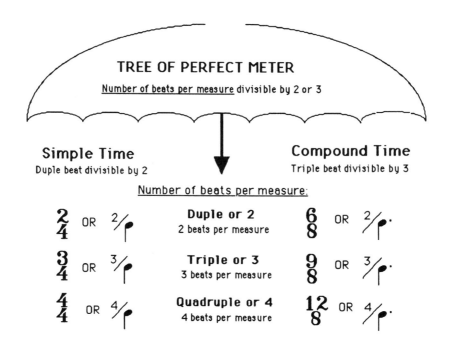

Perfect Meter categorizes all time signatures based on their *numbers of beats per measure* and NOT the type of beat in use.

Any time signature where the *number of beats per measure is divisible by 2 OR 3 without a fraction* falls within Perfect Meter. Since the numbers 2, 3, and 4 meet this criteria, all time signatures covered thus far in both simple and compound time automatically fall under the category of Perfect Meter.

TERMINOLOGICAL CLARIFICATION: There are now two uses for the words **duple** and **triple**. There are duple and triple beats AND duple and triple measures (the number of beats per measure). Make a mental note of this. It will now be possible to have duple beats in triple measures and triple beats in duple measures:

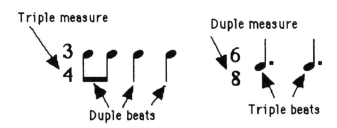

 Maxim #61: Perfect Meter refers to any time signature where the number of beats per measure is divisible by 2 or 3 without a fraction.

4.4 Comparisons: simple versus compound

Within the category of Perfect Meter we can now compare the similarities and differences between Simple and Compound Time signatures:

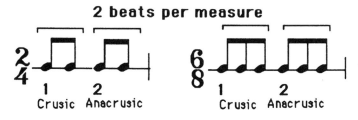

Similarities:

Both 2/4 and 6/8 are duple time signatures, since both have two beats per measure. Both are felt with one crusic and one anacrusic beat per measure.

Differences:

The beat in 2/4 is **duple** (two equal divisions) while the beat in 6/8 is **triple** (three equal divisions). 2/4 is therefore referred to as a "simple/duple" since its beat is duply-divided and it has 2 beats per measure. 6/8 is therefore a "compound/duple" since its beat is triply-divided and it has 2 beats per measure.

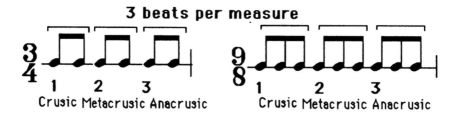

3 beats per measure

Similarities:

Both 3/4 and 9/8 are **triple** time signatures since both are comprised of three beats per measure. Both are felt with one crusic, one metacrusic, and one anacrusic beat per measure.

Differences:

The beat in 3/4 is duple (two equal divisions) while the beat in 9/8 is triple (three equal divisions). 3/4 is therefore referred to as a "simple/triple" since its beat is duply-divided and it has 3 beats per measure. 9/8 is therefore a "compound/triple" since its beat is triply-divided and it has 3 beats per measure.

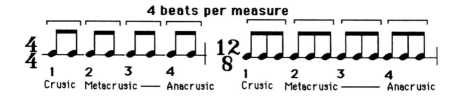

4 beats per measure

Similarities:

Both 4/4 and 12/8 are **quadruple** time signatures since both are comprised of four beats per measure. Both are felt with one crusic, two metacrusic, and one anacrusic beat per measure.

Differences:

The beat in 4/4 is duple (two equal divisions) while the beat in 12/8 is triple (three equal divisions). 4/4 is therefore referred to as a "simple/quadruple" since its beat is duply-divided and it has 4 beats per measure. 12/8 is a "compound/quadruple" since its beat is triply-divided and it has 4 beats per measure.

Now count each signature several times in a row:

$\frac{2}{4}$ 1 & 2 & $\frac{2}{\text{♩.}}$ 1 a da 2 a da

$\frac{3}{4}$ 1 & 2 & 3 & $\frac{3}{\text{♩.}}$ 1 a da 2 a da 3 a da

$\frac{4}{4}$ 1 & 2 & 3 & 4 & $\frac{4}{\text{♩.}}$ 1 a da 2 a da 3 a da 4 a da

> Maxim #62: The difference between Simple and Compound time signatures is *the division of the beat* and NOT the number of beats per measure. Both fall under Perfect Meter.

4.5   Rhythmic Identity and Transposition

Rhythm has the uncanny ability of sounding the same at any speed. The recognition comes from the fact that rhythm, like Morse Code, is based on combinations of long and short durations. Using the U.S. National Anthem again, the song gains its "rhythmic identity" from the following sequence of long and short durations:

Short short long long long long / Short short long long long long:

Oh-oh Say can you see by the dawn's ear–ly light
● ● ▬ ▬ ▬ ▬●● ▬ ▬ ▬ ▬

The anthem is in 3/4 and usually performed at about metronome 94 which would normally assign the quarter note to the beat. Should a composer wish to have the anthem performed "slower than normal", the half or whole could be selected as the beat, since musicians will generally interpret half notes more slowly than quarters. This procedure is called Rhythmic Transposition:

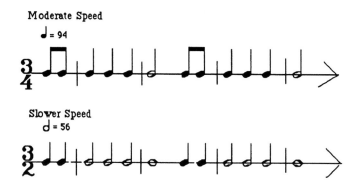

The time signature 3/2 is a triple meter like 3/4, each having 3 beats per measure. The difference is that the beating note in 3/2 is a half note: all the values in 3/4 are therefore moved DOWN the BOV, making them larger and longer.

- The 8th note pickups in 3/4 become two quarters in 3/2.
- The quarters in the 1st measure of 3/4 become three halves in 3/2.
- The half/two 8th combination in the 3rd measure of 3/4 becomes a whole and two quarters in 3/2, etc.

In both of the examples above, the rhythmic **construction** in each measure is identical. They "look" exactly the same:

Short/ short/ long/ long/ long/ long.
Short/ short/ long/ long/ long/ long.

Try this: Hold the previous page away from you and squint your eyes at the above 3/4, 3/2 example. There's no *rhythmic* difference. There are three beats in the first measure of 3/4 and of 3/2. The only difference is in the note values: a musician will play the 3/2 slower than s/he will play the 3/4 because the notes "look" longer.

 Sing the first four measures of the anthem to yourself from "Oh" to "light". Sing it once at m.m. 100 while looking at the 3/4 notation. Then switch to m.m. 60 and sing it again at the slower speed while looking at the 3/2 notation. The song will maintain its identity at both speeds, only it is slower in 3/2.

Lets look at the anthem using all beat assignments from 16th to whole note. Each transposition is EXACTLY THE SAME RHYTHM:

General principle: If the tempo of a composition is to be *slower than normal*, **increase** the size of all values by 100%, 200%, etc. If the tempo of a composition is to be *faster than normal*, **decrease** the size of all of note values by the same scale (move up the BOV to a higher number).

This procedure is similar to the method by which a photographer "reduces" or "blows up" a negative: *the picture remains the same*:

 This size is like selecting the 32nd or 16th as the beat.

 This size is like selecting the 8th or quarter as the beat.

 This size is like selecting the half or whole as the beat.

Here are three examples of the identical walking sequence, written with the 8th, quarter, and half as the assigned beating note. Although the rhythmic pattern is the same in all three, the tempo can vary considerably.

Notice that with the change of scale,
the dance score visibly communicates
increasingly slow performance.

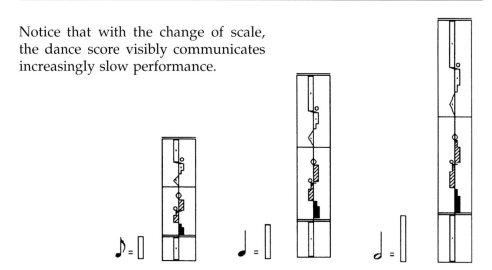

> Maxim #63: Rhythmic Transposition is a process in which
> note/rest values are changed to reflect a change in the assigned
> beating note.

4.6   Tree of Perfect Meter: expanded

By transposing the beat assignments throughout the BOV, we can
immediately see ALL of the possible time signatures that fall under the

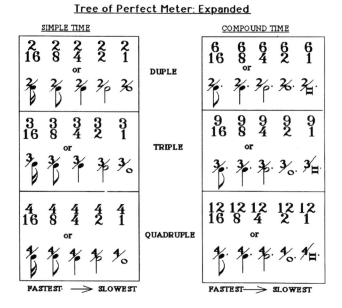

umbrella of Perfect Meter. Remember that transposing the beat effects **tempo** only: the metric characteristics *remain the same*.

 ### *MOVEMENT CONCEPTS*

4.7   Going into the Air

Going into the air is represented simply on the LN staff: when there is a **gap** in the support columns, *with no hold sign* to keep the dancer's weight on one or both feet, the dancer is **in the air**. Absence of support equals being in the air.

Beat 3: land in 1st pos.

"&": in the air

Beat 2: land in 2nd pos.

"&": in the air

Beat 1: Plié

Starting Pos.: 1st

 Maxim #64: No symbols or hold signs in the support columns means "go into the air".

Springs is the generic word used to describe actions that go into the air. "Jump" means something specific in LN movement analysis. There are, in fact, five forms of spring.

KINDS OF SPRINGS

1. **Jump.**   Take off from 2 feet and land on 2 feet.
2. **Hop.**   Take off from 1 foot and land on the same foot.
3. **Leap.**   Take off from 1 foot and land on the other foot.
4. **Assemblé.**   Take off from 1 foot and land on 2 feet.
5. **Sissonne.**   Take off from 2 feet and land on 1 foot.

Note: *"Assemblé"* and *"Sissonne"* are French words, borrowed by LN from ballet vocabulary since there are no English equivalents for these kinds of springing actions. Below are examples of the 5 kinds of springs.

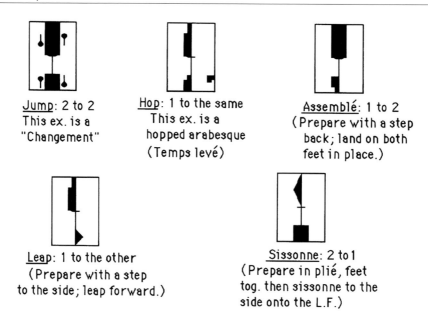

Jump: 2 to 2
This ex. is a
"Changement"

Hop: 1 to the same
This ex. is a
hopped arabesque
(Temps levé)

Assemblé: 1 to 2
(Prepare with a step
back; land on both
feet in place.)

Leap: 1 to the other
(Prepare with a step
to the side; leap forward.)

Sissonne: 2 to 1
(Prepare in plié, feet
tog. then sissonne to the
side onto the L.F.)

> Maxim #65: Spring is the generic word for actions in the air.
> There are 5 specific forms of spring.

Timing. Springs, as a rule, land **on** the beat. Because of this, springing actions mirror the crusic and non-crusic energies of a measure: the dancer is usually in the air on the anacrusis and lands on the crusis. Because of this, preparation spaces are used with movement combinations or choreography involving springs, to give the dancer time to go into the air **before** "1", so that he or she can land **on** the beat.

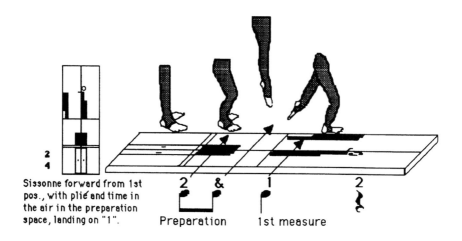

Sissonne forward from 1st
pos., with plié and time in
the air in the preparation
space, landing on "1".

Preparation   1st measure

Cancelling hold signs to go into the air.   If a dancer is holding on one or both feet, the hold sign MUST BE CANCELLED to permit a spring. There are 2 ways to cancel a hold sign, to allow a dancer to spring from the floor.

(1) *Write gestures* for the leg or legs that have been holding. If legs are gesturing, they are by definition not bearing weight and therefore can not continue to hold.

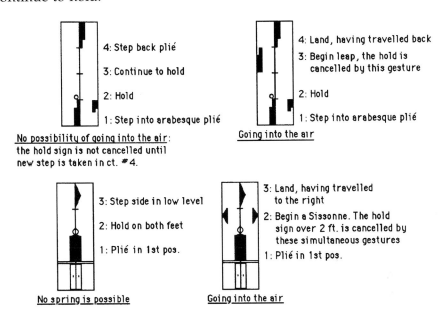

Maxim #66: Leg gestures may cancel hold weight signs, if the gesture is performed by the same leg that has been holding.

(2) The 2nd way to cancel a hold weight sign is with an ***action stroke*** or *'air line'*. This is a straight line, drawn in the leg gesture column, to indicate the leg is active in the air. An action stroke or air line indicates that the leg gesture has an unemphasized or undefined direction. In many cases the action stroke may be thought of as the equivalent of a "place low" leg gesture. Rather than write "place low" gestures repeatedly, 'air lines' can be used as a short hand. However, in the examples below, the undefined, unemphasized direction of action strokes is illustrated. They describe the legs gesturing below the body, but their exact position will be influenced by the direction of the take-offs and landings. In example (a), (b), and (c) the legs perform three different actions. In (d), place low gestures are emphasized.

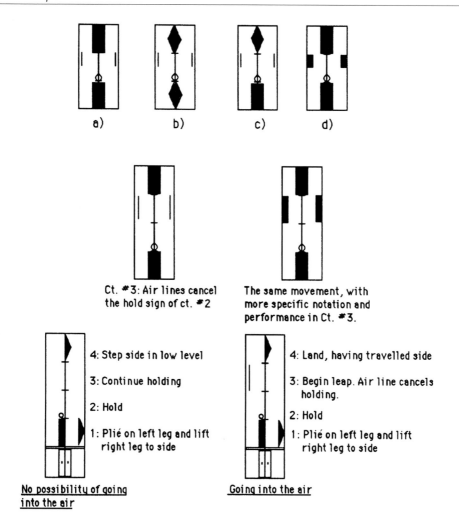

a)   b)   c)   d)

Ct. #3: Air lines cancel the hold sign of ct. #2

The same movement, with more specific notation and performance in Ct. #3.

4: Step side in low level

3: Continue holding

2: Hold

1: Plié on left leg and lift right leg to side

<u>No possibility of going into the air</u>

4: Land, having travelled side

3: Begin leap. Air line cancels holding.

2: Hold

1: Plié on left leg and lift right leg to side

<u>Going into the air</u>

 Maxim #67: Air lines, or action strokes, may cancel hold signs, if written for the same leg that has been holding.

4.8   Lengthening and Shortening: leg gestures

The symbols for "shortening" and "lengthening" as modifiers of steps can also be used with leg gestures.

X will bend a leg gesture slightly, shortening the distance between the free end and the fixed end of the leg (the foot and the hip).

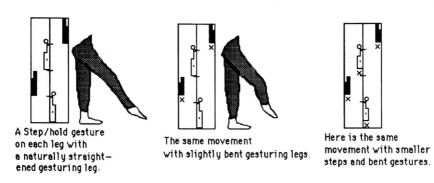

A Step/hold gesture on each leg with a naturally straightened gesturing leg.

The same movement with slightly bent gesturing legs.

Here is the same movement with smaller steps and bent gestures.

Backwards **N** will extend a leg gesture beyond the normal straight line of the leg, bringing the quality of "reaching" to the movement. Backwards **N** lengthens the distance between the foot and the hip (the leg's extremity and its point of attachment).

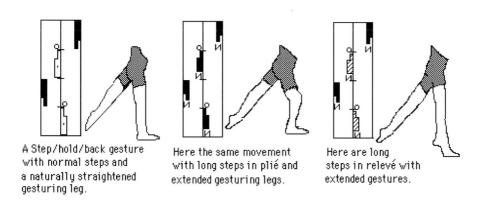

A Step/hold/back gesture with normal steps and a naturally straightened gesturing leg.

Here the same movement with long steps in plié and extended gesturing legs.

Here are long steps in relevé with extended gestures.

 Maxim #68: **X** and backward **N** can modify leg gestures in the same way as steps, shortening (bending) or lengthening (extending) the leg in the air.

4.9 Split-column Leg Gestures

The leg gesture column can be divided in two, to describe actions of the leg in which the thigh moves in one direction, and the lower leg in another. "Passé" and "parallel passé" are common actions of this type.

In passé, the thigh opens to the side, while the lower leg moves toward the body (toward the standing leg). Imagine passé with the left leg: the left foot drawn in to the right knee, with the leg turned out. In this position, the left thigh will be directed to the left side (middle level), while the lower leg will move to the right side (low level). The directions and levels for the thigh and lower leg are determined in the same way as with gestures for the whole leg: by comparing free end to fixed end. For the thigh, the free end is the knee and the fixed end is the hip. The free end for the lower leg is the ankle and the fixed end, the knee. The foot is usually carried along in line wih the lower leg, but since this is not always the case (as in a flexed-foot position), look at the ankle-to-knee relationship when describing the lower leg.

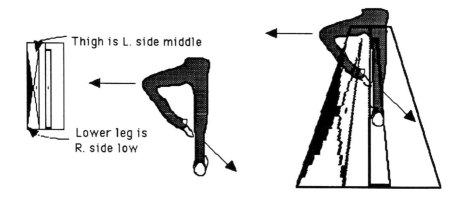

Notice that the leg gesture column is divided to accommodate 2 symbols for the leg. The symbol describing direction and level for the thigh (the heavier part of the leg, the part closer to the center of the body), is placed closer to the staff's center line.

The notation of "Passé" is nicknamed a "butterfly" because of its overall shape. Think of the butterfly as a movement cluster that will always signify "passé".

Pins are added to butterflies when it is necessary to indicate whether the lower leg will come in front or behind the supporting knee.

L. foot crosses
behind R. knee

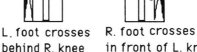

R. foot crosses
in front of L. knee

Low passé
(cou de pied)

"Parallel passé" (the gesturing foot drawn in to the knee of the standing leg with no turn-out) involves a different pair of directions for the thigh

and lower leg. Analyze this position and decide what these two directions are. Where is the thigh? The lower leg?

These examples of
divided-column nota-
tions should be me-
morized as symbol
clusters for ease in
reading:

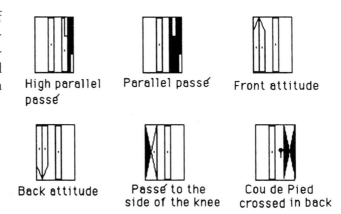

High parallel
passé

Parallel passé

Front attitude

Back attitude

Passé to the
side of the knee

Cou de Pied
crossed in back

 Maxim #69: Split-column leg gestures describe combined actions of the thigh and lower leg. The symbol for the thigh is
always written closer to the center line of the staff.

4.10   Lengthening and Shortening: arm gestures

X and backwards N can be used to modify gestures of the arms, in the
same way they are used with supports and leg gestures. X will shorten
the distance between the hand (free end) and the shoulder (fixed end),
bending or "contracting" the arm. The hand will remain in the same
spatial relationship to the shoulder as the arm bends, changing neither

direction nor level. The elbow will displace to allow the hand to draw closer to the shoulder.

Backwards N in the arm column will slightly lengthen the
distance between the hand
and the shoulder, adding the
quality of "reach" or extension
to a gesture.

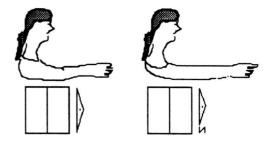

4.11   Split-column Arm Gestures

The arm column can be divided to accommodate direction symbols for the upper and lower parts of the arm in exactly the same manner as with split-column leg gestures. When the upper and lower parts of the arm move in separate directions, two symbols will split the arm gesture column. The free end of the upper arm (the elbow) is compared to its fixed end (the shoulder), and the free end of the lower arm (the wrist) is compared to its fixed end (the elbow). We can assume that the hand is carried in line with the lower arm, unless we are given separate information for it.

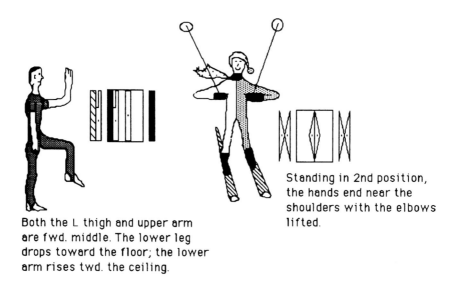

Both the L thigh and upper arm
are fwd. middle. The lower leg
drops toward the floor; the lower
arm rises twd. the ceiling.

Standing in 2nd position,
the hands end near the
shoulders with the elbows
lifted.

As with split-column leg gestures, the upper limb is written closer to the center of the staff (in this case, the upper arms).

NOTATION

 4.12 RN: compound time

A. The beat in compound time is larger than that in simple time, but all 8ths and 16ths within the beat are still beamed together. Note that secondary beams are still interrupted when 8ths, 16ths and rests are mixed:

B. The "look" of compound time is quite different than the "look" of simple time. For one thing, the quarter note is no longer a complete beat – it is only 2/3 of a beat in Compound time. Therefore, *all single quarter notes MUST be accompanied by an 8th note or its equivalent*:

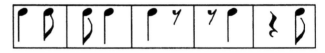

C. The dotted quarter rest may be used freely to express one beat. However, the quarter rest may never be used on the 2nd or 3rd 8th of a compound beat: it must be broken into 8th rests:

D. The dotted whole note fills an entire measure in 12/8 (the equivalent of 4 dotted quarter notes), and the dotted half fills an entire measure in 6/8 (the equivalent of 2 dotted quarter notes). However, the only way to express a full measure in 9/8 is to use a dotted half tied to a dotted quarter (or its rest equivalent):

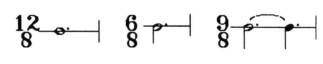

E. When an entire measure is to be silent, the whole rest is used. For example, in 3/4, the whole rest would be used IN PLACE OF the dotted half rest. A whole rest means "whole measure rest", and so is used in any measure in *any* time signature:

4.13   RN: complex resting

Along with complicated rhythms comes complex resting. When beats are broken into smaller and smaller pieces, rests, when needed, should be placed in such a way as to visually reinforce the natural divisions of the beat. In all cases, the correct solution to complex notational problems is "readability", or, the solution which most closely adheres to the divisions of the beat and/or measure.

For example, the last note of a composition is a 16th note on the attack of the second beat of a 4/4 measure. How will you "rest" the remaining beats in 4/4? Always start with the incomplete beat first:

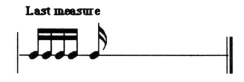

Thinking of the 2nd beat in two halves, place a 16th rest to complete the *first half* (or 8th note equivalent), so the eye can see the first "half beat". Then complete the second half of the beat with an 8th rest.

The second half of the measure must now be rested as well. Since the second half of the measure is silent, we can use a half rest (instead of two quarters):

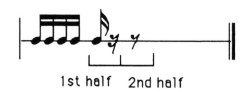

CLARIFICATION: There is another solution to the above example, using a dotted 16th rest in place of the 16th/8th combination: What is important is that BOTH SOLUTIONS ARE CORRECT.

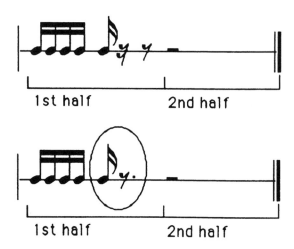

4.14   LN: springs and air lines

A. Preparation

Spaces. We have seen that movement sequences that begin by going into the air often use preparation spaces. The preparation allows the dancer time to get into the air before a landing on ct. "1" of the opening measure.

Assemblé en avant (travelling forward) lands on ct.1.

Preparation: plié & time in the air.

The length of time in the air in the preparation space will help determine the height of the opening spring. The longer the preparation space or the more time spent in the air, the higher the spring will be, or, the greater will be the distance travelled.

2-ct. prep. space will facilitate a high leap (grand jeté)

B. Air lines are drawn in the leg gesture columns, since they represent actions by the legs in the air, and serve to cancel hold-weight signs or other information in the support columns.

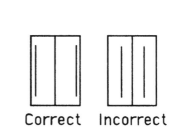

Correct   Incorrect

They can be of any length, depending upon the time spent in the air during a spring.

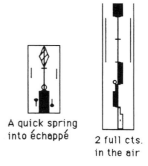

A quick spring into échappé

2 full cts. in the air

Air lines can also be used next to symbols in the support column when "lift" is desired in an action, with little actual release from the floor. The "Sous-Sus" is a good example of this. The example shows relevés and pliés in 5th position where the dancer lightly springs from position to position without actually jumping. The weight is lifted.

A common mistake is to over-use air lines, adding them to every springing action. Air lines are generally only needed to cancel hold weight signs. If no hold weight sign is present in a support column, the gap between direction symbols for the supports *is in itself* enough to take the dancer into the air.

Air lines cancel hold sign: jump occurs on beat 3.

Correct

Incorrect: no hold to cancel

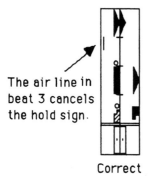

The air line in beat 3 cancels the hold sign.

Correct

Assemble begins on ct.3 without air lines

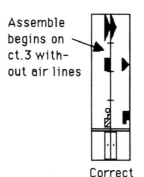

Correct

Air line here is not necessary: there is no hold to cancel.

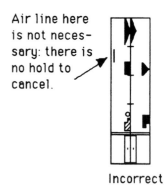

Incorrect

4.15   Split-column Symbols

Two notation rules apply to these hybrid symbols:

1. Never use 2 columns for these actions. Slim down your direction symbols so they can be squeezed into a single arm or leg gesture column:

2. Keep the 'chimneys' on fwd. & bk. direction symbols toward the center line of the staff:

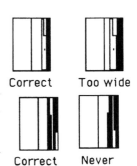

Correct   Too wide

Correct   Never

4.16 Repeated X and Backward N

As previously explained in Chapter 2, the pre-signs "X & backward N" modify the direction symbols with which they are paired. When sequential actions in a series involve contraction or extension, X & backward N will need to be repeated for each new action.

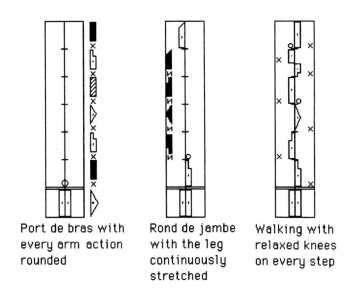

Port de bras with
every arm action
rounded

Rond de jambe
with the leg
continuously
stretched

Walking with
relaxed knees
on every step

Because this repetition can be cumbersome to write and read, the duration of X & backwards N can be extended with either a bracket or a hold sign. The use of brackets or hold signs drastically reduces the number of times the pre-signs need to be repeated. Either method is correct.

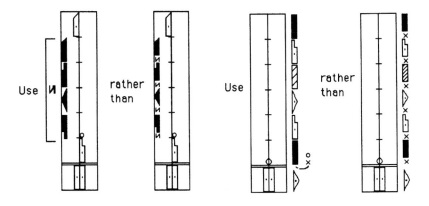

Use   rather
                       than

Use   rather
                       than

Notice that a bracket is self-cancelling;
when it concludes, so does the effect of
the X or backward N within it. Hold signs
with X or backwards N need to be specifically cancelled or they will continue in
effect indefinitely. The cancellations for hold signs are either the "return-
to-normal" sign or the "neither bent nor straight" sign, i.e., a return to the
natural state. Either is correct.

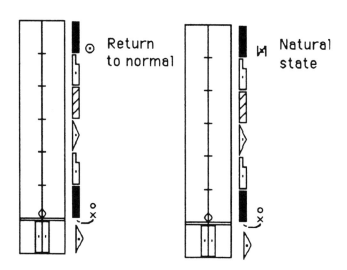

In this example,
the hold sign could
be cancelled with
either symbol, plac-
ed in the same col-
umn as the hold
sign, at the desired
point of cancella-
tion. In both cases,
the last arm gesture
will be naturally
straight.

Another use of hold signs as extensions of X &
backwards N is in the starting position, where a
particular stance can be specified. Here, the stance
for the entire dance (unless cancelled later on) is
with relaxed knees:

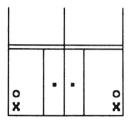

 Maxim #70: Hold signs in other columns of the staff obey the
same rule as those in the support columns; their effect lasts
until cancelled.

RHYTHMIC APPLICATIONS

4.17   Compound Code Words

Below are some of the most common rhythms found in Compound Time. Since the compound beat is larger, there are more rhythmic possibilities per beat than are found in Simple Time. Practice each pattern until its rhythmic identity becomes familiar.

The student should now begin to graduate from the use of all previous code words except for the purposes of analysis. Once a rhythmic pattern has been deciphered, it should be practiced and recognized as a sound pattern, with less and less dependence on code word help.

Should the above Compound rhythms be difficult to read at first, use the following new code words until these basic rhythms become familiar to the eye and ear:

- For the dotted quarter, use the word **ONE**

- For three 8th notes per beat use the word **HAR-MO-NY**

- For six 16ths within a beat, place an "&" in between the syllables of the word **Har-mo-ny**

Har & mo & ny &

Compound Code Word Analysis:

The following is an analysis using the compound code words:

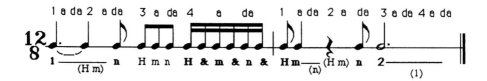

4.18   The Compound "Hand-el"

Three touches within a hand-el can be used to experience the three 8th divisions of **Har-mo-ny**. 16th notes can be "felt" in between the 8ths as the hand lifts away from the palm. Use this hand-el when reading all compound rhythms:

Here is the above example once more, with hand-els:

4.19   Re-grouping: advanced

It should now be possible to take a phrase containing sub-beat, full-beat, and thru-beat rhythm and regroup it into either simple or compound time. In either category, you must be aware of (1) the size of the measure, (2) the type of beat selected, and (3) the size of the individual note and rest values.

Remember that you are going to "take" from the original what the measures/beats require. It is therefore important to calculate, after you place each note, determining the amount of time remaining in the current beat or measure. *You must complete each beat before you can complete the measure – you must complete each measure before you can go on to the next measure.*

PROCEDURE (beat by beat/measure by measure):
Look at the first note (or rest) of the original. If it is:

- larger than the current measure, see rule **A** below.
- exactly the same size as the measure, see rule **B** below.
- smaller than the measure but larger than the beat, see rule **B** below.
- exactly the same size as the beat, see rule **B** below.
- smaller than the beat, see rule **C** below.

(A) Borrow exactly what is needed from the note to fill the entire first measure (with one symbol if possible), placing that note's remaining value in the next measure.

If the remainder is larger than the next measure, keep borrowing measure by measure, until the original note's value has been consumed. Then calculate the amount of time remaining in the last measure (if any) and go on to the next note of the original.

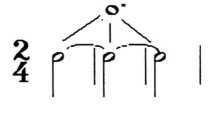

(B) Use the note or rest as is, then calculate the amount of time that remains in the measure (if any) and go on to the next note of the original. Exception: dotted rests that fall on a weak division of a beat should be broken down to reflect the beat's division.

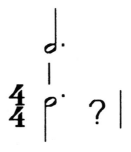

(C) Use the note or rest as is. Then calculate the amount of time remaining *in the current beat* and complete that beat before going on to the next beat. Remember to beam all 8ths, 16ths, etc. within the same beat.

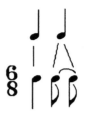

ORIGINAL

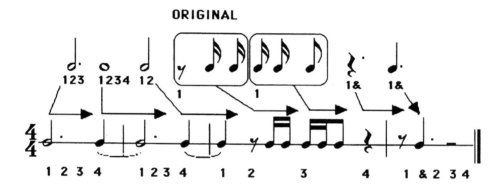

Notice how the re-grouped solution is easier to read since it visually adheres to the four duple beats of the measure.

1ST MEASURE: You are looking for four quarter note beats. The dotted half note occupies the first three beats of the measure without a problem.

With only one beat remaining in the measure, one quarter must be borrowed from the whole note of the original in order to complete the first measure.

2ND MEASURE: You are looking for four quarter note beats. The remainder of the whole note (3 beats) is placed as a dotted half and tied to the previous quarter in measure #1. One beat remains in the measure. A quarter note must be borrowed from the half note in order to complete the second measure.

3RD MEASURE: You are looking for four quarter note beats. The remainder of the half note (1 beat) is placed as a quarter note and tied to the previous quarter in the 2nd measure, leaving three beats

open in the measure. The 8th rest from the original is smaller than the second beat and is placed as the first half of the second beat ("Num"). There is still a half beat ("ber") needed in the second beat before the third beat may be begun. The first two 16ths in the original equal an 8th note, so can be brought into place to complete beat #2. The third beat becomes then a combination of the next two 16ths and the 8th note. These are beamed together since they now occupy the same beat. Finally, a quarter rest is borrowed from the dotted quarter rest which completes the third measure.

LAST MEASURE: You are looking for four quarter note beats. The  remaining 8th rest from the borrowed dotted quarter rest is placed on beat #1 which leaves a half beat open in the first beat. The dotted quarter note, being larger than a beat (rule B) is placed "as is" on the "&" of the first beat which sustains through the second beat. Having run out of original rhythm, a half rest completes the measure.

The same original in compound time would look as follows:

ORIGINAL

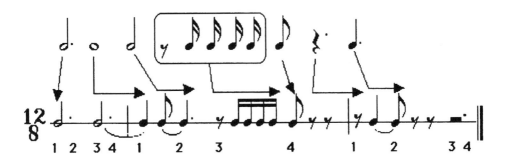

Notice the differences when the original is applied to different size beats. Especially notice that the half note and the dotted quarter needed to be broken, due to the fact that they did not fall on the beat.

MOVEMENT APPLICATIONS

4.20   Clusters: compound

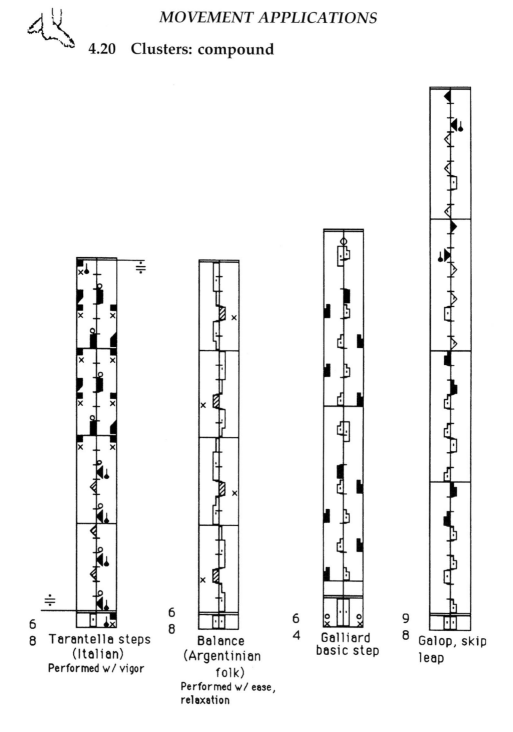

6
8   Tarantella steps
      (Italian)
   Performed w/ vigor

6
8   Balance
   (Argentinian
      folk)
   Performed w/ ease,
   relaxation

6
4   Galliard
   basic step

9
8   Galop, skip
   leap

4.21   Clusters: ballet springs

Note that the horizontal "connecting bow" between the leg columns means the legs are touching. Note: The ballet movements below are written with general timing indications.

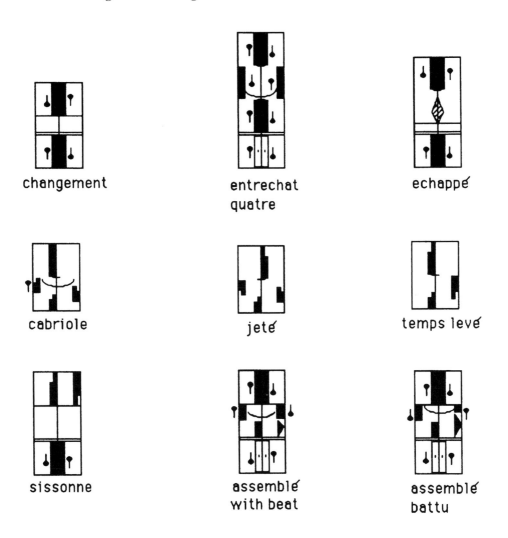

changement

entrechat
quatre

echappé

cabriole

jeté

temps levé

sissonne

assemblé
with beat

assemblé
battu

4.22   Clusters: folk and social

Note: Springing steps in folk and social dances are often written in middle level. The emphasis in these steps is not on vertical change, so little plié is necessary or desired on the take-offs and landings. (Look at the polka and

schottische below.) The mazurka, however, is one example
of a national dance step that is written in low level, to
communicate its weightedness and sense of being
"into the floor".

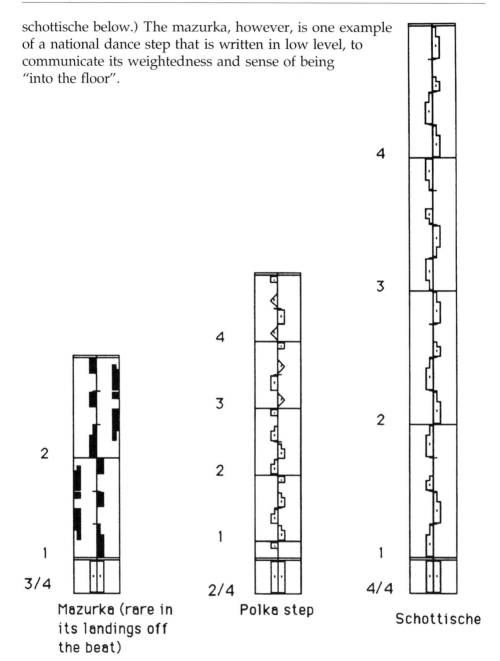

Mazurka (rare in
its landings off
the beat)

Polka step

Schottische

4.23 Clusters: modern

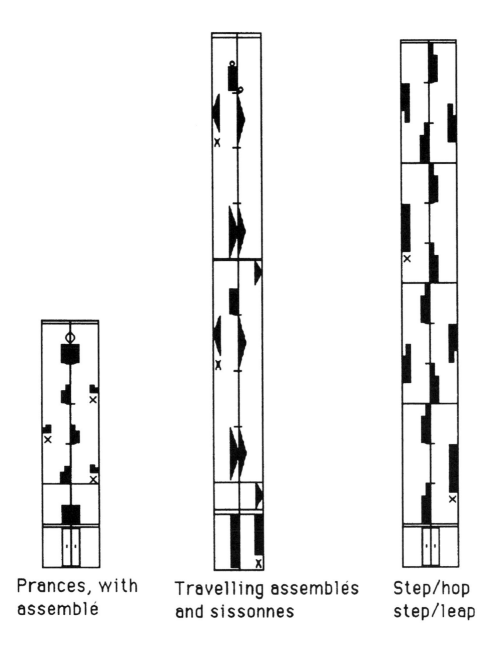

Prances, with
assemblé

Travelling assemblés
and sissonnes

Step/hop
step/leap

4.24   Compound Conducting Patterns

Conducting in compound time requires the "sub-division" of the basic conducting patterns (shown in 2.21) to reflect the triple division of the beat.

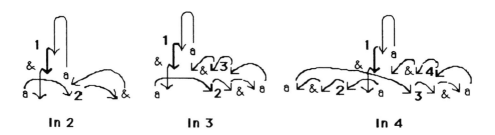

In 2   **In 3**   **In 4**

This type of conducting sub-division occurs only when the tempo is slow to moderate. In faster tempos, because the arm can not move quickly enough to reflect each beat's subdivisions, the basic simple conducting

In 6   In 9   In 12
8   8   8

patterns are used instead, with the triple feeling.
Remember as you practice to include the crusic, metacrusic, and ana-crusic beat qualities which are also present in compound meters.

- When conducting a compound "2", try saying:
  "PRESS a da LIFT a da".
- When conducting a compound "3", try saying:
  "PRESS a da OUT a da LIFT a da".
- When conducting a compound "4", try saying:
  "PRESSa da INa da OUTa da LIFTa da".

CHAPTER WRAP

4.25 RN Etudes

The following exercises are in compound time. Remember to use the new Hand-el and divide the beat into thirds.

#1.

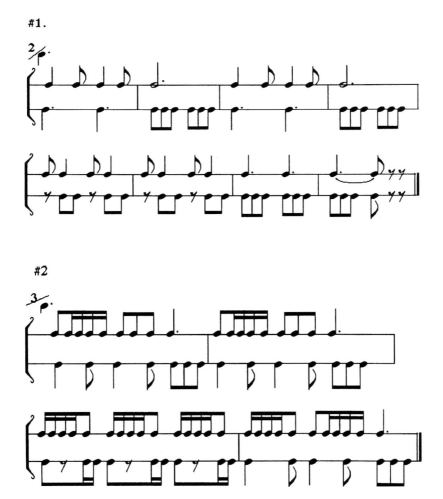

#2

#3

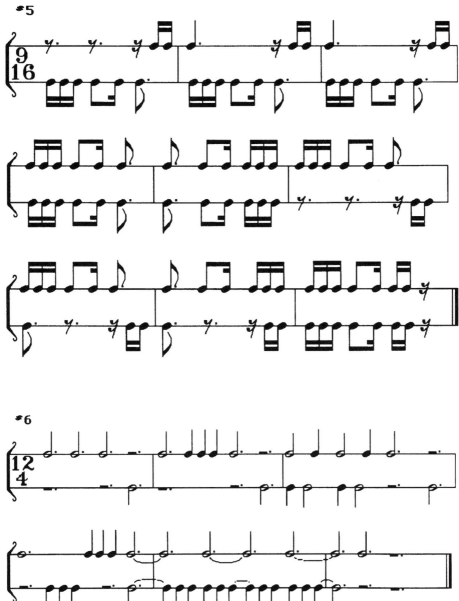

4.26   LN Etudes

1. Polka

Cue #14

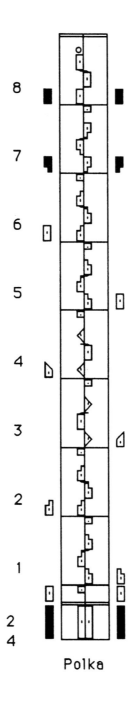

Polka

2. Port de bras (Vagonova Technique)

Half Port de Bras

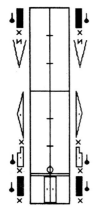

V = allongé,
breath in the arms
(see ch. 6)

[The arms gently
extend and the hands turn,
preparatory to lowering.
This is a shorthand
symbol combination.]

1st Port de Bras

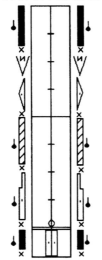

2nd Port de Bras

Face downstage left,
head turned slightly
to the right

3. Circle Dance in 6/8

Cues #15A and B

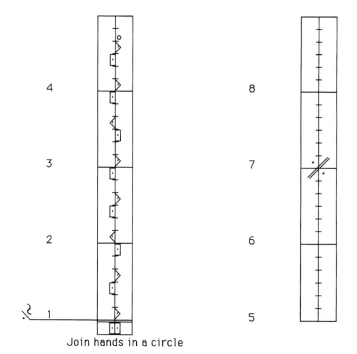

Join hands in a circle

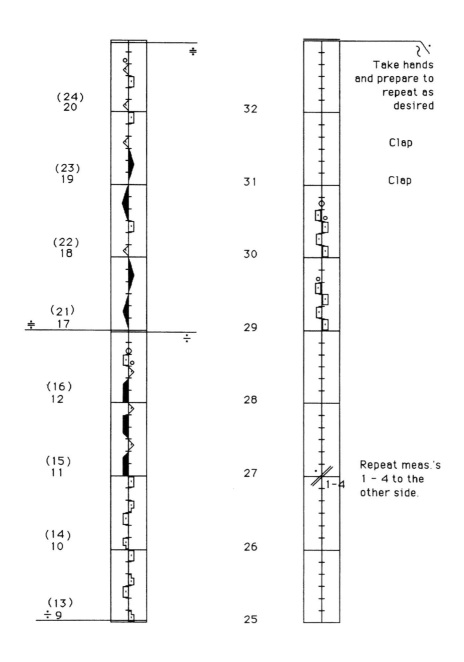

4.27   More Tricky Rhythms

Note that normal beat strokes have been removed from these examples. Lines have been inserted to help you see the principal compound beat divisions: 3 beats in 9/8; 4 in 12/8; and 2 in 6/8.

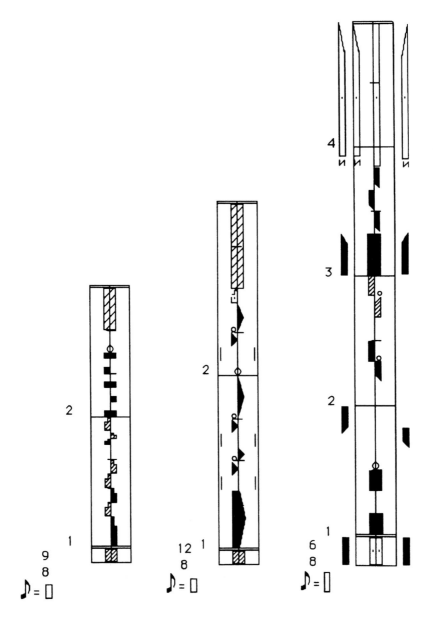

4.28 Suggested Assignments

Make 4 cards for each of the new Compound Code Words. Keep them in three separate decks at first: Quarters & 8ths; 8ths; and 8ths & 16ths. When you have attained equal proficiency with each deck, shuffle them together.

• Shuffle all of your Simple Code Word cards together into one deck and practice laying them out in rows of 2, 3, and 4, reading them at a slow, steady tempo. Increase speed as you are able.

• Re-organize the following original into 6/8, 9/8, and 12/8, then 2/4, 3/4, and 4/4. When reorganizing in Compound Time, remember that each beat must equal a dotted quarter and NOT a quarter. In all other respects the procedure is exactly the same as in Simple Time. Be sure to beam all 8ths and 16ths together within the same beat and add rests (if necessary) in last measures which require them:

• Align the following four parts together. The procedure is the same as in Chapter 3 except you must add one more line to the score. The parts are NOT aligned below. Do not reorganize: simply transfer to score paper and align, beat by beat:

Choreograph a trio in which each dancer performs the identical movement, but in which each is assigned a different beating note, affecting the tempo at which they move. One example would be to use 3/2, 3/4, and 3/8. Rehearse this trio with a metronome set to click the beat of the middle of the three time signatures. One dancer will then perform on the beat; one will be twice as slow; the other, twice as fast. The result will be three simultaneous presentations of the same movement that will appear both similar and different. The dancers will (of course) end at three different times.

Disperse your dancers in space, and then have them dance very close together. How does this affect the overall results?

After practice, experiment with the dancers *beginning* at three different times. View the results, then decide if you wish to introduce some pauses into one or more of the parts.

- Choreograph a solo of from 8 to 12 measures in 9/8. Write the rhythm of the steps in RN. Then re-group the rhythm into 2/4 in RN. Now perform the dance first with the original 9/8 rhythm; then with the re-grouped 2/4. (Sing the rhythms into a cassette recorder.) Allow the original choreography to bend to the rhythm in 2/4; then, fight the rhythm in 2/4, keeping the quality of its original 9/8. Which meter works better with your dance? Why?

- Read and perform the Taiwanese Tribal Dance. Because of the extended series of springs in this dance, none of them is taken high off the floor.

TAIWANESE TRIBAL DANCE

notated by Yun-yu Wang

This Taiwanese tribal dance is from the central part of Taiwan. It is a circle dance that was originally performed by men and women. The dancers stand side-by-side with hands joined. There is a 4-measure introduction in the music, during which the dancers bounce on the beat while raising or lowering their arms every 2 beats (while continuing to hold hands).

Cue #16

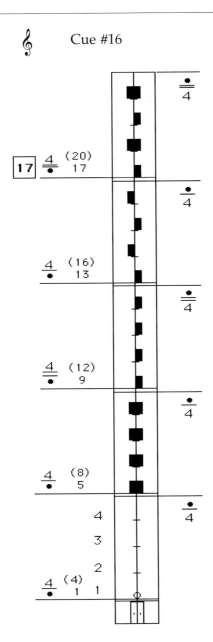

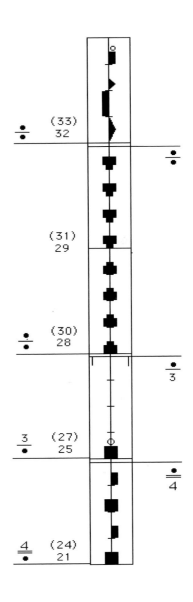

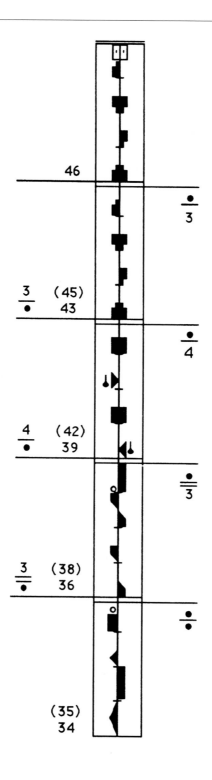

- Re-write the folk dance *Selyanchitsa* below using repeat signs. Ten measures would be an ideal solution.

- Perform *Selyanchitsa* with its music on the audio tape. What quality should the Kolo have, judging from its music?

Selyanchitsa (a Kolo from the former Yugoslavia)
Dancers join hands in a circle; the knees are relaxed throughout.

Cue #17

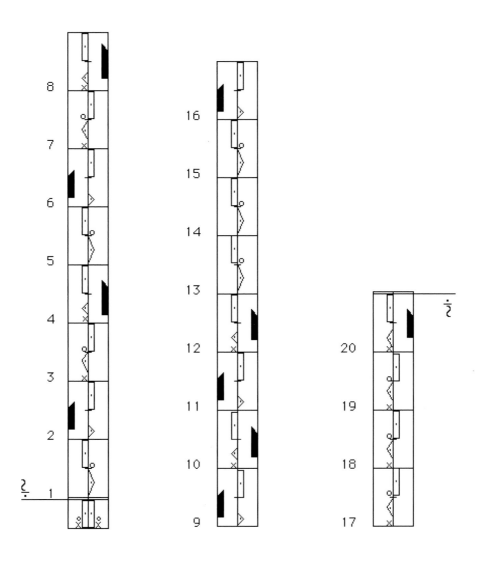

5
2's AND 3's

You have probably by now correctly deduced that 2's and 3's are the building blocks of Western rhythm. There are duple and triple beats (divisible by two or three); simple and compound note values (dotted values being triply divided); simple and compound time signatures (the 'beating note' divisible by two or three); and duple and triple time signatures (having two, three, or four beats per measure). In the above cases, the 2's or 3's are used consistently: you use either a simple or compound beat, a simple or compound measure, etc. As we enter this chapter, 2's and 3's will begin to come together WITHIN THE SAME MEASURE.

RHYTHMIC CONCEPTS

5.1   Irregular Meter

Irregular meter (also called Imperfect or Uneven meter) refers to any time signature in which the number of beats per measure is **not** divisible by two or three without a fraction. Consequently, the backbone metric patterns of Irregular meter are the odd numbers **5, 7, 11, 13,** and so forth. [**Note:** Numbers larger than 13, even or odd, can be divided Irregularly as well.] Since 5, 7, 11, 13 can not be evenly divided by two **OR** three (without a fraction), they can therefore be divided only by combinations of two and three TOGETHER. This fact leads to the primary difference between Perfect and Irregular meter, that *both duple AND triple beats can be used together in the same measures*. And, because of this "irregularity", there is a quality which is special to Irregular time signatures: they may be divided (or 'felt') in more ways than one.

   Maxim #71: Irregular Meter (large, odd-numbered time signatures) is defined as a number of beats per measure *not* divisble by two or three (without a fraction). Consequently, both duple AND triple beats can be used together in the same "Irregular" measures.

5.2   Long Beats and Short Beats

When one counts from 1 to 11 without inflection in a moderate, steady tempo, each count receives an equal emphasis, which we will call a "generic" eleven. Should you add emphasis to certain numbers within that eleven, you create internal 'sub-groupings' of various sizes. This we will call a "sub-grouped" eleven. Count steadily:

In this 'generic' example, there are 11 equal beats in the measure, with normal crusis on the downbeat, anacrusis on the upbeat (beat # 11), and 9 metacrusic beats (#'s 2–10).

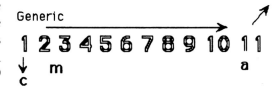

In the 'sub-grouped' example, there are **4** groupings in the measure: three "triple", (comprised of three numbers each), followed by one "duple" (comprised of two numbers). If we think of each grouping as a beat, we could say that this is a "quadruple 11": Crusis, metacrusis, growing metacrusis, and anacrusis.

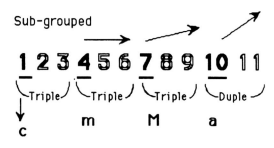

   Try this: Set a metronome to 80 m.m. and count the generic 11 several times in succession. As you do, move your arm from left to right, touching 11 points along the way. Then, count the sub-grouped 11, this time using the conductors arm beats in 4: **1** 2 3/**4** 5 6/**7** 8 9/**10** 11. Feel the difference?

These sub-groupings are called **Long beats** and **Short beats**, and, when present, determine how many beats there will be in a measure. In the previous example, the generic 11 has eleven *equal* beats, while the sub-grouped 11 has only four: three long beats (triple) and one short beat (duple). The reason a composer or choreographer divides an irregular meter has a lot to due with personal taste and *tempo*. Consequently, generic measures will usually occur at slower tempi while sub-grouped measures (fewer beats) will appear in faster tempi.

Here are some of the more common sub-groupings of Irregular measures:

Five digits are usually divided into a 3 followed by a 2 or vice versa:

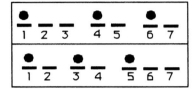

Seven is usually divided into a 3 followed by two 2's or vice versa:

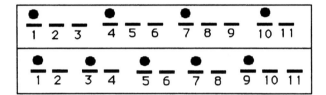

Eleven is usually divided into three 3's followed by a 2 or vice versa:

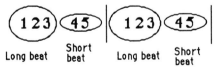

Thirteen is usually divided into three '3's' followed by two '2's' or vice versa:

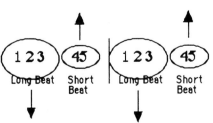

It is from the establishment of sub-groupings like those above that Irregular time signatures derive their "beats per measure": each sub-grouping taking on the role of a crusic, metacrusic, or anacrusic beat. At right, assuming a moderate to fast tempo, this '5' is sub-grouped into two beats per measure: one **long** beat followed by one **short** beat:

The long beat is performed as a down-beat since it is the first beat in the measure. The short beat will be performed as an upbeat since it comes after the downbeat:

Finally, as with any other time signature, long and short beats should be counted sequentially starting with "1" in each measure.

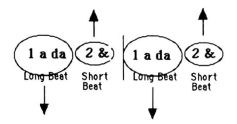

Sub-group Registration. Because 5's, 7's, etc. can take so many forms, a registration is usually placed above the time signature to help the performer see the intended sub-groupings and therefore perform with greater clarity. If a measure of seven is to be divided into a long beat followed by two short beats, the following registration should be placed over the time signature: **(3+2+2)**. If, during subsequent measures the division of the measure is changed, a new registration can be placed over the bar line where the change is to occur, or dotted lines known as "division marks" may be drawn between the new sub-groupings:

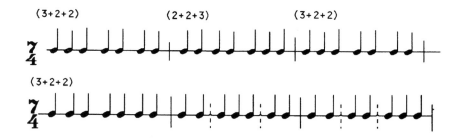

> Maxim #72: Long beats and short beats are terms describing the effect of duple and triple sub-groupings within measures of Irregular meter. Depending on tempo, each sub-group is usually felt as one beat.

5.3   The Tree of Irregular Meter

The following tree presents most of the "working" time signatures in Irregular meter. In addition to their generic values, they are shown with their sub-groupings (number of beats per measure). For example, a generic 7 becomes a triple measure when sub-grouped $3+2+2$.

Tree of Irregular Meter

SIMPLE   **COMPOUND**

5

$\frac{5}{16}$ $\frac{5}{8}$ $\frac{5}{4}$ $\frac{5}{2}$ $\frac{5}{1}$

Duple
(2+3) or (3+2)

$\frac{5}{\text{♩.}}$ $\frac{5}{\text{♩.}}$ $\frac{5}{\text{♩.}}$

or   or   or

$\frac{15}{16}$ $\frac{15}{8}$ $\frac{15}{4}$

7

$\frac{7}{16}$ $\frac{7}{8}$ $\frac{7}{4}$ $\frac{7}{2}$ $\frac{7}{1}$

Duple
(3+4) or (4+3)

Triple
(2+2+3) (3+2+2)
(2+3+2)

$\frac{7}{\text{♩.}}$ $\frac{7}{\text{♩.}}$ $\frac{7}{\text{♩.}}$

or   or   or

$\frac{21}{16}$ $\frac{21}{8}$ $\frac{21}{4}$

11

$\frac{11}{16}$ $\frac{11}{8}$ $\frac{11}{4}$

$\frac{11}{2}$ $\frac{11}{1}$

Duple
(6+5) or (5+6)

Triple
(4+4+3) (3+4+4)
(4+3+4)

Quadruple
(3+3+3+2) (2+3+3+3)
(3+2+3+3) (3+3+2+3)

$\frac{11}{\text{♩.}}$ $\frac{11}{\text{♩.}}$ $\frac{11}{\text{♩.}}$

or   or   or

$\frac{33}{16}$ $\frac{33}{8}$ $\frac{33}{4}$

13

$\frac{13}{16}$ $\frac{13}{8}$ $\frac{13}{4}$

$\frac{13}{2}$ $\frac{13}{1}$

Duple
(6+7) or (7+6)

Triple
(5+5+3) (3+5+5)
(5+3+5)

Quadruple
(4+3+3+3) (3+4+3+3)
(3+3+4+3) (3+3+3+4)

Quintuple
(3+3+3+2+2) (2+3+3+3+2)
(3+3+2+2+3) (2+3+3+2+3)
(3+2+2+3+3) (2+3+2+3+3)
(2+3+3+3+2) (3+2+3+2+3)

$\frac{13}{\text{♩.}}$ $\frac{13}{\text{♩.}}$ $\frac{13}{\text{♩.}}$

or   or   or

$\frac{39}{16}$ $\frac{39}{8}$ $\frac{39}{4}$

> Maxim #73: All irregular Time signatures can be felt generi-
> cally, or can be sub-grouped in a variety of configurations.

5.4   Polyrhythm: triplets and duplets

Another example of 2's and 3's occurring in the same beat/measure are
called *triplets* and *duplets*. The triplet refers to *"a 3" in the space where "a 2"
normally occurs.* They work on the principle of **compression**: that is, the
three notes in the triplet are compressed into a space of two. In effect,
each note is equally *reduced* in size.

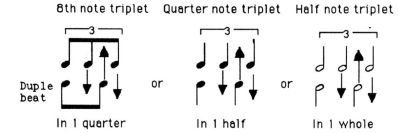

The duplet refers to *'a 2' in the space where 'a 3' normally occurs.* They work
on the principle of **expansion**: that is, two notes are expanded to fill a
space of three. In effect, each note is equally "expanded", allowing the
two notes of the duplet to become equally increased in size.

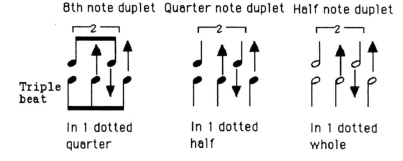

The primary difference between duplets and triplets is the same as that
between simple and compound beats: *Duplets (2's) proceed in a linear,
square-like manner, and triplets (3's), more curvilinear.* Triplets may be
thought of as curves within a straight landscape and duplets as straight
lines within a curved landscape. Therefore, a triplet or duplet is introduced
into a rhythmic pattern when a movement or moment in the music is to

feel "rounder" or "straighter" than the surrounding beats. *Generally triplets will occur in simple measures and duplets will occur in compound measures.*

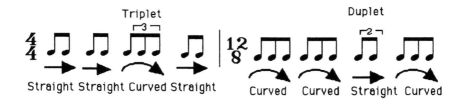

The code word for triplets can be **Trip-el-et** or **"3-of-them"**, or **"Har-mo-ny"**. The code word for duplets can be **"Dup-let" or "2-Things"** or **"Num-ber"**, whichever feels best to you.

Below are listed some of the triplet configurations you will encounter in your reading and composing:

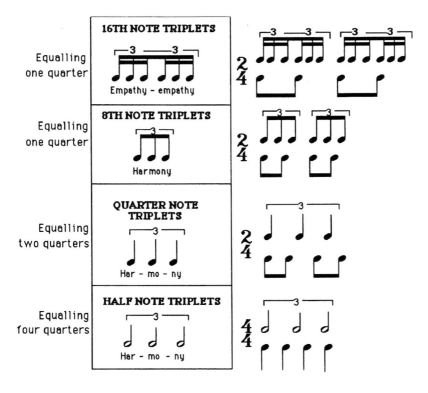

Below are some of the duplet configurations you will encounter in your reading and composing:

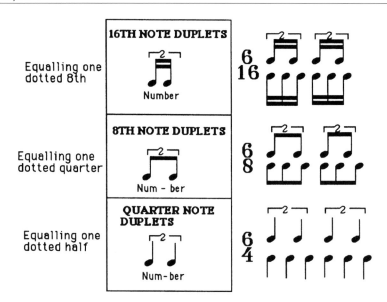

 Maxim #74: Triplets may be thought of as curves within a straight landscape and duplets as straight lines within a curved landscape.

5.5   Polymeter: "two against three"

Polymeter is a term meaning two meters occur at the same time, one common polymeter being the simultaneous playing of a duple and a triple meter, called *2 against 3*. Because the common denominator of two and three is six, the time signature 3/4 is used to represent the 3, and 6/8 to represent the 2, since each has six eighth-notes per measure. Lets look at an example: six can be divided into three groups of two, or two groups of three. Imagine the numbers below to the eighth-notes: the bottom x's represent three quarter notes in 3/4, the upper x's represent the dotted quarters in 6/8.

In the 3/4 below, the quarter notes would be felt as the basic beat with the dotted quarters felt as a "superimposition" of a "**2 against the 3**". In the 6/8 to the right, the reverse is true: there are 2 basic beats with the "superimposition" occurring in the three quarters, creating "**3 against the 2**".

There is no special notational symbol used to denote the presence of 2 against 3. Instead, in 3/4, two dotted quarter notes AUTOMATICALLY suggest the presence of "a 2 against the 3". In 6/8, three quarter notes AUTOMATICALLY suggest the presence of "a 3 against the 2".

To practice 3 against 2
Say the following sentence several times in the rhythm indicated:

Go and get her

Now say the same sentence, first emphasizing the basic "2" (stems down) and then the superimposed "3" (stems up):

Go   and   her

Go   get

Now try it with both hands in 6/8:

- Count to six out loud a few times in a slow tempo.
- Let the left hand emphasize 1 and 4 while the right hand lightly taps the superimposed 1 3 5.
- Practice each hand separately, then together. Then alternate hands.

```
       6
       5  x her
get x  4
       3  x and
       2
Go  x  1  x  Go
    L.H.   R.H.
```

To practice 2 against 3
Say this sentence a few times in 3/4.

She's on her way

Now, say either the notes with stems up or down.

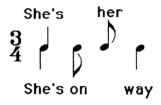

Now try it with both hands:

- Count to six out loud a few times in a slow tempo.
- Let the left hand emphasize 1-3-5 while the right hand lightly taps the superimposed 1-4.
- Practice each hand separately. Then together. Alternate hands.

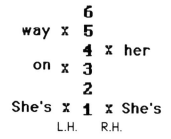

 Maxim #75: "2 against 3" and "3 against 2" are terms for the simultaneous juxtaposition of duple and triple metric patterns WITHIN THE SAME MEASURE.

One way to physicalize these two polymeters is to "walk" your hands down your body from shoulder to knee as shown below. Allow each arm to arch out through space (away from the body) between touches. Experience the distance from the body that each arm travels as it moves to its next touch:

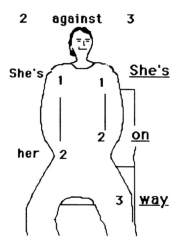

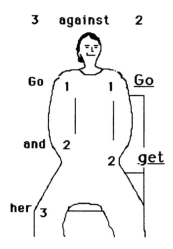

MOVEMENT CONCEPTS

5.6 Pivot Turns

Pivot turns cause the body to revolve around its vertical axis, whether turning to the right or left (clockwise or counterclockwise). "Turning",

"pivoting", and "swiveling" can all be used to describe the action of revolving while standing. The symbols for turning are parallelograms, whose top and bottom edges slant upwards in the direction of the turn.

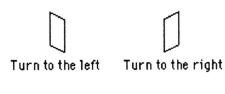

When turning on 2 feet, a turn sign is placed in both the support columns.

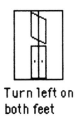 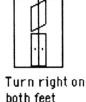

Turn left on both feet   Turn right on both feet

When turning on one foot, a turn sign is placed in the appropriate support column.

Turn right on the right foot   Turn left on the right foot   Turn right on the left foot   Turn left on the left foot

---

 Maxim #76: The shape of a turn sign indicates which way to turn, and its placement on the staff indicates whether a turn is on 1 or 2 feet.

The *length* of the turn sign tells how long it takes to do the turn:

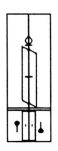 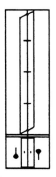

Turn in 2 cts.   Turn in 4 cts.

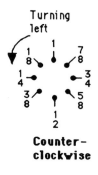

Turning
left

Counter–
clockwise

A *pin* inside the turn sign tells the dancer how much to turn. These diagrams illustrate how pins show degrees of turn by where they point within a clockwise or counter clockwise circle.

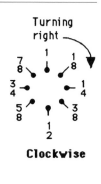

Turning
right

Clockwise

 This pin indicates
1/2
turn

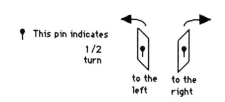

to the
left

to the
right

Maxim #77: The *length* of the turn sign indicates timing, and pins within turn signs indicate the *degree* of turn.

Levels in turn signs

The only time level shading appears in a turn sign is when a change of level occurs during a turn. Otherwise, turns are performed in the same level as the steps or preparations that precede them. It is important to notice *when* a change of levels occurs in a turn sign.

Level change at the beginning of a turn

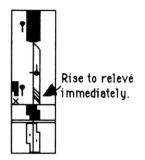

Rise to relevé immediately.

Notice that the high level stripes follow the shape of the turn sign. This is the only exception to the rule that high-level stripes ascend from left to right.

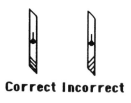

Correct Incorrect

Level change at the end of a turn

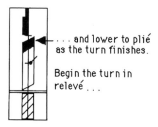

. . . and lower to plié as the turn finishes.

Begin the turn in relevé . . .

Gradual level change throughout a turn

IMPORTANT: Turn signs are never completely shaded, since it would then be impossible to see the degree-of-turn pin.

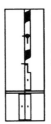

... but take the entire turn to reach low level.

Begin to plié at the start of the turn ...

 Maxim #78: No level in a turn sign means to stay in the level of the previous step or preparation. Partial shading within a turn sign indicates a change of level DURING the turn.

1/2 turn to the left on both feet, in relevé.

Step in mid. level, then plié as 1/8 turn to left begins.

Step RF diag. low; do a complete turn, coming to mid. level as the turn ends.

Step LF diag. mid; turn 1/2 to left, coming to relevé as turn ends.

Step fwd. high, then turn 1/4 to R in same level.

Step side low, then turn 3/8 to L in same level.

Step side low, then turn 3/8 to R, remaining in plié.

IMPORTANT: In all of the previous examples, the step and turn are considered *separate* actions: the step occurs and THEN the turn occurs. Steps and turns together (as single combined actions) are covered later in this chapter.

Front Signs

After every turn there will be a facing pin in the dance score that tells the dancer where to face at the end of the turn, in relation to the space in which the dance is taking place. Front signs are made up of 2 parts: a square that represents the stage or performance area; and a pin that points to where the dancer ends facing. Front signs are also commonly referred to as stage facings. Front signs are placed to the left of the starting position to indicate the dancer's facing at the start of a dance. Thereafter, a front sign is placed to the left of the staff **at the conclusion** of every turn, to re-orient the reader as to the new facing in the performance space.

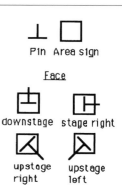

Pin   Area sign

Face

downstage   stage right

upstage   upstage
right   left

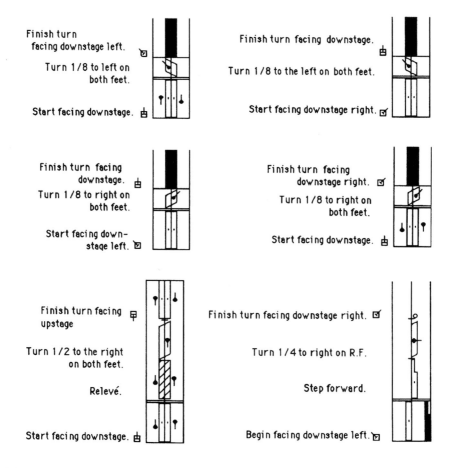

Finish turn facing downstage left.

Turn 1/8 to left on both feet.

Start facing downstage.

Finish turn facing downstage.

Turn 1/8 to the left on both feet.

Start facing downstage right.

Finish turn facing downstage.

Turn 1/8 to right on both feet.

Start facing down-stage left.

Finish turn facing downstage right.

Turn 1/8 to right on both feet.

Start facing downstage.

Finish turn facing upstage

Turn 1/2 to the right on both feet.

Relevé.

Start facing downstage.

Finish turn facing downstage right.

Turn 1/4 to right on R.F.

Step forward.

Begin facing downstage left.

Maxim #79: Front signs after every turn give the dancer's new stage facing direction.

5.7   Applying Ties to Steps and Turns

A vertical tie will connect steps or preparations that are linked to a turn in time,
indicating that *the step and turn are to be
performed as one smooth action* instead of
two distinct and separate actions. Without a tie, turns are performed with some
sense of separation from the steps that
lead into them.

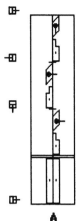
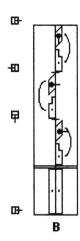

A   B

Ex. A: Steps and turns as separate actions.
Ex. B: Steps and turns as combined actions.

Notice that ties connecting steps and turns cannot begin at the start of the
step, to allow for the step direction to be established. This is exactly the
same logic as the step-gesture rule; it is **the step-turn rule**. Ties may
extend as far through the turn sign as necessary, and the length of the tie
will affect blending or "overlap".

Most often, steps ands turns overlap completely; i.e., as soon as the
dancer has begun transfering some weight onto the stepping foot, turning
begins. A very short tie is used as a shorthand for this complete overlap,
to avoid the space and consuming overlapping bow.

Sometimes the overlap is less than complete, in
which case the tie changes to show the exact
timing:

Begin blending into
the turn toward the
end of the step.

Maxim #80: Ties are used to blend steps and turns. *Where* the tie starts and ends tells how far tranference of weight extends *through the turn.*

5.8   Turns in the Air

For a turn to go into the air, a turn sign must be drawn across both support columns, and must be accompanied by 2 leg gestures or **air lines**. Recall that air lines are action strokes in the leg gesture columns. (See 4.14.)

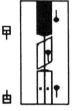

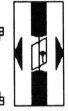

Half-pivot on the ground

Half-turn in the air. Air lines added to the turn sign release the legs from the floor.

Half-turn in the air with the legs opening to the side low in the air. The 2 leg gestures release both legs from the floor.

Actions in both leg gesture columns will cancel the support implied by the turn sign, in the same way they cancel hold signs. Notice that the turn sign appears over BOTH support columns for turns in the air, since no single leg is pivoting or can complete an air turn on its own.

 Maxim #81: Turns in the air are notated with a turn sign over both support columns, plus a release from the floor indicated with air lines or leg gestures.

5.9   Turns that Begin or End in the Air

Turns that go into the air sometimes start with a turn on the floor, or finish with one. In the following example, the dancer begins with a step to the side, and a pivot on the right foot. Part-way through the turn, the dancer goes into the air. At this point in the notation, the turn sign expands to cover **both** support columns, and air lines appear. The dancer lands on both feet after having done one full revolution.

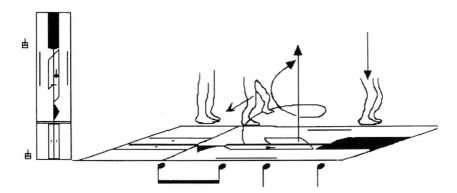

In the opposite case, i.e., a turn that begins in the air and finishes on the ground, *a landing always comes between the two turn signs.*

The landing is tied to the half-turn on the ground, to indicate that there is no break between the turn that began in the air, and the continuation of the turn upon landing.

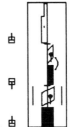

4: Step fwd.

3: Land on R.F. and keep turning, another 1/2 turn on the ground.

2: half-turn in the air.

1: Preparation.

 Maxim #82: Turns that begin in the air and continue on the floor use ties to connect the landing with the continuation of the turn. The landing and 2nd turn sign are joined.

5.10   Retentions in Space ("space holds")

Some movements require that a part of the body retain a spacial direction while the rest of the body turns. In effect, the body part that is NOT turning is thought of as "holding its spacial direction" while the rest of the body turns. A symbol called a space hold is used to maintain the position of the body part not involved in the turn.

The symbol for the space hold is a white diamond. One example of a turn employing a space hold is the "fouetté arabesque," a basic step from the ballet vocabulary, and performed in other dance styles. In a leg gesture column, the space hold keeps the leg in the same direction during the half-turn for the body as a whole. As a result of the space hold, the leg finishes behind the body (in arabesque) at the conclusion of the turn.

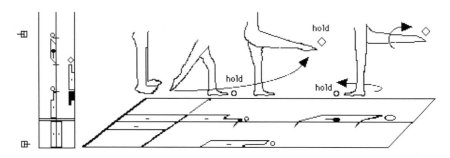

The same holds true for arm gestures:

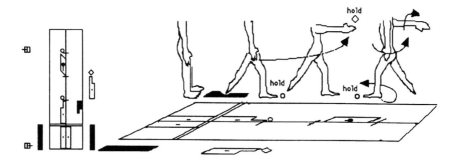

Notice that the right arm would stay in front of the body throughout the turn without the space hold:

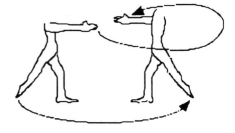

Space holds are always written opposite turn signs. Therefore, if a gesture continues during a turn, the space hold will be placed *inside* the gesture, as illustrated here. The direction the gesture moves in is judged from before the turn.

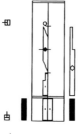

Arm moves continuously during the turn, finishing to the right of the body.

OR

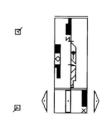

Leg lifts throughout the turn, ending fwd. of the body.

> Maxim #83: Space holds keep a part of the body in the previously stated spatial direction while the rest of the body turns.

5.11 Transitional and Non-swivel Turns

Turns that are unimportant to choreography, other than as a means of bringing a dancer to face a new direction, are often quick actions that immediately precede a major action or phrase. Transitional turns, as these actions are called, should be recognized for what they are in the score: *unemphasized* moments leading to something more important.

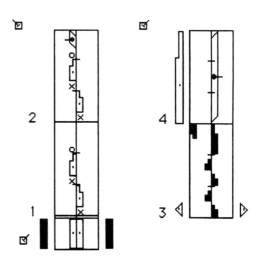

Above, the turn at the end of measure #2 is a transitional turn, bringing the dancer to face downstage left for a series of quick runs to that corner. The turn itself is unimportant. The turn in measure #4 is a more important, independent action.

Transitional turns often occur as preparations:

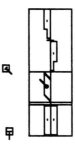

Non-swivel Turns. Some turns are choreographed so that the foot does not swivel on the floor as the body turns; it retains its previous spatial direction. These turns, in which the entire body turns without the supporting foot or feet moving, are called "non-swivel" turns. A space hold symbol is used to notate non-swivel turns. The space hold is placed in the leg gesture column *of the turning foot*, where it prevents the leg from rotating as the body turns to face its new direction.

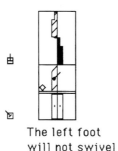

The left foot will not swivel as the entire body turns.

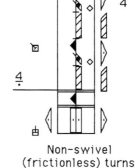

Non-swivel (frictionless) turns on the right foot.

Maxim #84: Transitional turns are unemphasized actions that change a dancer's facing in preparation for a more major action. These often take the form of non-swivel turns that use space holds on the standing leg to prevent the foot from swiveling.

NOTATION

5.12   RN Rules

A. To aid the eye in "seeing" the intended long and short beats within each measure, beams should be employed to maximum effect. In the following example, a combination of beaming plus good spacing allows the eye to recognize that there is one short and three long beats in the measure. Without the appropriate spacing and beaming, it would be impossible to tell what sub-grouping was intended:

B. Triplets and duplets must always be accompanied by an identification bracket. In places where more than one triplet or duplet is to be

performed in a row, each triplet must be bracketed, although in some scores the bracket is omitted and the 3 itself is sufficient.

5.13   Front Signs: stage facings

Where you place a front sign on the staff is important. Because the dancer's facing is changing constantly during a turn, it makes no sense to place a stage facing pin in the same count or part of a count as a turn sign. The new front sign is established **after** turning has stopped. So, *front signs are placed immediately after turns*, even at the end of a staff.

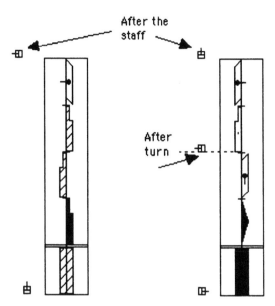

5.14   Pins in Turn Signs

Pins in turn signs should be placed where they are most easily seen. Avoid putting them directly on the center line. A good general rule is to place pins for right turns to the right of the center line, and vice versa. This makes reading easier, and reinforces the direction of the turn.

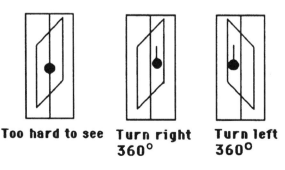

Too hard to see   Turn right 360°   Turn left 360°

When more than one turn is performed, a pair of pins can be placed in the turn sign. There's a principle of logic to notice here. Since LN is read from bottom up, the reader should encounter important information about the **amount** of turn at the bottom of the turn sign. So, the "whole turn" pin is always placed at the beginning of the turn sign, with the remaining fraction of the turn following it.

Numbers are used for 2 or more turns, with pins added as necessary for fractions.

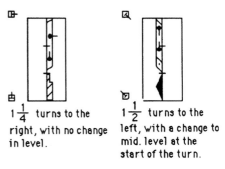

$1\frac{1}{4}$ turns to the right, with no change in level.

$1\frac{1}{2}$ turns to the left, with a change to mid. level at the start of the turn.

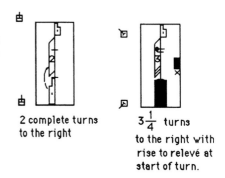

2 complete turns to the right

$3\frac{1}{4}$ turns to the right with rise to relevé at start of turn.

5.15   Turn Signs: leg gestures

Turn signs can appear in the leg gesture columns to describe a particular stance or rotation of the legs, such as turn-out, turn-in, or parallel. These turn signs do not affect the facing of the performer, since they do not appear in the support column(s). However, they do rotate (turn) the legs from the hips, affecting how they are placed or held as they step or gesture.

 Standing feet together, with the legs rotated outward. Turn signs that point out, away from the center line of the staff, describe <u>Turn-out</u>.

 Plié in 1st position, with the legs rotated inward. Turn signs that point in toward the center line of the staff describe <u>Turn-in</u>.

 Feet together in relevé, in parallel stance. A "composite sign" (a combination of both R and L turn signs) is used to describe this neutral stance, with the legs rotated <u>neither</u> in nor out.

Maxim #85: Turn signs in the leg gesture columns describe parallel, turned-out, or turned-in rotations of the legs.

If a particular degree of turn-out or turn-in is desired, pins are added to the turn signs for the legs. The pins are different from those used in the support columns, and are called 'open' or 'white' pins. The open pins reinforce the fact that these turns are different from those for the entire body, and that they affect only one body part. White pins indicate how much to turn the leg in or out from parallel position (feet pointing forward).

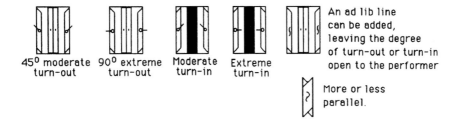

45° moderate turn-out   90° extreme turn-out   Moderate turn-in   Extreme turn-in

An ad lib line can be added, leaving the degree of turn-out or turn-in open to the performer

More or less parallel.

When turn signs appear in the leg gesture columns in a starting position, *all movements* will be performed with the stated degree of turn-in or turn-out, unless or until other turn signs appear in the leg columns to cancel the previous rotations.

The sequence at right begins in parallel stance, and all actions will be performed in parallel until measure #3, when the legs rotate out in cts. 1 and 2. The subsequent rise and plié will be performed with turn-out, until parallel stance resumes on ct. 3 of meas. #4, in preparation for the repeat.

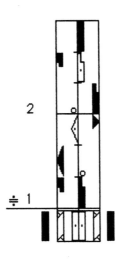

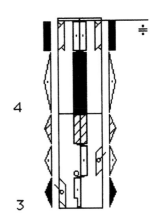

Maxim #86: White or "open" pins are used to specify the degree of turn-out or turn-in for the legs. Leg rotations that appear in starting positions last until cancelled, as do all turn signs in the leg gesture columns.

5.16   Hold Signs on Gestures

In general, hold signs are not necessary on arm or leg gestures. However, hold signs may be added to arm or leg gestures during turns if the "design" of the body is to be especially retained while turning. During turns, arms/legs will normally maintain their position and be "carried along". When extra attention is to be paid to keeping the body's design intact while turning, a hold sign may appear.

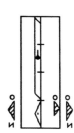 Here, hold signs emphasize the importance of keeping the leg side-high, and the arms in lengthened side-high reaches during this slow promenade turn:

5.17   Tables of Hold Signs and of Cancellations

The following table summarizes usages of space holds and circular hold signs in the support and gesture columns. Notice in the table that maintaining a position does not always require a hold sign.

TABLE OF HOLD SIGNS

	SUPPORTS	ARM GESTURES	LEG GESTURES
HOLD SIGN ○	Maintain weight	Maintain body design exactly	▶
SPACE HOLD ◊	Non-swivel turn ◊---	Maintain direction & level of gesture while rest of body turns	▶ (written here)
OPEN SPACE WITH NO HOLD SIGN	Spring in the air	No movement: stay in previous position.	▶

TABLE OF CANCELLATIONS

	SUPPORTS	ARM GESTURES	LEG GESTURES
HOLD SIGN ○	Any step; air lines or leg gestures on the held leg(s)	Any new arm movement	Any new leg movement
SPACE HOLD ◇	Effect is auto-maticically cancelled at end of non-swivel turn	Automatically cancelled at end of the action the hold modifies.	⟶

5.18   Air Lines with Turns

These are drawn in the leg gesture column(s). They may be drawn longer or shorter, depending upon the duration of the turn in the air. Care should be taken in drawing these air lines, since the point at which they begin establishes the precise moment for leaving the ground.

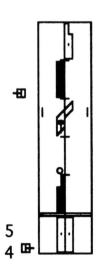

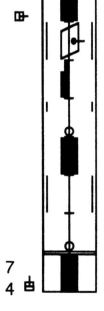

RHYTHMIC APPLICATIONS

5.19   Irregular "Hand-els"

When reading rhythms in irregular meter, it will become necessary to switch back and forth between duple and triple hand-els to follow the long and short beats within each measure.

For example, in the "7" at right, the hand-els should be Number/ Number/Harmony:

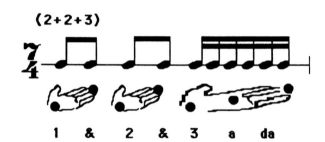

5.20   Re-grouping: irregular

The procedure for re-grouping in irregular meters is identical to re-grouping in Perfect meters. However, you must be particularly careful when deciding what is the most "natural" solution regarding which note and rest values are to be divided within uneven measures. For example, a whole note which falls on beat #1 in a measure of 5/4 can be written in several ways depending on the structure of the measure: 3+2; 2+3; 4 + 1; etc.

Although both notations are correct, you must be extra clear when notating the subtle divisions of irregular meter.

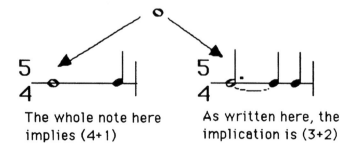

The whole note here implies (4+1)

As written here, the implication is (3+2)

To further illustrate the complexities of re-grouping in irregular meters, the following "original" is re-written in 7/8, sub-grouped into (3+2+2). Watch the re-beaming as well:

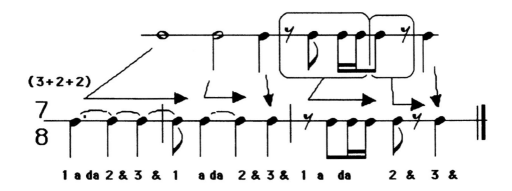

Note that in the 1st measure, it is possible to combine the 2 quarters into a half:

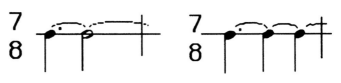

Both solutions are correct

The same original re-grouped in 4/4 would look (and feel) very different:

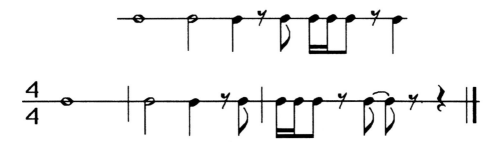

MOVEMENT APPLICATIONS

5.21   Clusters: turns

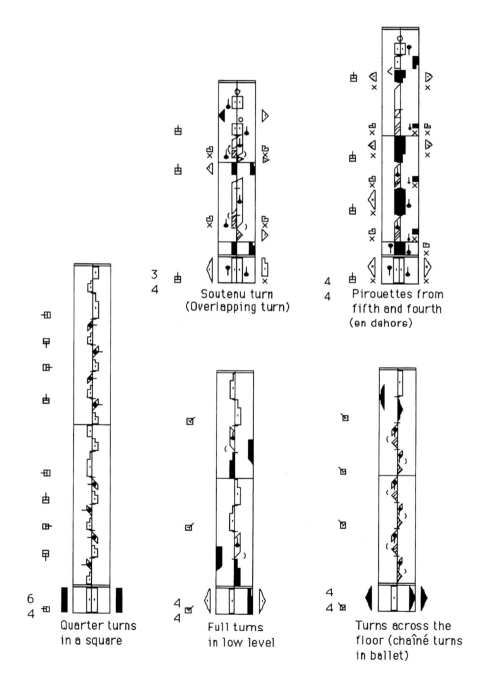

$\dfrac{3}{4}$ Soutenu turn
(Overlapping turn)

$\dfrac{4}{4}$ Pirouettes from
fifth and fourth
(en dehors)

$\dfrac{6}{4}$ Quarter turns
in a square

$\dfrac{4}{4}$ Full turns
in low level

$\dfrac{4}{4}$ Turns across the
floor (chaîné turns
in ballet)

5.22   Clusters: irregular

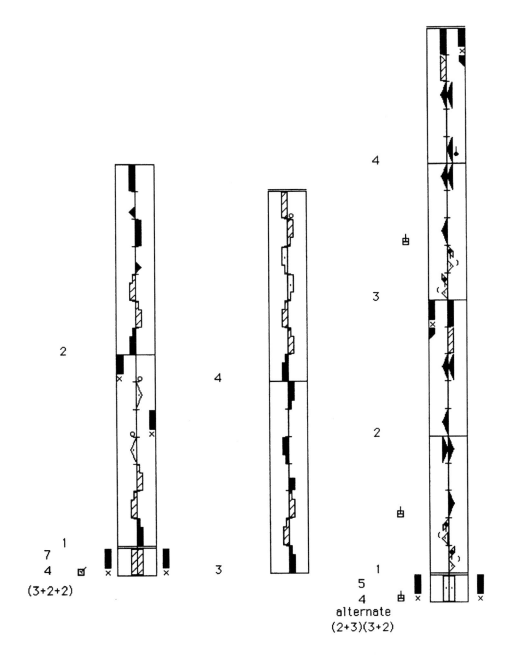

5.23   Conducting Patterns: irregular

When beating 5's and 7's in a moderate to slow tempo, the pattern is divided between the long beats on one side and the short beats on the other.

When the tempo is fast, or when there are especially large measures in use, conductors will modify the pattern to indicate only the essential sub-groupings, reducing the pattern to as few strokes as possible. Although there are literally hundreds of possible patterns in use, it should be sufficient to show just a few examples:

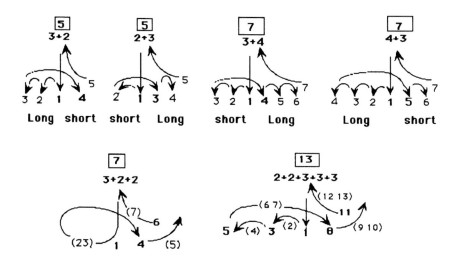

At the left above is a "3-stroke seven" which visually indicates ONLY the attack of the long beat (1), and the two short beats (4 and 6). The non-articulated values (2, 3, 5, and 7) are not displayed but are hidden within the pattern's long, curving strokes.

At the right above, the "5-stroke thirteen" displays only the two short beats (1 and 3) and the three long beats (5, 6, and 11) in five strokes. The non-articulated values (2, 4, 6, 7, 9, 10, 12 and 13) are not displayed but are hidden within the pattern's long, curving strokes.

CHAPTER WRAP

5.24 RN Etudes

*1

*2

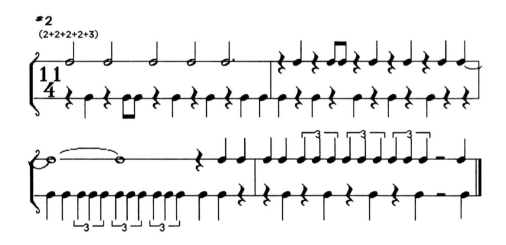

Eleven's Song

Thirteen's Song

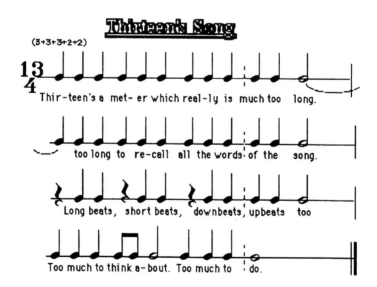

When to Use Triplets

Try to use one trip-pe-let in each measure.   How a-bout here on the first beat?

Now try one on the second. My favorite place is here on the third beat. But don't get too

fus-sy a - bout where you write them | Trip-pe-lets work at the start of a - ny beat!

When to Use Duplets

Du-plets are great when you've got to em-pha-size words which re - qui - re a deep - er meaning

I love you True-ly.   I could kill you! Please stop your cry-ing! Stop it! Stop it!

Duplets work best when they're giv - en a rest so don't use too man - y in a   row.

FIVE JIVE

5.25 LN Etudes

Turning in the air

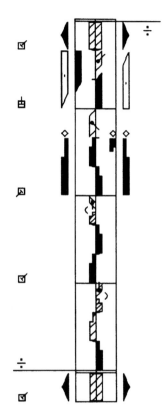

3
4

Turns in different
levels and space holds

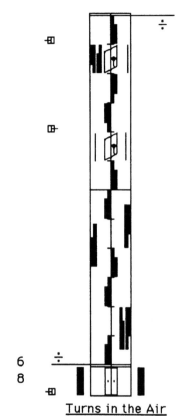

6
8

<u>Turns in the Air</u>
* Judge the direction of landings
from <u>after</u> the turn

Polonaise

This dance is done in couples with the woman standing at the man's R side. This is written as a solo for the woman, with the man doing the opposite.

PREPARATION: Step back R, L, transfer weight forward onto RF, leaving LF pointed back, facing front. Arms to sides, as though laying left hand on partner's right. 1 measure.

I

MEASURE COUNT

1 1 Brush LF forward,
    with small *plié* on R
  2 Step L forward
  3 R forward

2 1 Step L, brush R forward
    simultaneously with left *plié*
  2 Step R forward
  3 Step L forward

3 1, 2, 3 Repeat measure
    2 other side

4 1, 2, 3 Repeat measure 2

5 1, 2, 3 Repeat measure
    2 other side

6 1, 2, 3 Repeat measure 2

7 1, 2 Repeat measure 2 other side
  3 Complete L circle 7/8
    around to end upstage
    center on measures 2 to 7

8 1 Cross L over R
  2 Turn on balls of both
    feet to R (*tour de Basque*)
  3 Drop weight back on
    LF, bend forward,
    with a slight bow

II

9 1 1/4 R turn on L as R slides
    forward

MEASURE COUNT

  2 Step forward R, bring LF to 1st
    position
  3 Step forward R

10 1 Point LF forward to stage R
  2 Point LF back to stage L
  3 Hold

11 1, 2, 3 Repeat measure 9 other side

12 1, 2, 3 Repeat measure 10 other side

13 1 Brush forward R leg, *plié* left
  2 Step forward R, close LF to 1st
    position
  3 Step forward R

14 1, 2, 3 Repeat measure 13 other side

15 1 6 quick steps forward: R, L
  2 R, L
  3 R, L

16 1 Step R. 7/8 turn R
  2 Drop weight back onto LF, body
    facing corner 2 (downstage L), leav-
    ing RF pointed, R forward diagonal
    to corner 2, L arm front, R arm back,
    bowing slightly forward from the
    waist

NOTE: On the last two measures – 15 and 16 – the man brings heels together and bows forward from waist.

Polonaise

Cue #18

Choreography
adapted from a dance
by TED SHAWN and
notation by
Ann Hutchinson Guest

Arranged for partners.
(Women is to man's right to begin.)

Style notes:

1. Join inside hands to begin.
   Release hands at the end of
   meas. #7.

2. Lean & turn slightly toward
   gesturing leg in meas. 1–7.

3. Circle the room once

   counter-clockwise in
   meas. 1–7.

4. Meas. #8 ct. 3 to the end, the man
   (or one of the partners) does the
   reverse of the other's movements.

5. The hooks on the leg gestures in meas.
   10 & 12 mean that the toe touches the floor.

6. Ending position: leave the right toe on the
   floor as you step back and stretch the right
   leg. Lean slightly toward the left forward
   diagonal.

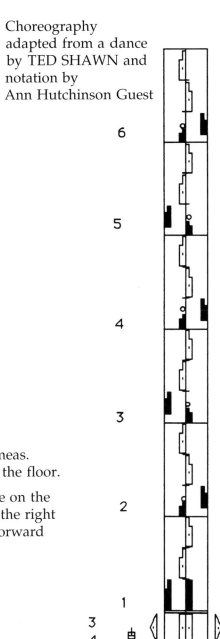

W, M

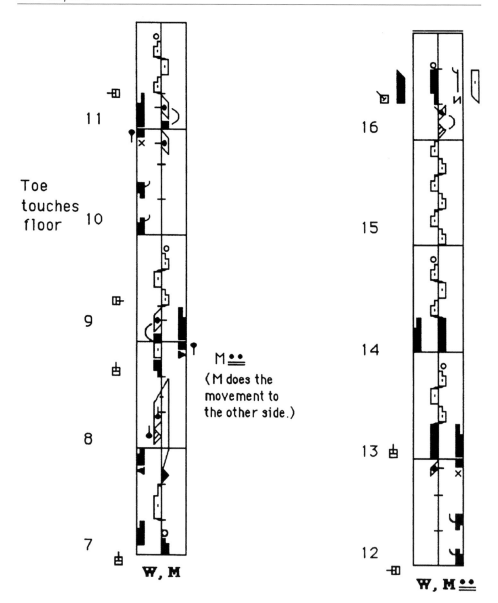

Toe
touches
floor

M ••
(M does the
movement to
the other side.)

W, M

W, M ••

5.26 More Tricky Rhythms

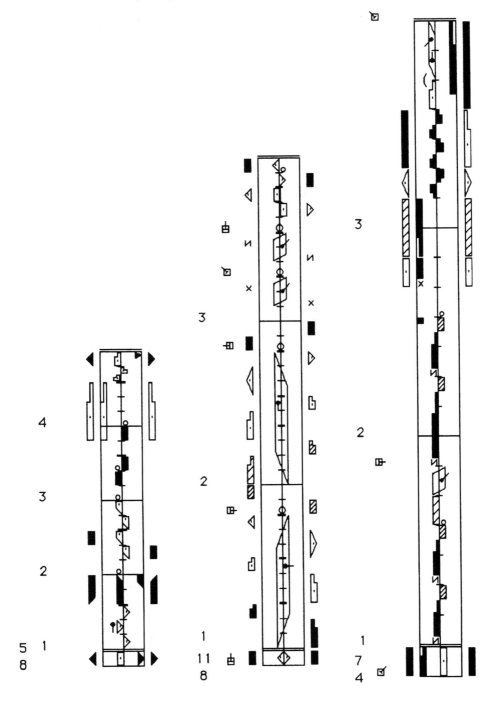

5.27   Suggested Assignments

 Take one of the Tricky Rhythms from 5.26, write the rhythm out in RN, then choreograph a new movement phrase on the rhythm with pivot turns and turns in the air. When finished, write the new exercise in LN.

- Take the 7/8 etude #1 from 5.24 and choreograph a duet based on its rhythms. Incorporate as many types of actions as you can from previous lessons (i.e., gestures, springs, turns, and steps of different sizes).

- Since the *Polonaise* was your first experience reading an entire dance based on a historical form, it is an opportune time to begin linking contextual knowledge of a dance with performance practice. To better support your performance of Ted Shawn's *Polonaise* (5.25), research the history and social context of this dance form. In what country did it originate? What qualities or attributes does it express of the people who created it? What composers have written Polonaises? In what specific ways can your historical understanding of the dance affect your performance?

 3 against 2. Walk across the floor in a rhythm of steady dotted quarters while clapping quarter notes with your hands. This is 3 against 2. Now switch, clapping the dotted quarters with the hands and marking the quarter notes with the feet. This is now 2 against 3.

- Select clusters or etudes from earlier chapters and introduce turns into them. Perform the originals and new versions as theme and variations.

- Choreograph a 3-part study. In part #1, include several pivot turns. In part #2, take these turns into the air. In part #3, use space holds to introduce arm and leg gestures of special interest during either air or pivot turns. Write this study in LN.

6

UPSETTING THE BALANCE

RHYTHMIC CONCEPTS

6.1 Syncopation

"Syncopation is a violent distortion of a normal accentual (metric) pattern. A car crash. Falling down stairs. A sudden stop on a train. An angry outburst. All these are examples of syncopation in life."* In rhythm, a syncopation occurs when a heavy accent falls on a weak beat or weak part of a beat, and comes in two types: those that sound *too soon* or those that sound *too late*. Meter has a sense of balance: **syncopation upsets that balance.**

A rhythm can be considered to be syncopated if it emphasizes a weak division, and non-syncopated if it emphasizes a strong division. For example, when you say the word Albatross, its non-syncopated natural rhythm is the Anapest (short/ short/ long):

Albatross
● ● ▬

The word becomes syncopated when the weak syllable 'ba' receives greater length (accent) than normal, becoming an Amphibrach:

Al ba tross
● ▬ ●

In rhythmic notation (notice the use of an accent mark to inform the reader to 'bring out' the syncopation):

Al-ba-tross Al-ba-tross

 Maxim #87: Syncopation is a violent distortion of a normal accentual (metric) pattern. Any rhythm that heavily accents those divisions of a measure (or beat) which are metrically weaker is syncopated.

---

*Dr. Robert Abramson, in a lecture at The Juilliard School, 1992.

6.2   Syncopation: upbeat (*contre-temps*)

By far the most common type of syncopation is caused by the shifting of emphasis from the downbeat to the upbeat, called *contre-temps*. Try this:

(1) Set your metronome to 80. Clap the beat while saying number:

(2) Stop saying "Num" while continuing to clap and speak "ber":

(3) Stop clapping and continue saying "ber" while "feeling" the missing claps. If you experience a physical reaction where the claps used to be, you are feeling a syncopated, upbeat rhythm. *Note that accents are mandatory on all syncopation.*

Imagine that the black boxes represent four beats in 4/4, the white ovals representing four quarter notes which occur "on the beat", counting "1-2-3-4":

By inserting an 8th rest on the down-beat, all of the quarters will displace (shift) to the right by one half-beat, thereby creating **a syncopation by displacement** (successive accented upbeats).

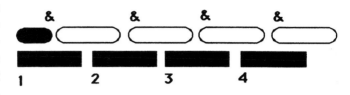

The same two examples in RN look as follows:

Non-syncopated   **Syncopated**
(Can be written either way)

Since the beat in Compound time is triply-divided, an upbeat syncopation can occur on either the second or third division of the compound beat:

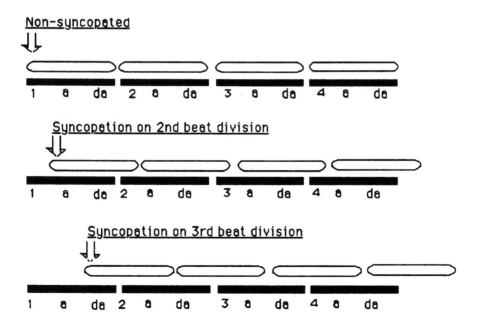

The same three examples in music notation look like this:

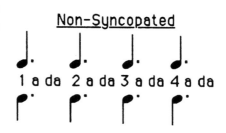

Non-Syncopated

1 a da 2 a da 3 a da 4 a da

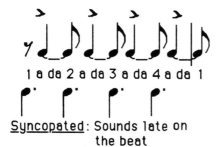

Syncopated: Sounds late on the beat

1 a da 2 a da 3 a da 4 a da 1 a

Syncopated: Sounds early on the next beat

6.3   Syncopation: off-beat

Rhythms which accent weak divisions of the beat *other* than the upbeat are known as "off-beat syncopations". The code word "A-IC" is a perfect example:

The rhythm "a-ic" **becomes** syncopated because it throws a conflicting, heavy emphasis onto the weakest parts of the beat.

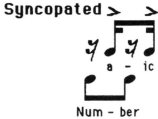

STYLISTIC NOTE: Rhythms (such as those at right) which do not show accent marks may not be performed with enough force to make the syncopation effective. Remember – **accent your syncopations, ON paper as well as IN performance.**

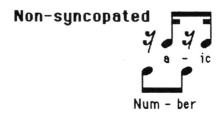

An off-beat syncopation which occurs for only one beat is referred to as a "one-beat syncopation". Those longer than a beat are called "a two-beat syncopation"; "a 3-beat" etc. Those as long as or longer than a measure are referred to as "a 1-bar syncopation"; "a 2-bar" etc.

One-beat Syncopations. Below are syncopations which occur in one beat. Some you have previously seen as Code Word rhythms, although the syncopation was not stressed.

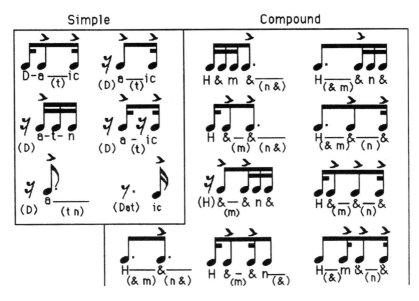

Multi-beat Syncopations. Syncopations rarely last for just one beat. Music is frequently constructed on long syncopated passages that continuously repeat from measure to measure. The backbone of jazz and "scat" melodies, multi-beat syncopations are among the most intense rhythms in music.

Procedure:

(1) Take a simple one beat syncopation like "Di-a-ic" and place several side by side, into *successive syncopated beats*:

(2) By tieing the ends together, from "ic" to "Di", a "chain" of one-beat syncopations occurs ("a-ic") which emphasizes the **off-beats** and de-emphasizes the on-beats:

There is also a syncopation which occurs when larger note values begin on off-beats and **overlap** into the next beat, shifting the focus again away from the on-beats. For example, the quarter note can frequently fall on either "a" or "ic":

• When it falls on "a" it **sounds late** as it enters just after the on-beat.
• When it falls on "ic" it **sounds early** as it enters just one 16th before the next on-beat.

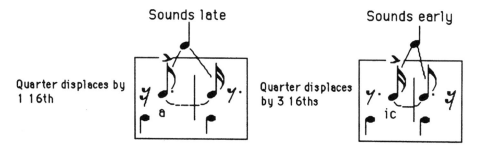

Metric Syncopation. In addition to the single and multi-beat syncopations listed above, whole measures can be syncopated as well. The rules are the same, stressing weaker over stronger divisions. This refers to the weaker beats of the measure. One of the most common full-measure syncopations in 2/4 is the stressing of the '&' of beat #1. Here are several variations:

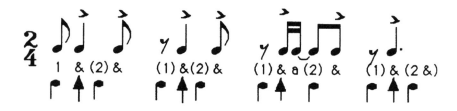

In 3/4, stressing the '&' of beats 1 and 2 is also quite common:

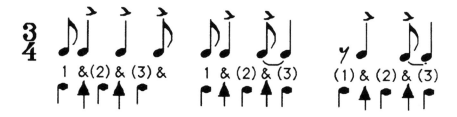

In 4/4, stressing the '&' of beat #2 is the most common form of syncopation.

6.4   Syncopation: styles and use

For as long as there has been a steady beat, there has been the thrill of escape, and thus syncopation has been around for a long time. From the Monkey Chants of Indonesia to the early polyphonic works of Machaut, to Bach, to Scott Joplin, to Gershwin, syncopation has been known to most cultures. The listener's response to syncopation is often a very physical one. While we're not usually compelled to tap our feet to Mozart, we're compelled to do so to jazz. Today, it would be difficult to find many popular songs which are not in some way syncopated; in fact, saying "syncopated jazz" is being redundant. To get an idea of how syncopation works, details follow on a few of the most common styles of syncopation, those which you're probably hearing on a daily basis.

- *Swing Style*. There are two common approaches to performing jazz music: **Straight** and **Swing**. Straight style is exactly what you have been learning in this book up to now: the exact reproduction of rhythmic values *as they are written*. Swing style is quasi-improvisational: the rhythms are notated in simple time but are performed in compound. In other words, the performer turns all duple beats into triples. Triplets swing/8th notes are "straight." Swing uses a very cool type of off-beat accent that is not written unless a stronger 'push' is desired.

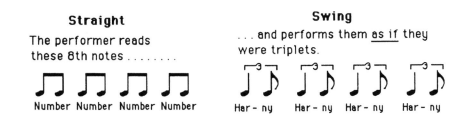

You can experiment with swing style by singing the children's song Twinkle Twinkle Little Star:

The song is usually performed "straight". But by simply adding the registration *Swing* at the start of the song, a performer will sing the piece in triplets, *AS IF IT HAD BEEN WRITTEN IN 12/8*.

- *Melodic syncopation* implies that a syncopated melody is at work above a generally non-syncopated accompaniment (here, a 'walking bass').

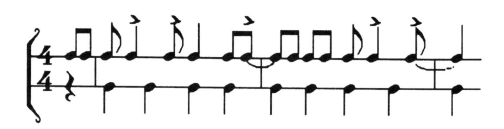

- The opposite of the above is also common, a *non-syncopated melody over a syncopated accompaniment*:

• *Syncopated patterns* quite frequently appear in popular songs: syncopation alternates with non-syncopation, creating a pattern of tension and release. In the Rolling Stones song *I Can't Get No Satisfaction*, the syncopated text alternates with rests, allowing the beat to peek through. The song progresses in "surges". Clap a steady beat and chant the example below with lots of accent. That's syncopation!!!

> Maxim #88: Syncopated rhythms which do not show accent marks may not be performed with enough force to make the syncopation effective. Remember – **accent your syncopations, ON paper as well as IN performance.**

6.5   RN Dynamics

> A note on "musical language". The official language of music is widely accepted as being Italian, and much music (regardless of the nationality of the composer) is therefore written with instructions for dynamics and tempo in Italian. However, composers will also give instructions in their native languages when expression and execution are involved. Therefore, Italian is usually inter-mixed with other languages within the same score. It is wise to own a copy of the *Harvard Dictionary of Music* to help you interpret foreign instructions.

Dynamics are those notational markings within a score which indicate to the performer the relative "volume" of sound and intensity to be produced at a given moment or beat in time. As with dance, the addition of dynamics to a composition requires the performer to spend more or less energy at specified times, energies which go along with the changing of volume and intensity.

More energy = more volume/intensity
Less energy = less volume/intensity

The following table of dynamics is simple: at one end there is **extremely loud,** and at the other, **extremely soft.** Between exist the gradations of volume which make up the full range of audio volume:

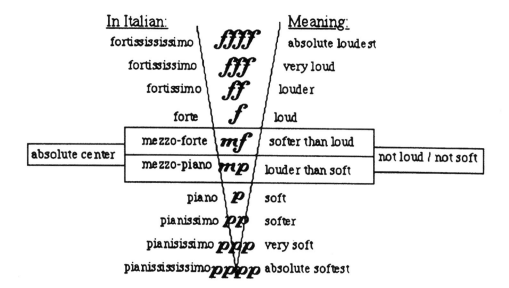

Further subtleties between dynamic symbols are made possible with the commonly used Italian words **poco** (little), and **più** (more), as in

poco piano (a little softer but not quite pianissimo) or
più forte (a little louder but not quite fortissimo).

There are generally two ways in which the dynamics of a composition may be changed – suddenly and gradually. For sudden changes, one need only to place a new dynamic marking under the notation and the volume change will be made instantaneously by the performer:

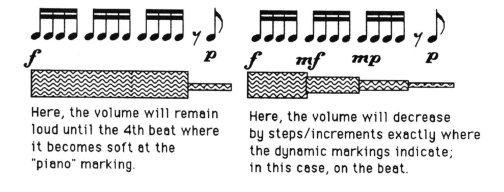

Here, the volume will remain loud until the 4th beat where it becomes soft at the "piano" marking.

Here, the volume will decrease by steps/increments exactly where the dynamic markings indicate; in this case, on the beat.

For gradual increases and decreases in volume, the crescendo and decrescendo (or diminuendo) "wedge" is employed:

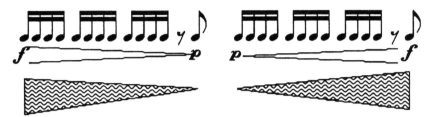

Here, the volumne of sound will <u>gradually</u> diminish from loud to soft.

Here, it will <u>gradually</u> increase in volume from soft to loud.

There is no limit as to how long a crescendo or diminuendo can last. There are often instructions which accompany those that are more than a few beats long: poco a poco (little by little) and molto (much):

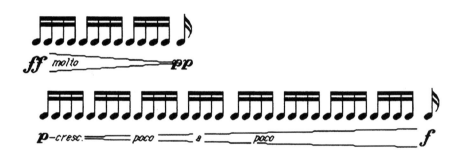

Also common are the use of the dynamic terms themselves, syllabically extended with dashes for the intended duration of the change of volume:

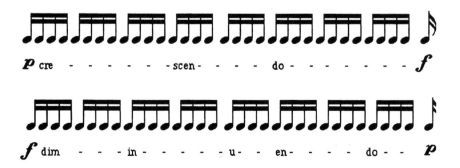

> Maxim #89: Dynamics are notational markings within a score that indicate to the performer the relative "volume" and intensity of sound to be produced at a given moment or beat in time.

MOVEMENT CONCEPTS

6.6   LN Dynamics

The *Crescendo & Diminuendo* symbols are also used in LN to increase or decrease any quality over a period of time. To the right are the general symbols for increase and decrease; symbols for the specific quality or movement elements that are changing will be placed within them.

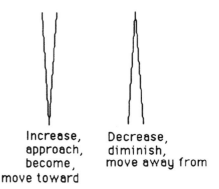

Increase,
approach,
become,
move toward

Decrease,
diminish,
move away from

Notice the similarity of these symbols for gradual increase & decrease to those used in RN. The LN symbols are in effect music symbols flipped to the vertical. Symbols describing quality, direction and level, or scale can be placed within these two symbols.

A. Movement Qualities: Below is a selection of symbols for qualities that can be used in combination with "increase and decrease." Nuance and subtlety in movement performance are captured with such qualitative descriptions. *Qualities* are elements of performance and style; they suggest how and with what dynamics to perform a movement sequence.

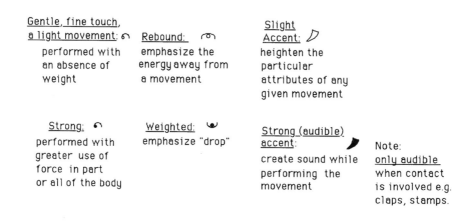

Gentle, fine touch,
a light movement: Rebound:
performed with   emphasize the
an absence of   energy away from
weight   a movement

Slight
Accent:
heighten the
particular
attributes of any
given movement

Strong:
performed with
greater use of
force in part
or all of the body

Weighted:
emphasize "drop"

Strong (audible)
accent:
create sound while
performing the
movement

Note:
only audible
when contact
is involved e.g.
claps, stamps.

For example, this dynamic would indicate that a particular movement would be performed with increasing gentleness: or increasing heaviness: or increasing uplift:

B. General statements of direction: Direction symbols placed within crescendo and diminuendo symbols describe gradual changes of overall direction and/or level. Depending on the column in which these symbols are placed, this change can be for part or all of the body.

Low or "sinking"   High or "rising"

Movement is performed while gradually sinking:

The movement gradually gets lower (lower than before)

C. Recall that the general statements of scale are:

Χ
Small, contracted

Very small, very contracted

Extended, long or large

Very extended, very long or large

Placed within the symbols for increase or decrease, X and backwards N will gradually alter either the scale of movement, or the extension of a part of the body, depending on the column in which they are placed and to what they refer.

When written in combination, the symbols for increasing or decreasing, and specific movement qualities or elements, should affect the motivation for movement and the performance of choreography. They offer suggestions for interpreting movement that can help shape phrasing, or extend dynamic range within a dance. Some examples follow.

As the dancer walks quickly in plié, the arms move in a generally rising direction. This could be interpreted as increasing upward "reaching", or as producing a lift that makes the action increasingly light.

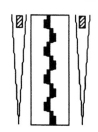

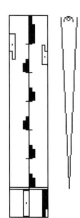

It could also the interpreted strictly as an increasingly vertical lift for the arms, which would contrast with the forward (horizontal) momentum of the movement.

This series of travelling springs, moving from step-hop to step-leap to a larger step-leap should be performed with increasing lightness.

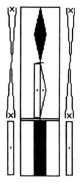

Contraction decreases then increases in the arms as the dancer steps to 2nd pos., then pliés:

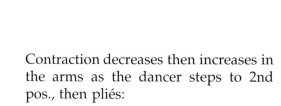

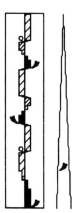

The initial stamps in this sequence will be louder (produce more sound) than those following. The stamps gradually diminish.

Maxim #90: The crescendo (increase) & dimenuendo (decrease) symbols can be used in combination with a variety of other symbols to change the dynamics of a movement or phrase.

Impulse vs. Impact. Two highly expressive symbols, for movements that begin with an impulse or that end with an impact are formed by combining the phrasing bow with accent symbols. By attaching an accent to the beginning of a phrasing bow, "impulse" is communicated. This means that the movement or sequence is initiated with increased energy. Then energy ebbs to normal level in the course of the action(s). The opposite configuration communicates "impact". Accents attached to the ends of phrasing bows mean that energy peaks as a movement or sequence ends.

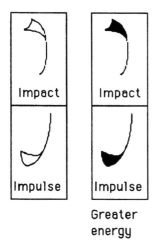

Greater energy

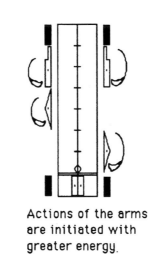

Actions of the arms are initiated with greater energy.

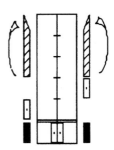

Energy peaks as the arms reach the forward high diagonals, the greater attack coming at the end of these gestures.

6.7 Stage Area Signs

In choreography with complex or precise stage placement of dancers, stage area signs can be used to give important supplemental information. They are placed to the left of the staff, just beyond the dancer's stage facing. Stage area signs are shaded to designate a particular part of the stage.

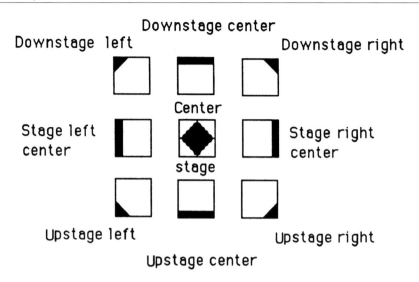

Placed in the starting position, a stage area sign describes where a dancer is standing onstage before the dance begins.

Begin upstage center,   Begin upstage R,   Begin in the
facing downstage   facing downstage L   downstage L corner,
                                              facing stage right

6.8   Entering and Exiting

Stage area signs can describe entrances and exits when they are attached to the double bar lines that begin and end a score.

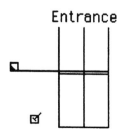

As movement begins, the performer appears in the upstage left corner. In the starting position, the performer prepares by facing downstage right.

The logic here is that, since the first stage area sign appears attached to the double bar line indicating "movement begins," the dancer will become visible onstage for the first time *as the dance begins*. The starting position is therefore an offstage preparation, prior to entrance.

Exit

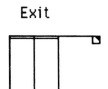

As movement ends, the performer is seen for the last time, in the downstage right corner.

The opposite logic is true for exits. Attached below the double bar line signifying "end of movement," the stage area sign gives the dancer's last location *on* stage before the exit concludes the dance.

6.9   Floorplans

Floorplans are graphic representations of onstage travel that align with the LN score. They clarify how much and in what direction(s) dancers travel as they perform particular measures of movement. A floor plan's basic format is a 3-sided rectangle:

The open side, at the top, represents the front of the stage, open to the audience. Notice that the floorplan is drawn from the performer's point of view (with the audience in front), to make it easier for dancers reading a score to place themselves on the stage.

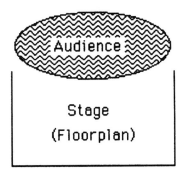

There are two alternatives to the basic floorplan format. One is "director's plans," which are drawn from the audience's perspective, and the second is a closed rectangle used to represent performance areas which are not proscenium stages.

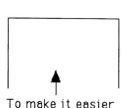

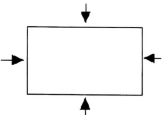

To make it easier
to read from a direc –
tor's viewpoint, "downstage"
is at the bottom of the floorplan.

For court, social, traditional,
or folk dances in which the
audience may be placed around
the room or dancing space, or
for dances with a divided front.

Numbers are drawn at the base of each floorplan, indicating the measures in the LN score to which the floor plan corresponds:

1
This floorplan will
describe the movement
in measure #1.

5 - 8
This floorplan will
describe the movement
which starts in measure
#5 and continues through
measure #8.

Numbers are some-times refined to indi-cate specific counts as well as measures:

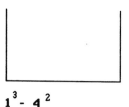

1 ^{3} - 4 ^{2}

Here, the floorplan will
picture the travel
from count #3 of meas. #1
to count #2 of meas. #4.

Floorplans are only provided for measures in which there is significant travel on the stage or across space. When the dancers move in place or only slightly, floor plans will not appear.

Maxim #91: Numbers under floorplans correspond to measures and/or counts within the LN score.

6.10 Floorplans: placing the dancer on the stage

Dancers are represented on floorplans with round pins or tacks, some of which are gender-specific. Although the round pins are preferred, the two sets of pins can be used in combination to help follow the actions of different groups on stage at the same time.

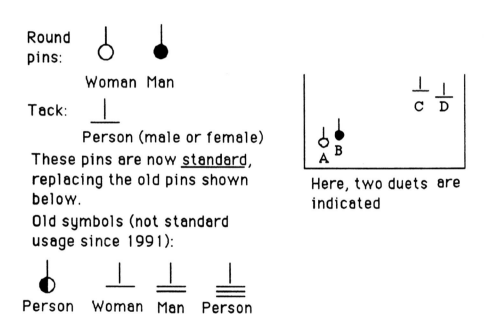

Round pins:

Woman Man

Tack:

Person (male or female)

These pins are now <u>standard</u>, replacing the old pins shown below.

Old symbols (not standard usage since 1991):

Person Woman Man Person

Here, two duets are indicated

Notice that letters can be placed at the base of the pins to identify dancers further. "Person" pins are used when movement is not "gender-specific", and either a man or woman could perform the movement, such as dancer "A" in this trio:

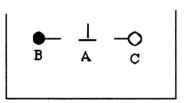

When pins are placed on a floorplan, they must be a clear illustration of where the dancer is located on the stage, and where they are facing at the start of a travelling sequence. The actual path of travel is shown with a line that ends with an arrow. The arrow shows the point on stage at which the sequence ends, but DOES NOT say anything about where the dancer ends facing.

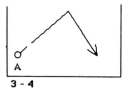

3 - 4

Dancer A (a woman) is in the upstage left corner, facing downstage right. Throughout meas. 3 & 4, she will travel on an angled path, ending in the upstage right corner.

To know a dancer's facing direction at the end of her travel, the reader must refer to the specific measure in the LN score, or use wedges or show facing at the end.

Use △ for a woman, ▲ for a man, or ◭ for a person, with the wedge pointing in the direction of the facing on stage.

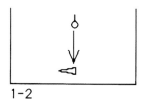

1-2

Female dancer travels upstage in meas.'s 1-2, ending her path facing stage left.

Sequential floorplans need to agree as to the stage placement of dancers and flow smoothly one into the next. The following plans show 8 measures of travel for 2 dancers, each floorplan picking up where the other stops. In measures 3 & 4, the woman does not travel:

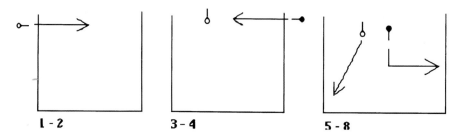

l - 2   3 - 4   5 - 8

Maxim #92: Pins, often in combination with letters, identify dancers on floorplans and show facings on stage. Lines and arrows show the path and extent of travel; wedges show the final facing.

6.11 Floorplans: duets and groups

Lines and arrows change slightly to accommodate travel for more than 1 person. In measures 9–12 below, the woman passes in front of the man. Her dominant path is shown with an unbroken line; his yielding path is shown with a broken line. In measures 13–16, the pair dances together. The double arrow in the path reinforces that this is joint travel:

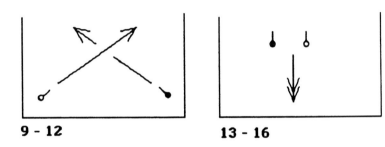

9 - 12   **13 - 16**

When more than 2 people trace a path together, the arrow changes to a solid shape:

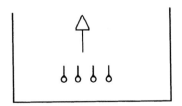

 Maxim #93: Floorplans must follow one another with clarity and exactness as to dancers' placements on stage. Modifications to lines and arrows describe travel for more than one person.

NOTATION

6.12   RN Rules: syncopation

A. Since the nature of syncopation is to 'escape' the beat, this can also be reflected in the way a syncopation is notated. Rather than notating 'by the beat', the notation can visually encourage the performer to syncopate by placing the longer values ON the weak divisions. Therefore, notated syncopations can look as different as they sound:

In the 2/4, the quarter note visually syncopates the division between beats one and two. Both are correct:

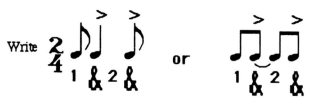

In the 3/4, the two dotted quarters look more like 6/8; however, because of the time signature, the reader is encouraged to syncopate. Both are correct:

In 4/4, the successive quarter notes encourage the performer to "ride over the top" of beats 2, 3, and 4. Both are correct:

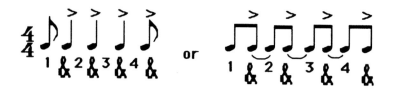

Here, in 4/4, the notation makes it perfectly clear that the syncopation involves the first 3 beats of the measure; beat #4 is non-syncopated and is clearly notated as such. Both are correct:

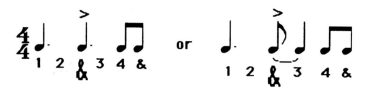

B. In places where complicated off-beat syncopations are involved, 'by-the-beat' notation is sometimes easier to read. The operative phrase here is "which is easier to read?":

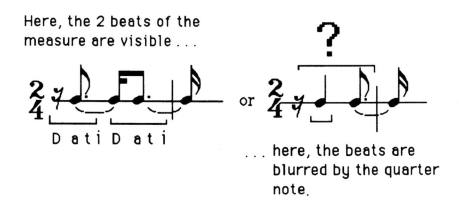

In this case, both will be used by composers depending on style, taste, or some other mediating factor.

    6.13   LN Rules: floorplans

(A) *Placement of floorplans in a score*
Floorplans can be placed along the bottom of the page of notation to which they refer, or they can be arranged in a vertical stack on the right side of the page close to the movement they illustrate. When at the bottom, floorplans read from left to right; when stacked vertically, they read from bottom to top.

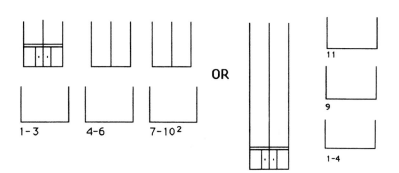

(B) *How many floorplans to use?*
The decision of how many floorplans to use is open to the notator. What is important is that they be easy to follow and clear to read. Putting too much information in one floorplan can make score reading difficult. Using too many floorplans requires that the reader's eye "jump" more than necessary, scanning several representations of the stage. This may slow down score reading.

Too much information for
a single floorplan:

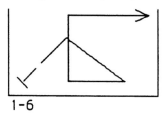

1-6

Too many floorplans for the same sequence:

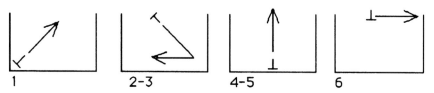

1   2-3   4-5   6

A clearer, simpler use of floorplans:

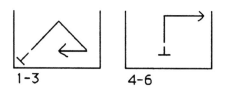

1-3   4-6

(C) *Retracing steps on floorplans*
When a dancer's path retraces a previous line of travel, two kinds of indications are possible. One uses a double arrow, to show that movement progresses and then retreats along the same line. The other places a smaller line within the arrow of the initial path, indicating that the primary line of travel is re-used. Either method is correct.

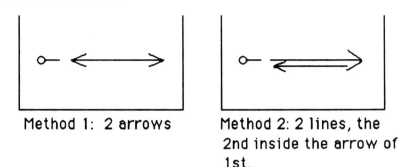

Method 1: 2 arrows   Method 2: 2 lines, the
2nd inside the arrow of
1st.

(D) *Not for pivots*
The action of pivoting, swiveling, or turning is NOT drawn on a floorplan. However, if a turning sequence 'travels', a plain line will illustrate this.

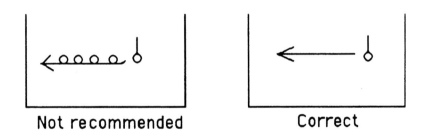

Not recommended   Correct

RHYTHMIC APPLICATIONS

6.14 Re-grouping: moving between simple and compound meters

It is sometimes necessary to transpose a rhythmic passage from a simple meter to a compound meter, and vice versa. This process is identical to the re-groupings in previous chapters.

For example, the following passage in 2/4 needs to be rewritten in 6/8. In 2/4 there are 8 quarter note beats divided into 4 measures. To re-group this into 6/8, the numbers of beats AND measures will have to be changed WHILE NOT changing the original arrangement of notes and rests.

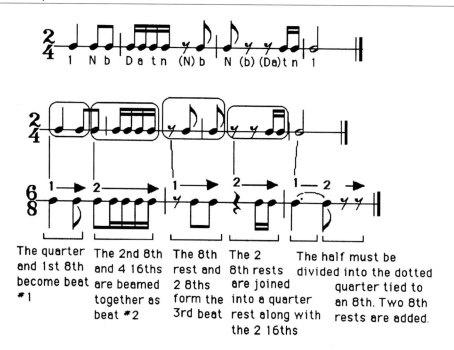

The quarter and 1st 8th become beat #1

The 2nd 8th and 4 16ths are beamed together as beat #2

The 8th rest and 2 8ths form the 3rd beat

The 2 8th rests are joined into a quarter rest along with the 2 16ths

The half must be divided into the dotted quarter tied to an 8th. Two 8th rests are added.

Finally, it can be seen that while in the 2/4 there are 8 beats in 4 measures, the 6/8 solution provides 6 beats in 3 measures. Fewer beats, less crucis, and a rounded compound beat will make a performance of the 6/8 feel very different than the 2/4. This is yet another example of the influence of meter over rhythm. (See below.)

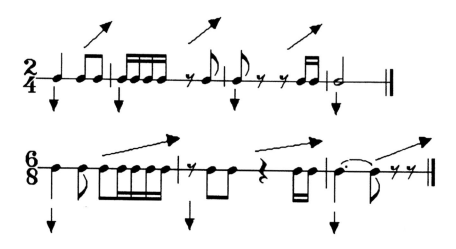

In a reverse process, the following rhythm in 9/8 will need to be "chopped down" to fit into 2/4:

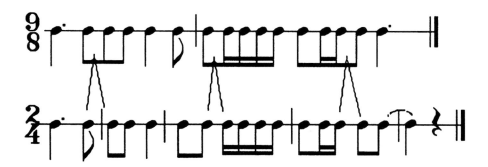

The 9/8 has 6 beats in 2 measures, while the 2/4 has 10 beats in 5 measures. Notice that the compound beaming in 9/8 had to be re-formatted to accommodate the smaller quarter note beat in 2/4. Also notice where re-beaming took place to accommodate the quarter note beat in 2/4 (measure #3).

6.15   Re-grouping: moving between perfect and irregular meters

In a process similar to the one described in 6.14, it is also sometimes necessary to transpose rhythms between perfect and irregular time signatures. While the procedure is the same, there is more adjustment necessary due to the irregular nature of the beats in 5's, 7's, etc. Let's re-group from a simple rhythm in 4/4 to 5/8, with the 8th notes being equal (8th = 8th):

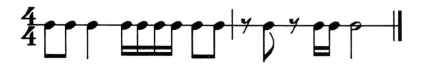

The 1st step is to count each one of the five 8th-note sequences within the 4/4:

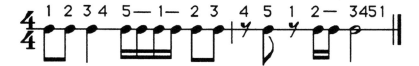

Step #2 is to re-group the rhythms of the 4/4 into 5/8, changing the bar lines where necessary:

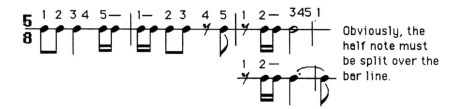

Obviously, the half note must be split over the bar line.

And finally, certain decisions must be made concerning how the "5" is to be felt, which will affect the beaming and groupings within each measure.

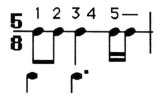

In meas. #1, the (2+3) approach is obvious, and a slight separation between the 2nd 8th note and the quarter will aid in seeing that the short beat comes first, followed by the long beat:

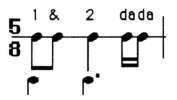

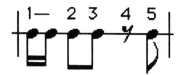

Measure #2 has two solutions, either of which is correct. Select either a (2 + 3) or a (3 + 2), depending upon artistic consider-ations. The beaming will reflect this:

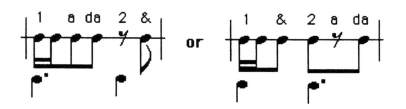

or

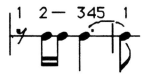

Measure #3 needs only a slight separation between the 2nd 16th note and the dotted quarter to bring out the natural (2+3) grouping:

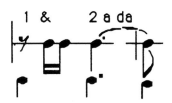

Finally, since the last measure will be comprised mostly of rests, you may decide how they are to appear, either (2+3) or (3+2):

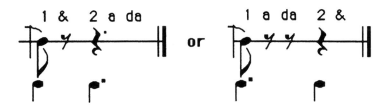

One possible solution:

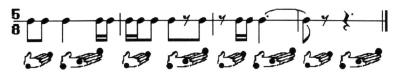

Due to the regular nature of beats in perfect meter, the reverse process is simpler since you will not need to determine the "feel" of each beat. For example, when moving from 7/8 to 2/4, each beat in 2/4 is the same size. All you need to do is count each set of two 8th-notes throughout the 7:

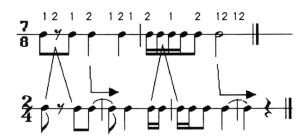

Note: Sing the 7/8 above, and then the 2/4 solution. The rhythm in 7/8 IS NOT syncopated, but when regrouped in 2/4, the second measure becomes extremely syncopated.

MOVEMENT APPLICATIONS

6.16   Clusters: syncopated

Prances, with
accents off the
beat

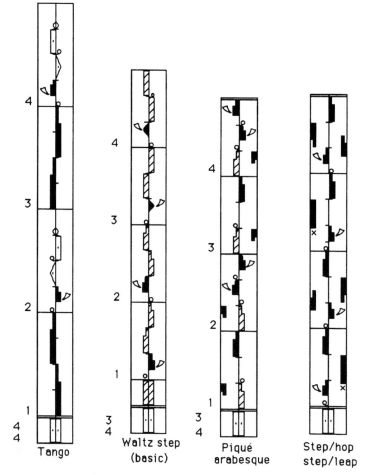

Tango

Waltz step
(basic)

Piqué
arabesque

Step/hop
step/leap

6.17   Clusters: dynamics

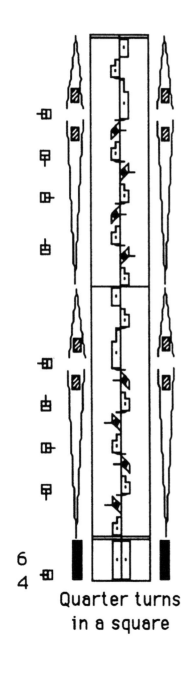

Quarter turns
in a square

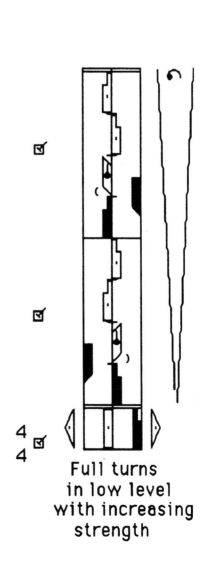

Full turns
in low level
with increasing
strength

CHAPTER WRAP

6.18   RN Etudes

1 - Successive upbeats in bass

#2 - Syncopated vs. non-syncopated parts

#3 - Syncopated melody vs. non-syncopated "walking bass"

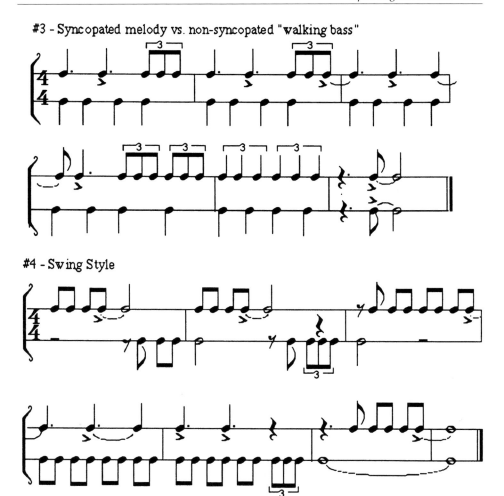

#4 - Swing Style

Hey you!

6.19   LN Etudes

Perform this variation on Ted Shawn's "Polonaise", which shifts the timing of some actions to create syncopation. (Complete style notes for the dance can be found on page 240.) What is the effect of the syncopation on the movement? On the dance as a whole?

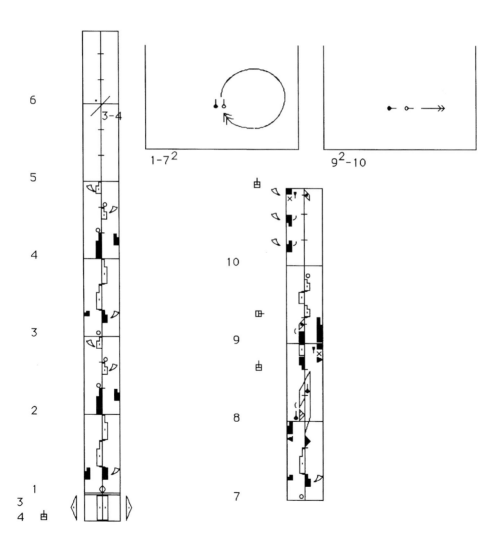

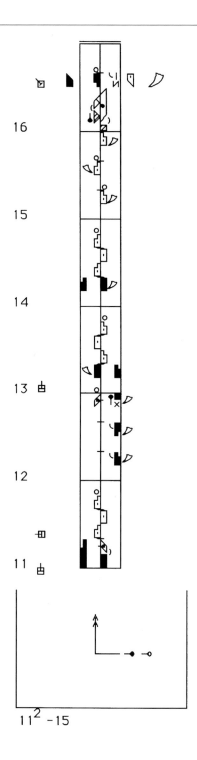

6.20 More Tricky Rhythms

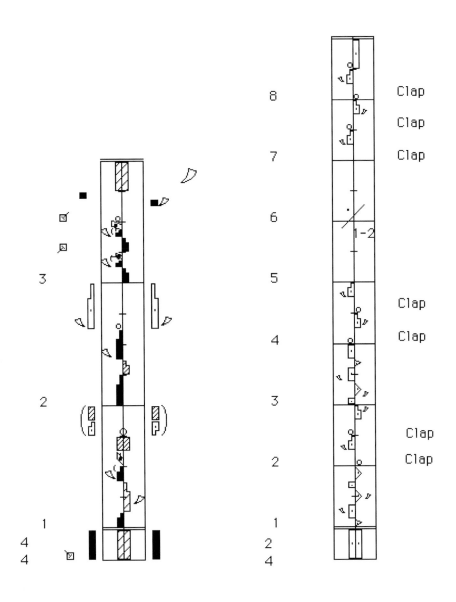

6.21   Suggested Assignments

 Rewrite the RN etudes from Chapter #2 to include syncopations before and/or after the beat. Perform them first in their original non-syncopated state, then as syncopated.

- Make a list of 20 syncopations which occur in life (sports, work, etc.). Then make a list of 20 non-syncopations which occur in life. Compare the lists and discuss in class.
- Regroup the following Irregular original into the suggested new time signature. Then perform both with appropriate crusic, metacrusic, and anacrusic beat qualities. Can this possibly be the same rhythm?

 Select a variety of clusters from previous chapters. Change their rhythms to employ syncopation before or after the beat. Practice performing the clusters in their original non-syncopated rhythms, then with syncopation. How does the syncopation affect the performance of each type of movement you have chosen?

- Write 2 or 3 of the clusters in the above assignment in LN, showing their new syncopated rhythms.
- Create a duet with unison movement. Have one dancer perform the movement with syncopated accents while the other performs "on" the beat. What is the effect of this division in the use of time in the dance?
- Create a solo movement phrase which displays non-syncopated movement in the lower body and syncopated movement for the upper body. Then reverse the process, sending syncopated rhythms to the lower body while the upper body maintains a non-syncopated rhythm. Which is more difficult to do? Which is more interesting visually? Notate your favorite results in LN.

Write an 8-measure phrase in an Irregular meter incorporating RN dynamics. Choreograph 2 sets of movement
for this rhythm. In the first, make the movement qualities
sympathetic to the dynamics in the RN. Verify that the
aural and visual results of this composition are complementary. In the second, use opposing qualities to introduce contrast between the RN and LN dynamics. Which is more
difficult to perform? Which (do you think) is the more interesting
viewing experience? Notate your favorite results in LN.

7

CHANGING TIMES

One of the predominant characteristics of 20th-century music has been the tendency to be unpredictable rather than predictable, one aspect of musical predictability being the establishment of a downbeat at "regular" intervals. A salient feature of modern music/choreography is the frequent changing of time signatures to create uneven phrasing and accent.

RHYTHMIC CONCEPTS

7.1 Metric Registration

When moving from 4/4 to 3/4, the beat in both measures is the same. You simply change the count at the new measure.

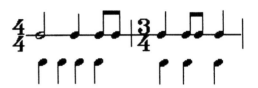

The quarters in 4/4 are the same as those in 3/4.

However, when a new time signature is introduced that has a *different beat assignment*, the composer must indicate to the performer **what** is the relationship between the two meters.

For example: should a measure of 2/4 follow a measure of 3/8, how would the performer know the relationship between the two measures? The dotted quarter beat in 3/8 and the quarter beat in 2/4 are different sizes:

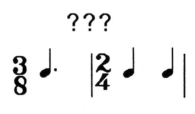

The answer to the above example is that 3/8 and 2/4 can relate on several levels:

(1) Proportionally. The 8th note is common to both measures. (Recall "8th equals 8th".) Since the 8th note in each measure has the same value, it can be used as a common denominator. This process maintains the original BOV proportions of note values:

At a moderate tempo, tap a steady 8th-note pulse and sing several times in a row:

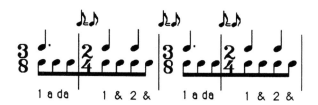

(2) Non-proportionally, A conversion process may be used in which the new beat value is **modified** to *assume the size of the previous beat value.* By using the formula "dotted-quarter-equals-quarter", the new quarter note in 2/4 is *expanded to the size of the previous dotted quarter in 3/8.*

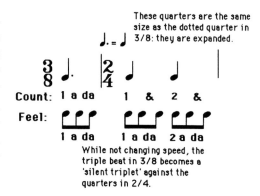

These quarters are the same size as the dotted quarter in 3/8: they are expanded.

While not changing speed, the triple beat in 3/8 becomes a 'silent triplet' against the quarters in 2/4.

Note: When switching from 3/8 to 2/4, the performer experiences 2 against 3 while adjusting to the new beat (see 5.5).

A registration mark is mandatory each time the beat assignment changes size. This is placed above the bar line where the change is to occur:

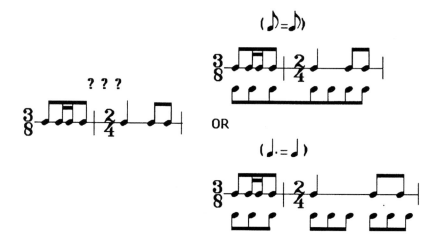

In another example, suppose you move from 4/2 to 4/4. Would a registration be important here? Although both measures are simple/quadruple and have the same number of beats, they **do** differ in the assigned beating note. The common denominator in this instance will usually be the quarter note **(quarter=quarter)** which, like **(8th=8th)** maintains the proportional relationship between quarters and halves. However, you may also see the non-proportional registration of **(half=quarter)**, which means that the new quarter becomes the old half note: the quarters become twice the size, making the 4/4 sound and act **as if it were 4/2**:

Proportional: quarters remain the same

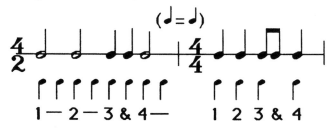

Non-proportional: quarters become halves

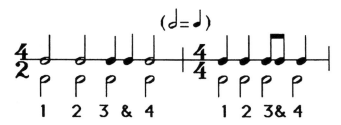

Although the non-proportional example above may seem strange, it is an effective way of establishing a slower quarter note WITHOUT a change in tempo.

 Set the metronome to 90 clicks and perform each example above several times. In the proportional example, each click will represent a quarter note. (The halves will be sung as thru-beats in the 1st measure.) In the non-proportional example, each click represents a half note in the 1st measure **and** a quarter in the 2nd. (There will be no change; the quarters will become halves.) In fact, the old half and the new quarter notes will sound the same.

> Maxim #94: Metric Registration is a process in which the common denominator between time signatures of differing beat assignments is displayed above the bar line between the change.

7.2   Variable (Mixed) Meter

Variable (mixed) meter allows for the constant changing of time signature whenever a shift of emphasis is desired. Variable meter allows the natural weight of the downbeat to be placed anywhere that crusic stress is required, or, more accurately, wherever you need to feel "ONE". Variable meter is an extremely useful phrasing tool for choreographers who deal with full-body and partial-body movements requiring varying amounts of time, space, and energy to execute. **Each measure can be specifically crafted for each movement phrase or gesture.**

Any time signature can be placed adjacent to any other time signature in a composition, being careful that the proper registration mark is present to indicate the common denominator. (See 7.1.) In the following example of mixed meter, note that *there is no need for metric registration* since each measure uses the same quarter-based beat:

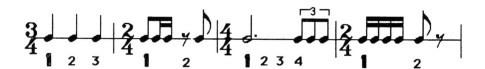

The above would be counted 123 12 1234 12. The phrase moves between different size measures: long (3/4) to short (2/4) to longest (4/4) to short (2/4). The time between downbeats is irregular, uneven, and thus unpredictable, like much modern music and traditional music from Eastern Europe and the Middle East (Israel, Greece, Bulgaria, etc.).

> Maxim #95: Variable Meter refers to the changing of time signature at places where the natural crusic weight of the downbeat is desired. Any time signature may be placed adjacent to any other.

7.3 Alternating Meter

Similar to variable meter, alternating meter allows two different time signatures to switch back and forth from measure to measure in a recurring pattern of alternation. When writing an alternating time signature, both time signatures are written side-by-side at the start, separated by a plus (+), which indicates the presence of the alternation. This 'double signature' eliminates the need to write a new time signature in each measure. Instead, the performer knows to switch back and forth **without** the visual reminder:

IMPORTANT: It's the **meter** that alternates. The **rhythm** in each measure usually varies from measure to measure.

One metric registration will suffice throughout the entire alternation:

When the pattern of alternation is broken for one or more measures, it is then necessary to indicate each new time signature(s) normally. If the alternation re-appears at a later time, the double signature is then re-applied:

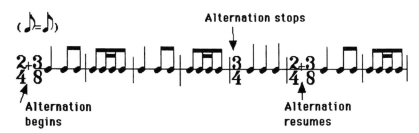

When shifting from measure to measure involves going from simple to compound time, the performer is encouraged to "flip a switch" and feel one metric quality, then the other:

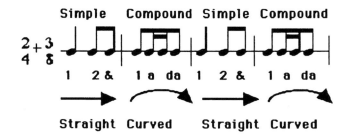

It is also possible to have a third and (rarely) a fourth time signature as part of an alternating pattern. In the example below, note that there are three downbeats per repetition of pattern:

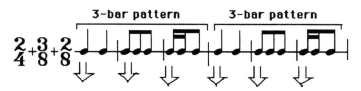

> Maxim #96: Alternating Meter refers to two (or more) time signatures that switch back and forth in a pre-arranged alternating pattern.

7.4   Monometer: 1-beat measures

Another type of meter (similar to Variable) is the Monometer, in which each measure is based on a continuous pulse (frequently the 8th note). Unlike variable meter, each measure is thought of as having just one beat, no matter how many 'pulses' occur within. Consequently, each measure consists of one downbeat with as little anacrusisis as possible, suggesting an immense amount of downward crusic accent. Monometers are considered to be one of the most propulsive, agitated, and aggressive meters in existence. It is therefore particularly necessary to accent the Db of each measure.

Procedure:
Begin with the establishment of a "pulse base", in this case, a series of 25 uninterrupted 8th notes:

The 8ths are then divided into groupings of varying amounts. Note that some groupings consist of five pulses and others, only one:

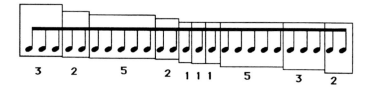

These groupings are then translated into measures which are "8th-note based". By counting the number of 8ths in each grouping, we arrive at a time signature that uses the 8th note as the assigned "pulse". The resulting pattern is comprised of 10 measures in the metric sequence:

3   2   5   2   1   1   1   5   3   2.

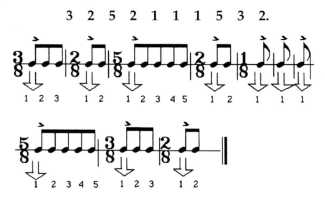

Remembering that each measure is felt as having one beat only, with supressed upbeats, the above phrase would be counted as follows:
Down 2 3 Down 2 Down 2 3 4 5 Down 2 Down Down Down Down 2 3 4 5 Down 2 3 Down 2.

The same example could be transposed to a 16th pulse-base, or any other pulse-assignment. There should be absolutely no difference in the rhythm: only the **speed** will be affected by the faster pulse:

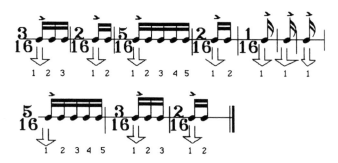

> Maxim #97: Monometer (single-beat measures) refers to the dividing of a steady pulse-base into measures, *each of which acts as if it contains only one beat, regardless of the number of pulses in the measure.*

7.5   Additive Measures

When Western musicians notate Afro-Cuban rhythms, metric patterns will internally re-arrange as they attempt to reflect the off-beat, syncopated nature of some of the most intricate improvisational rhythms in the world. Since these rhythms basically defy notation, the western notation system attempts to capture them through irregular and/or unorthodox groupings within each measure, called additive measures. The example below shows two additive measures in 4/4. When the eye sees the measure on the left, it sees three beats: a duple beat followed by two triple. On the right, there is a triple/duple/triple construction. In both cases, the performer will play as if there were three beats while still feeling the basic 'time-line' in 4. This is poly-meter at its best.

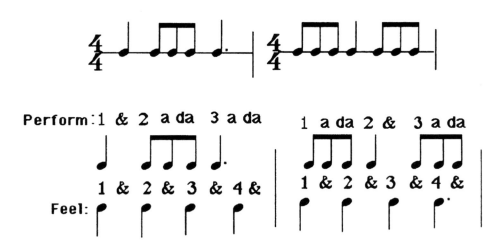

Try walking the above quarters while clapping the additive rhythms.

> Maxim #98: Additive measures refer to standard time signatures that are divided in unorthodox ways.

MOVEMENT CONCEPTS

7.6 Paths: straight

Path signs are symbols written to the right of the staff that describe travel, the paths that movements carve through space. As symbols recorded on the staff tell dancers how to move their *bodies*, path signs explain or reinforce the *spatial design* of travel. Path signs can describe linear (straight) or curving (circling) travel.

Straight path signs. These symbols are flat at both ends. Travel begins and ends precisely at the ends of the path sign.

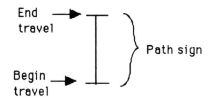

Straight path signs are generally not complete without a direction symbol inside them, telling whether the path moves forward, side, back, etc. (Since the levels of the body's actions are given on the staff, direction symbols in path signs DO NOT NEED LEVEL. They only state the direction of travel.)

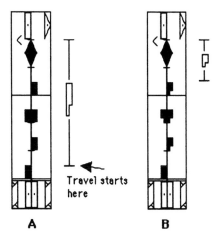

A   B

Examples A & B above are different descriptions of the same movement. In A, the path sign provides a strong visual impression of travel throughout the springing combination. Although the springs in counts 1–4 are written with landings in place, they will travel steadily backwards because of the path sign.

In B, the springs on one foot and in the closed position (parallel 1st) are written with back direction symbols in the support column. That eliminates the need for a path sign with those actions. However, the spring to 2nd cannot be written differently in the support column. *Open positions have to be written with direction symbols that describe stance.* (Here, the feet are to each side of the center of weight.) **The only way to describe a traveling spring in an open position is with a path sign.**

You can decide which notation description of the above combination you prefer. Both are correct. Below are some further examples of straight path signs. Notice that, to enhance the sense of extended travel for a movement sequence, a straight path sign can be modified with backwards **N** or **double backwards N.** Amount of travel can be diminished with **X** or **double X.**

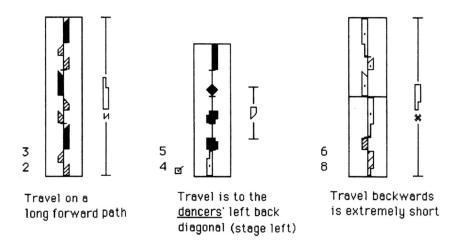

Travel on a long forward path	Travel is to the <u>dancers</u>' left back diagonal (stage left)	Travel backwards is extremely short

In the following examples, stage area signs are used with path signs to clarify the location on stage at which the dancer must arrive, or approach.

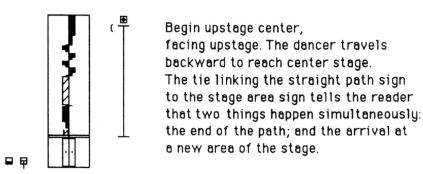

Begin upstage center, facing upstage. The dancer travels backward to reach center stage. The tie linking the straight path sign to the stage area sign tells the reader that two things happen simultaneously: the end of the path; and the arrival at a new area of the stage.

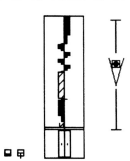

Here, the dancer travels less, approaching center stage without actually arriving there. An area sign within the symbol for "approach, become, increase" – inside the path sign – implies that a part of the stage gains in importance, i.e., is approached.

Maxim #99: Straight path signs appear outside the staff, to the right. They describe linear travel by incorporating direction symbols or stage area signs.

7.7 Paths: circling

Circular path signs describe curving travel through space. They are a combination of two symbols: the straight path sign and the turn symbol.

Straight path sign merged with right turn symbol results in path sign for circling clockwise.

Straight path sign merged with left turn symbol results in path sign for circling counter-clockwise.

The slanting ends of circling path signs are read in the same way as turn symbols; they indicate the direction in which to circle. However, with circles it is generally easier to think in the terms of *clockwise* or *counter-clockwise* travel, as opposed to curving to the right or left.

Also similar to turns is the use of pins with circling paths, to describe the amount of circling that is to be performed.

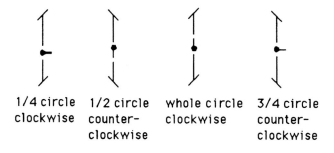

1/4 circle clockwise   1/2 circle counter-clockwise   whole circle clockwise   3/4 circle counter-clockwise

Although there are similarities in the ways turns and circles are read, it is important to be clear about the difference between these two kinds of actions. Turning is synonymous with pivoting or swiveling, with the action of the turning foot creating sliding friction against the floor. In circling, the primary emphasis is on carving a path through space, on creating a curving or arcing shape with traveling steps. Swivelling of the foot against the floor is absent or minimal as dancers move on the periphery of their circles.

Reading circular paths.   In the examples below, try to notice these three things sequentially:

    1 – Direction of travel in the support columns
    2 – Direction of the circular path
    3 – Amount of circling and final facing

Then, combine this information in a performance of the movement. Use the floorplans to verify your results.

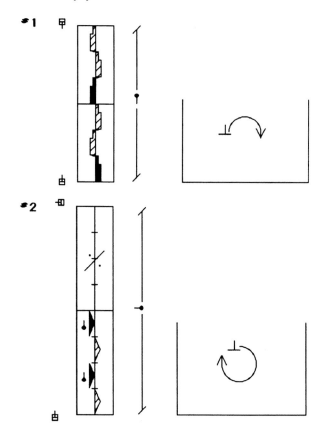

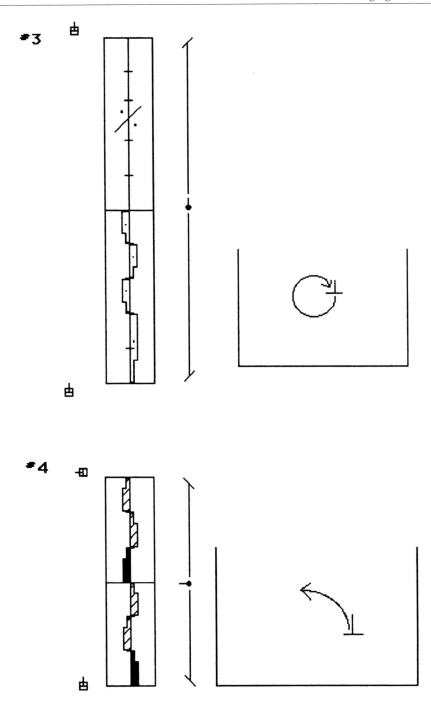

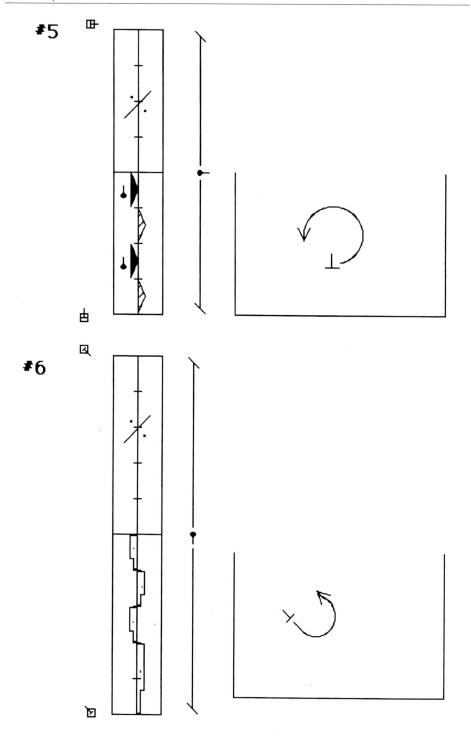

Maxim #100: Circular paths describe curving travel. The direction of *travel* is given in the support columns. The direction and amount of circling is shown by the path sign.

7.8 Focal Points

When an entire dance, or a significant part of it, is performed in a circle, the notation score may use a device known as a focal point to simplify the spacial orientation of the dancers. The need for a simplifying tool becomes obvious if a group of people stands in a circle. The example to the right shows a possible arrangement of 5 performers:

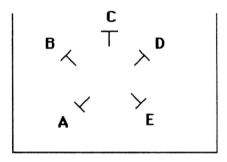

If we were to set up a typical starting position for these dancers, each one of them would need a different stage facing. And where exactly *is* each dancer facing? **A** roughly faces downstage right; **B** faces upstage right; **C** directly upstage; **D** faces upstage left; and **E** faces downstage left, On a staff, this array of stage facings would be daunting:

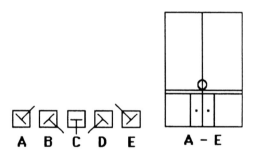

The combination of all these facings does nothing to give the impression that these dancers are in a circle, which is in fact the most important thing for the reader to know. What the notation should tell us about this group of 5 is that they are all facing the same way: *toward the center of a circle*.

In circle dances, Front Signs are supplanted by a description of where the dancers face in relation to the center of their circle. The circle center is referred to as the *focal point* and the symbol for it is a large dot: •. If the dancers have the focal point in front of them, they will be facing in, toward the center of the circle. With the focal point behind them, they will be facing out, or "backs to the center." The focal point may also be to their right of left, if they are facing around the circle with one side toward the center. Below is the notation for these examples:

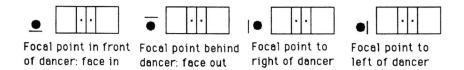

Focal point in front of dancer: face in   Focal point behind dancer: face out   Focal point to right of dancer   Focal point to left of dancer

A "meeting line" is used in conjunction with the focal point. The meeting line represents the dancer. Where the focal point is placed in relation to this line is where the center of the circle is located vis-a-vis the performer.

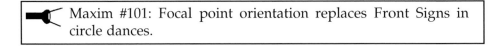

Maxim #101: Focal point orientation replaces Front Signs in circle dances.

An older method of showing the dancer's relation to the center of the circle was by using the focal point with a *composite turn sign*, which, as its name implies, is a combination of both turn signs, superimposed one over the other. In the starting position of older scores, the composite turn sign is an immediate signal that the dance is arranged in a circle. Please note that this is an older method than the meeting-line described above, but one that you will encounter in many scores.

Composite turn sign

In the starting position, dancers have their backs to the center of a circle.

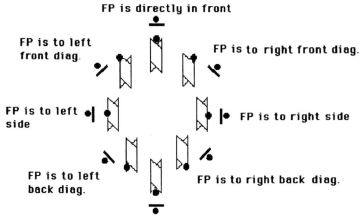

FP is directly in front

FP is to left front diag.

FP is to right front diag.

FP is to left side

FP is to right side

FP is to left back diag.

FP is to right back diag.

FP is directly behind

Let's set up a circle dance, beginning with everyone facing the center.

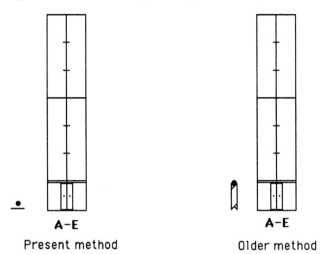

A–E

Present method

A–E

Older method

As our dance begins, notice that focal points have replaced pins in the turn signs. The degree of turn has been made LESS IMPORTANT than the new orientation of the dancer to the center of the circle. The turn description does not tell you how far to turn; it tells you where you must end in relation to the focal point. With the air turn in measure #2, the dancers hop and turn until the focal point is to their left. (Left side faces in to the circle.) In measure #4, the pivot on 2 feet reorients dancers to the circle center, ending with the focal point in front of them (facing in).

Notice that the dancers' new facing in relation to the center of the circle is reinforced with a meeting line and a focal point placed to the left of the staff after each turn, where a reader would normally look for a stage facing.

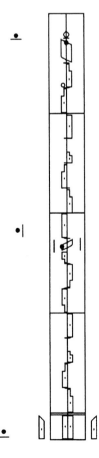

Maxim #102: Focal points can replace pins in turn signs. When they do, the new orientation to the focal point will also appear outside the staff in place of Front Signs, to reinforce the end result of the turn.

7.9   Path Signs: combination

The principal symbols for traveling on a path, or for changing Front Signs, can be combined in a variety of ways. Each combination describes a particular way of moving, to accommodate myriad choreographic possibilities. Below are some examples:

Revolving on a Straight Path

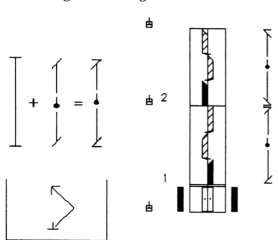

The straight path sign is the dominant sign in this combination, dictating travel in a straight line. The direction of travel is given in the support column. All the steps, regardless of the fact that there is also circling in the path, are written to give the direction of the straight line of travel.

The circling sign within the straight path sign indicates that the performers will *revolve* around themselves as they travel.

The term 'revolve' is used here, as opposed to 'turn', because of the *minimal sliding friction* against the floor in circling. Performers should keep swiveling to a minimum.

Turning on a Straight Path

Here the straight path is again dominant. All the turn symbol tells us is that while moving *on our straight path*, it's necessary to turn (pivot) a half-turn, to end facing the opposite direction. The timing should be

Turning on a Straight Path

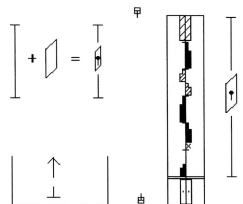

distributed throughout the path, and *the feet can swivel*. If the turn were designed to happen all at once at a particular moment in the sequence, it would be written in the support column.

Note that revolving (circling) on a straight path and turning on a straight path are similar actions. Both are about linear travel with change of front. The crucial difference is that turning involves swiveling, and revolving (circling) aims for non-swivel turns.

Spiraling In and Out

Circling, while approaching the focal point = Spiraling In. (The center of the circle is getting nearer.)

Circling, while moving away from the focal point = Spiraling Out.(The center of the circle is receding.)

In these examples, three symbols are combined: circling; crescendo (moving toward or approaching) or diminuendo (moving away); and focal point. Read the examples below in the same sequential order as plain circular paths (1. supports, 2. direction of circling, 3. amount of circling), adding a spiral towards or away from the center. Use the floorplans to verify your results.

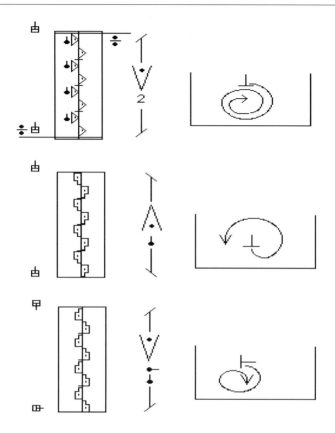

NOTATION

 ## 7.10   RN Rules

The rules concerning correct notation for the new meters introduced in this chapter are accompanying the illustrations in sections 7.1 through 7.5. Please refer to these pages for solutions to notating in those meters.

7.11   Cross-beaming

To facilitate the writing of pieces that ask one performer to perform 2 or more parts/instruments at a time, cross-beaming permits the use of beams **between** parts. For example, a percussionist is often called upon to play several instruments simultaneously. Imagine that each line below represents five individual drums. By allowing the beams to cross from line to line, it becomes easier to maintain *rhythmic groupings* while moving from drum to drum. The first example is harder to read as the notes tend to blur together:

Cross-beaming can make the coordination between any 2 parts (for example, clapping and speaking) much easier to read since the rhythmic groupings appear clearer and, as long as a note is sounding in any one part, *rests are not necessary* in the other part(s).

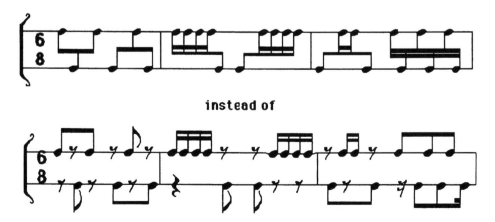

Note that stems can be drawn up or down from beams that lie between parts.

RHYTHMIC APPLICATIONS

7.12   Code Word Combinations

By now your code word cards should be well mastered and your sight-reading skillful in all Perfect meters. Now, try this method of practice, which will present new challenges in Imperfect and more contemporary meters.

Procedure:
Take all the compound and simple code word cards you currently have, shuffle them together into one deck, and lay them out in rows of at least four cards per row. Set the metronome to 120 and use it as an "8th note pulse". Sight-read, allowing two clicks for simple cards and three clicks for compound cards. Allow yourself to switch back and forth between the simple and compound cards, changing "hand-els" when necessary.

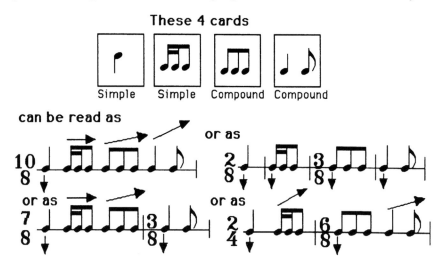

MOVEMENT APPLICATIONS

7.13   Circle Centers

In reading or writing circular paths, locating the center of the circle to be drawn on the page or in space is crucial. Otherwise, the shape of the movement or floorplan may distort the choreography. There is a simple rule to follow: *the center of your circle will always be at 90 degrees to your direction of travel.*

By keeping your notation (or travel) equidistant from the center of a circle, you can best maintain the shape of a path. A common error in performance is to "loose the center" part-way through a circle, with performers turning around themselves at the end of their travel. A good way to avoid this is to practice circling paths in all directions with a partner. Place one person in the center of the planned circle, and have the other travel around them maintaining a constant distance.

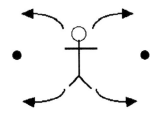

Forward and back circles will have centers to the right and left of your starting point, depending on whether travel is clockwise or counter-clockwise.

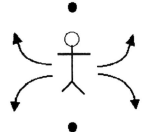

Sideways circles will have centers in front or in back if your starting position, depending on whether travel is clockwise or counter-clockwise.

7.14   Floorplans for Circling

The amount of space any given circle uses is determined by the number of steps written for it in the support column, and whether the steps are modified by **X** or backward **N**, making them shorter or longer than normal. There is no standard size for a 1/4, 1/2, or whole circle. Even the level of steps can affect the size of a circle, with steps in plié extending a circular shape beyond what would be expected of steps in relevé. When reading circular paths, use the floorplan to help you gauge the amount of space to cover. If you are drawing a floorplan for a circular path, take into account the number and size of steps involved in travel, and draw your floorplan to scale.

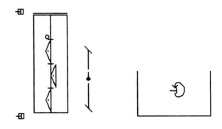

Whole circle with only 3 steps

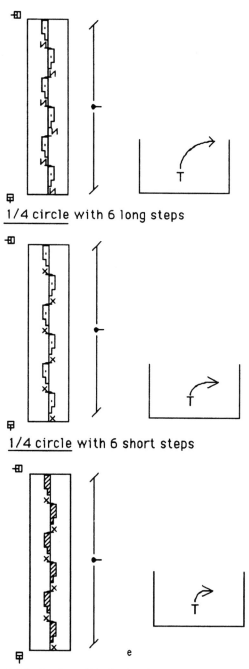

1/4 circle with 6 long steps

1/4 circle with 6 short steps

1/4 circle with 6 short steps in relevé

7.15 Clusters with Floorplans

Cue #19

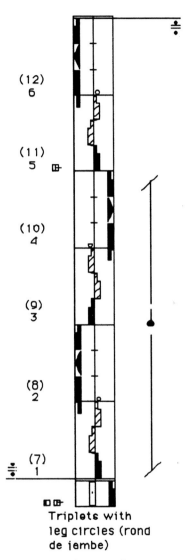

Triplets with
leg circles (rond
de jambe)

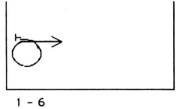

1 - 6

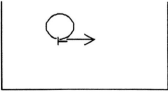

7 - 12

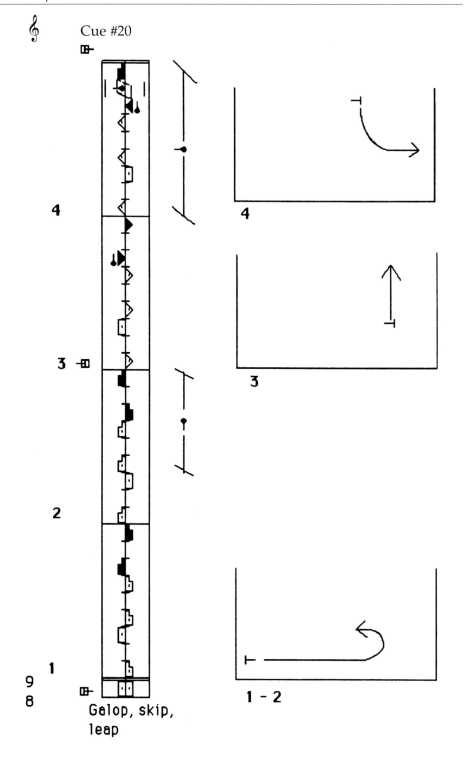

Cue #20

4

3

2

1

9
8

Galop, skip,
leap

4

3

1 - 2

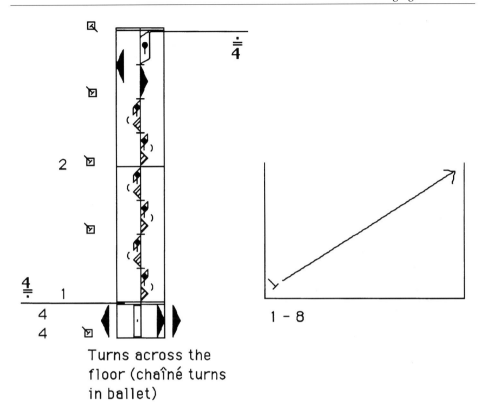

Turns across the
floor (chaîné turns
in ballet)

1 - 8

CHAPTER WRAP

7.16 RN Etudes

Variable Meter

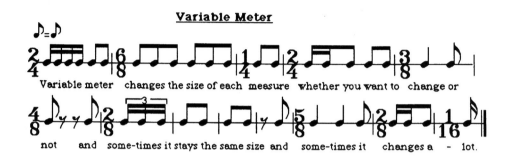

Variable meter changes the size of each measure whether you want to change or not and some-times it stays the same size and some-times it changes a - lot.

#2 – Variable meter

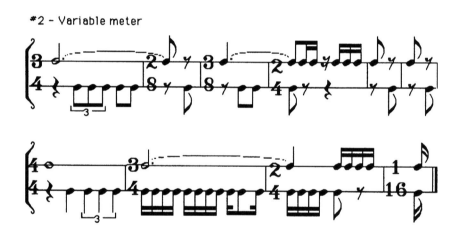

Alternating Meter

Monometer

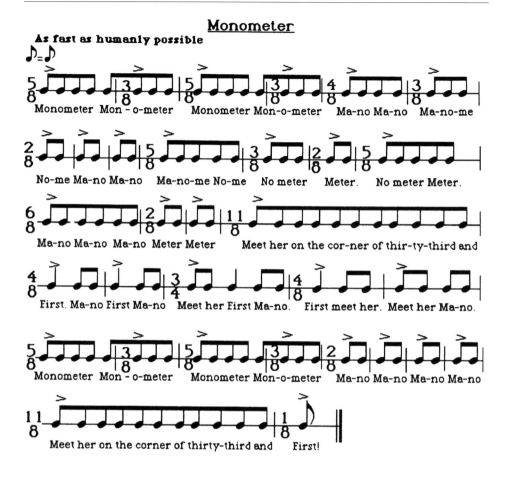

7.17 LN Etudes

Alta Regina, **an Italian Renaissance Dance** (15th and 16th centuries)

In Italy, where the Renaissance began and flourished, dancing was a skill required by all of the members of the ruling class. Dancing was a central part of the balls that celebrated all important events at court. The nobles used these occasions to exhibit their distinct qualities: quick thinking; elegance; and the complete self-assurance that came from power and wealth. They could make this display, with dignity, while dancing.

The richest courts maintained their own dancing masters, who were responsible for creating new dances, offering lessons, and instructing children in good manners as well as in dancing. Many of the nobility who resided at Court practiced dance performance on a daily basis. Dancing masters reached out to students beyond the Court by writing dance manuals, instruction books that circulated the most popular dances and that all dancers could use to help them practice. It is thanks to these dancing manuals that we possess actual choreography from the Italian Renaissance. If dancing masters had not taken the time to write books and notate dances, the choreography of their time would have been lost.

Nobiltà di dame is one of these dancing manuals that was printed at the end of Renaissance, in 1600, by Fabritio Caroso. Caroso was an influential dancing master who taught at some of the great Courts of Italy, and he recorded in *Nobiltà* 49 dances, with the music for each. His book, which offers instruction on the names and correct execution of steps, and rules of behavior for ladies and gentlemen at a ball and elsewhere, is a wonderful guide to the etiquette and choreography of the Italian Renaissance.

Alta Regina (*Great Queen*) is the third dance in Caroso's book. The style of the dance was in part determined by the fashions worn at the time. The gentlemen's quilted *pourpoint* (a padded vest) and the lady's boned corset encouraged everyone to maintain a noble, straight posture. The elaborate hats and many layers of clothing, topped by a cape for the gentleman and with false, hanging sleeves for the lady, made arm gestures while dancing awkward. Arms, therefore, were carried quietly, staying gracefully extended by the sides of the body. However, ladies would sometimes dance with a handkerchief or fan in one hand, and gentlemen, who wore their swords in public (in case they should be needed), kept these weapons steady with their left hand, and their capes sometimes tucked under their left elbow, while they were dancing.

Although most dancing was done in couples, many dances incorporated solo sequences for the lady and gentlemen to perform, offering them the opportunity to flirt and display their skill. Notice that the 3rd and 4th "playings" of *Alta Regina* (the 3rd and 4th time through the tune) are solo sections. The solos begin with a moment of rhythmic complexity: the movements in the first two measures are polyrhythmic as the dancers move in duple beats against the triple meter of the music. To aid in reading this "2 against 3", *dancer's counts* are placed to the left of the staff. These counts are in parentheses to reinforce that they concern the choreography, not the music.

When performing *Alta Regina*, recall that it was a social dance, with pleasant interaction between partners. One indication of the social nature of the dance is its frequent use of reverence. In the 1st playing, reverence is the opening movement. In every subsequent playing (2–6), reverence comes at the end, paired with a forward and back swaying step called the stopped-step. Together these movements occupy the concluding 8 measures of those 5 playings, creating a repeating, terminating cadence for the sections of the dance.

Alta Regina, notated by Rachelle Palnick Tsachor

GLOSSARY

L = Lady   G = Gentleman

 Circling path continues from one staff to the next.

 Scuff forward with the heel.

 Pull back to place, hitting the ball of the foot on the way.

 Step and turn simultaneously

 On the step and rise, turn until the focal point in on your left.

Note that high level steps are performed with the heel just off the floor, in this example just high enough to be able to place the toes of the right foot under the left heel.

Stylistic Notes

General notes applying to the entire dance:

- High level steps and springs are performed with the heel just slightly off the floor.
- Steps in general are small, and pliés are moderate.
- The feet (ankles) would have been flexed slightly in all leg gestures, to keep the chopins (slippers without heel straps) on the foot.
- Although there was no movement of the shoulders in the dance, because upper body movement was restricted by the corsets and neck ruffs that were in fashion, partners did follow one another in the dance with their eyes, and with glances over the shoulder. As a matter of style, partners should gaze at one another whenever desirable or practical during the dance.
- Overall performance style is fairly vigorous, while maintaining poise.
- Note that focal points are used in the dance when circling occurs, or when the partner becomes a focal point (for example, in the solos in the Third and Fourth Playings). Front signs are used when room directions take on more importance.

FIRST PLAYING

- Measures 1–4: Partners begin the dance with a reverence. During this movement, the gentleman removes his hat, and replaces it.
- Measures 5–12: Partners circle each other, flirting. The step they perform four times is called a "broken sequence."
- Measures 13–16: Partners move toward each other, then teasingly move away. The step they perform twice is the "sapphic step."
- Measures 17–20: Swagger slightly in the "stopped steps."
- Measures 21–24: The four stamped sequences of the dance style known as "Canary" are performed playfully, teasingly.

SECOND PLAYING

- Measures 1–8: The "broken sequence" step repeats in a circling pattern, performed flirtatiously.
- Measures 9–16: "Stopped steps" forward, and "half reverences" are paired.

- Measures 17–24: Swagger slightly in the "stopped steps" and conclude the Second Playing with a full reverence. The Second through Sixth Playings of the dance conclude with this 8-measure pattern of "stopped steps" and reverence.

THIRD PLAYING

- Measures 1–16: The gentleman shows off to the lady, who watches to see how well he dances.
- In measures 1–2 (and 9–10), the step performed is "the knot," in which the gesturing foot and lower leg cross behind and wrap around the supporting leg.
- The step in measures 3–4 (and 11–12) is the "flourish;" the springing actions in measure 5 (and 13) are "falling jumps." The "sapphic step" reappears in measures 7–8 (and 15–16).

FOURTH PLAYING

- Measures 1–16: The lady shows off to the gentleman, who watches with admiration.

FIFTH PLAYING

- Having displayed their individual skills, the partners dance together in a mixture of "flourishes," "falling jumps," and "sapphic steps."

SIXTH PLAYING

- Measures 1–16: A sideways traveling step, called "reprise," is paired with "falling jumps" and the "sapphic step" to create an angular path of travel.
- Measures 17–24: In the final reverence, a gracious acknowledgement of the pleasure of the entire dance is expressed.

Cue #21

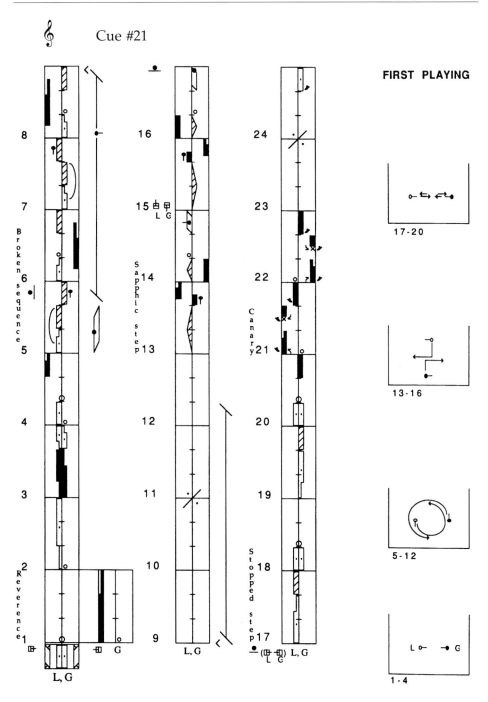

FIRST PLAYING

17-20

13-16

5-12

1-4

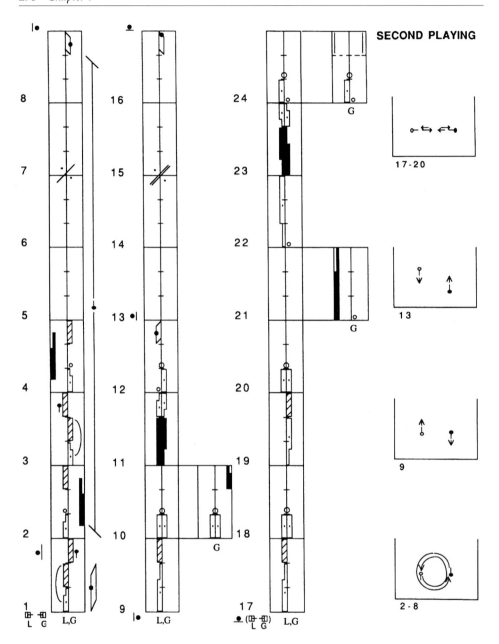

SECOND PLAYING

THIRD PLAYING

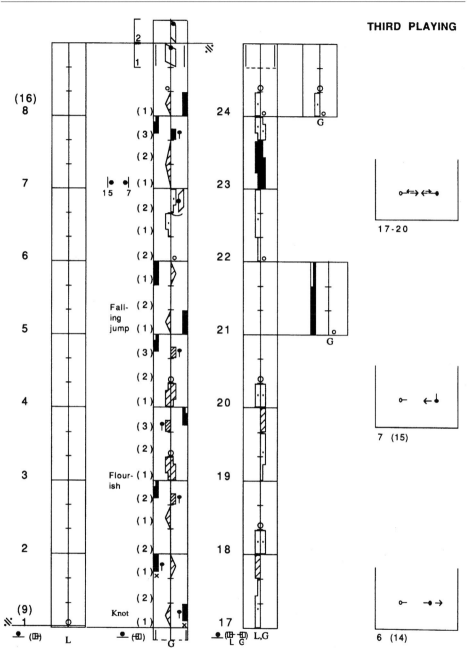

17-20

7 (15)

6 (14)

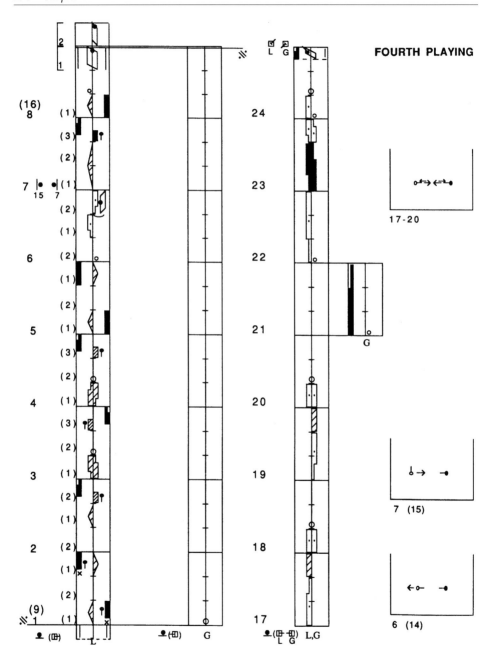

FOURTH PLAYING

17-20

7 (15)

6 (14)

FIFTH PLAYING

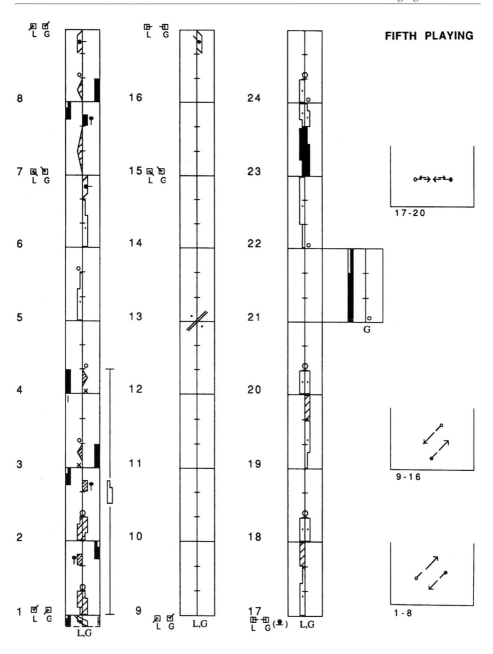

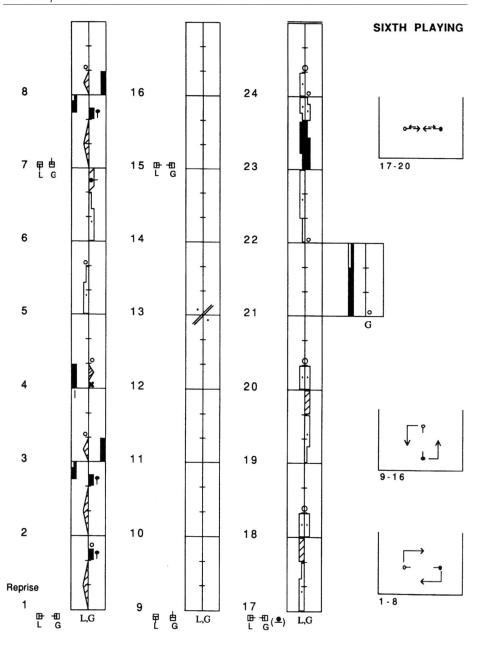

SIXTH PLAYING

7.18 More Tricky Rhythms

Notice that changes of meter, marked outside the LN staves to the left, appear *just prior to* measure(s) in a new meter. This placement warns score readers of imminent change, preparing them for a different meter as they cross the bar line.

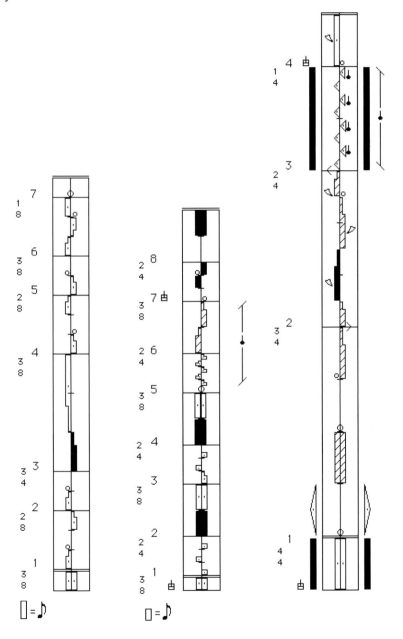

7.19   Suggested Assignments

 Pick one RN etude from each of the previous chapters and re-write it with cross-beaming.

 Establish a monometric pulse-base of thirty 8th-notes. Divide them into at least 8 measures, then write them out in RN with the appropriate time signatures. Choreograph a movement phrase that reflects the changing weight and accents of the meters. Perform this with an accompaniment consisting of the same rhythm played on a drum.

• Recite the following numeric pulse-base several times, in a steady 8th note pulse: 12 123 12 1234 12345. Then, once you have memorized the pattern,

(1) Walk steady quarter notes while reciting it.
(2) Clap your hands on each #1 of the pattern while walking the quarters.
(3) Try to change direction every 2 steps, every 3 steps, every 4 steps, etc.
(4) Now, try stepping on each "1" of the pattern while counting the quarters out loud from 1 to 8.

 Create an 8-measure sequence based on the "2-step". (See Cluster in 2.20.) Add turns and additional movements as desired, and follow these floorplans.

1 - 4	5 - 6	7 - 8

• Choreograph a 16-measure duet that uses the following focal point orientations, with the focal point being your performing partner.

Measures

	1,2	3,4	5,6	7,8	9,10	11,12	13,14	15,16
Dancer A	•	•	•	•	•	•	•	•

	1,2	3,4	5,6	7,8	9,10	11,12	13,14	15,16
Dancer B	•	•	•	•	•	•	•	•

𝄞   Cue #22

- Practice performing *Alta Regina* (7.17) with the alternate musical accompaniment provided on the accompanying audiotape. The new accompaniment will probably affect your perception of and ability to perform the movement. In the first playing, the music will be helpful to the choreography, but it will progressively challenge the choreography with each new playing. Perform the six playings as one continuous dance, allowing the music to change around you.

Variation #1: Do not at all allow the music to influence the original "style" of the choreography. Maintain a consistent performance throughout.

Variation #2: Adapt the performance of each playing to changes in the music. Identify the changes in the music (i.e., meter, rhythm, tempo, dynamics, etc.) and plan creatively how these changes can impact the movement.

Finally, be very clear in your evaluations of the effectiveness of variations 1 & 2 as you see them performed by others. Which do you prefer, and why?

8

CONCLUSIONS

Polymeter requires the existence of two or more simultaneous parts. When there is more than one metric pattern in play at the same time, the effect is "polymetric". Since polymeter assumes more than one part at a time, new notational practices also come into play.

RHYTHMIC CONCEPTS

8.1 Polymeter: superimposition

When metric patterns are placed against each other and one is considered to be dominant or 'base', the effect is called *Super-Imposition*. Literally, this means "imposing" one metric pattern atop or against another. When choreographers superimpose, they sometimes use the phrase "putting a 3 against a 4" or "putting a 2 against a 3." The operative phrase here is "putting against": the overall effect is one of competition of friction. It is sometimes helpful to imagine a draftsman's transparency sheets: the bottom sheet might contain a grid of city streets, while each "overlay" adds the trees, buildings, bridges, etc. to complete the total picture.

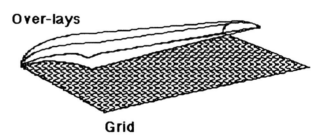

Over-lays

Grid

PROCEDURE:
To superimpose, you must first establish a base time signature to provide a steady metric pattern: in our example, we will use 4/4:

In order to "put a 3 against" the base 4 above, there are several options from which to choose. You could superimpose 4 groups of three quarters. While the base meter executes three downbeats in "4", the superimposed pattern will execute four downbeats, AS IF IT WERE IN 3/4:

OPTION #1

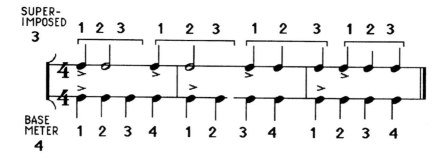

Note the use of brackets that aid the eye in seeing the superimposition of 3/4 written in the time signature of 4/4. Bar lines vertically connect both parts, observing the 4/4 metric division. The performance will accent both the "4" and the "3", with the "3" getting lots of **push**. There is a very real "argument" between the two parts: this type of friction can be *very exciting*.

 Try this. Set the metronome to 90. While sitting in a chair, tap your thighs on "1" (•) and clap 2, 3, 4(X).
[• XXX • XXX • XXX]. This represents 3 measures in 4/4. Now do it again while counting to three out loud, loudly accenting each "1".

Count	1 2 3 1	2 3 1 2	3 1 2 3
Clap	• X X X	• X X X	• X X X

You are now polymetric between your speech and your movement. Try this also while walking in 4 and clapping the 3, or vice versa.

OPTION #2
Eight groups of three 8th-notes (or 3/8) could be superimposed against 3 measures of 4:

Beams are drawn across the bar lines (where necessary) to reinforce visually the super-imposed 8th note patterns.

With the metronome still set at 90, try this:

| 1 2 3 | 1 2 3 | 1 2 | 3 | 1 2 3 | 1 | 2 3 | 1 | 2 3 | 1 2 3 | 1 2 3 |
| • | X | X | X | • | X | X | X | • | X | X | X |

You are again polymetric as you superimpose eight groups of three 8th notes against three groups of four quarters. Notice how the two parts will recycle again in measure #4.

OPTION #3
You could also superimpose sixteen groups composed of three sixteenth-notes against the same three measures of 4/4:

*** Note**: If necessary, due to page borders, beams may be broken, stretched off the right margin and continued on the next line(s) as seen here.

Now try this at the same 90 m.m.:

| 123 123 123 123 123 1 | 23 123 123 132 123 12 | 3 123 123 123 123 123 |
| • | X | X | X | • | X | X | X | • | X | X | X |

You are again polymetric, this time between a very rapid speech pattern and a 4/4 which now feels quite slow (although the tempo has not changed).

In addition to these options, there are endless combinations of superimpositions possible, far too numerous to indicate here. Just remember that *polymeter requires 2 metric patterns at work against each other.*

 Maxim #103: Superimposition refers to the over-laying of one metric pattern on another within the *same* time signature.

8.2   Polymeter: mixed

When more than one time signature occurs simultaneously in separate parts, and neither is considered "dominant", and neither part changes time signature once started, you have *the simultaneous mixing together of different time signatures*. Essentially, the matter falls under the category of alignment. As there is no 'base' time signature, each part receives its own time signature and maintains its own metric characteristics. What holds the parts together is their common denominator, in many cases, the 8th note. For example, the top part below is in 6/8 while the bottom is in 4/4.

Bar lines do not connect the parts except where both parts share a simultaneous downbeat. Above, notice that in a hypothetical 'next' measure, the downbeats would once again coincide.

As seen above, brackets may also be placed above and below the measures for visual reinforcement.

 Maxim #104: Mixed Polymeter refers to the simultaneous mixing together of *different* metric patterns in *different* time signatures.

8.3 Polymeter: mixed variable

Similar to mixed meter, mixed variable meter allows for the independent changing of time signature in each part.

Note and rest values NEVER align with time signatures: the alignment is *stretched* to allow for the placement of new time signatures **between** note/rest values:

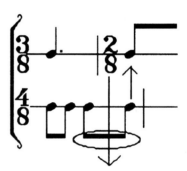

When one part moves to a new measure individually, the bar line is short and written across only that individual part:

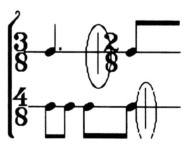

When two or more adjacent parts change meter at the same time, a long single bar line is drawn to connect both parts, serving as a visual cue to the players that they are entering a new measure simultaneously:

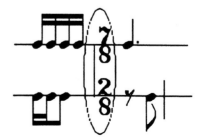

There is technically no limit to the number of "mixed" parts that can occur simultaneously. Below, two more parts have been added to the previous example:

Note that dotted "cue" lines have been drawn to connect simultaneous downbeats that are not adjacent to each other. This is a common notational practice since players in contemporary music ensembles prefer to play from the score (rather than from individual parts). They can stay together by seeing each other's position at each given "cue" point.

If the above example looks a bit frightening, think of it as a bit of creative brick-laying:

 Maxim #105: Mixed polymeter refers to the simultaneous occurrence of different time signatures, in different parts, which may independently change meter at any time.

8.4 Special Effects

The following is a list of "ornamental devices" which, in various ways, are used to alter the color, texture, and "motion" of the sound of any single note of group of notes:

Grace notes
Grace notes are the fastest decorative pickups to a beat. Whether a single 8th note or a group of two or three 16ths notes, they are written in a smaller size than standard notes. The single grace note is written as a small 8th note with a slash through the stem and flag; double and triple grace notes are written as small groups of 16ths or 32nds.

Grace notes are further broken into two categories, depending on whether they fall *on* or *before* the beat, referred to as either "**accented**" or "**unaccented**". Accented means that the grace note(s) will "steal time" from the beginning of the current note; unaccented means they will "steal time" from the end of the previous note. Grace notes have no real time value of their own: they are performed as fast as possible in relation to the current tempo and are said to live by the "grace of the note they steal from".

In the accented example to the right, the quarter note would be robbed of its full duration to make room for the grace note ON the beat. In the unaccented example, the grace note steals from the previous quarter note's duration, squeezing into the last millisecond of the measure BEFORE the next beat occurs.

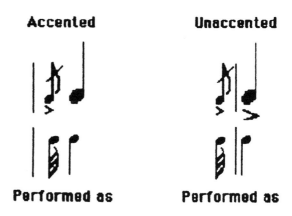

The differences in sound between an accented and unaccented grace note are described in the table below:

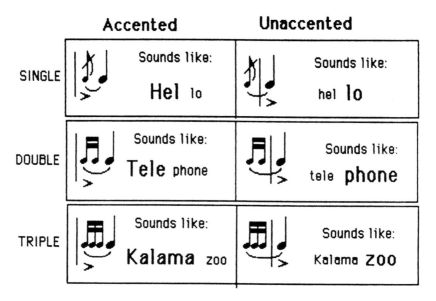

Flam
The term **flam** refers to a grace note performed by a percussionist.

Trill
Trills are very rapid oscillations between two adjacent notes (lower to upper or vise versa). They are therefore, as are grace notes, tonal in nature. Their rhythm is usually non-specific (performed as fast as possible) in relation to the current tempo, but it is sometimes desirable to write out the exact number of trill repetitions. In movement terms, a trill might be thought of as the rapid waving or fluttering of the hand:

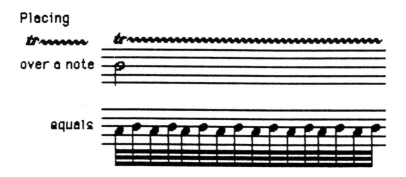

Rolls

These are non-tonal trills for percussionists. For example, the "growl" of a military drum just before the cannon goes off is the sound of a percussionist's roll:

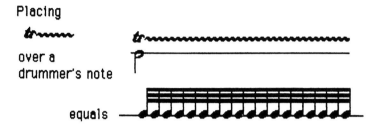

Placing

over a
drummer's note

equals

Tremolo

Very much like a trill, the prime difference being that where trills affect only **adjacent** notes, tremolos affect either the same note or two **non-adjacent** notes. There are two types of tremolo: single note and double note. The single note tremolo is a very rapid, uncontrolled pulsation ("to tremble") on one note, like the percussionist's roll. The double note tremolo involves two non-adjacent pitches that are alternated as rapidly as possible. Notationally, the number of beams placed between or beside the note values is determined by the tempo of the music:

a slow tempo requires a faster tremolo which calls for three beams; a fast tempo requires less tremolo, which calls for two beams:

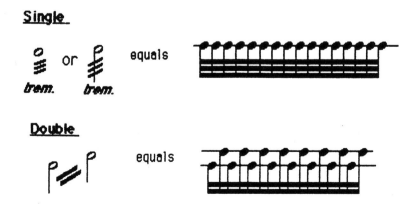

<u>Single</u>

or   equals

trem.   *trem.*

<u>Double</u>

equals

Note: The duration of a tremolo equals the affected note itself: above, it would be that of a half note.

Glissando

This ornament involves sliding from one note to another (tonal) either up or down in pitch, in a "siren-like" manner. A glissando can last for any length of time, depending on the duration of the notes involved. Notationally, a glissando is indicated by a slanting line connecting the two involved notes, accompanied by the word "glissando" or "gliss" or "gl.". Depending on the distance between the outer-most notes, the "interior" notes (those between the outer notes) are not individually articulated. Instead, they are "glossed over", creating the "sliding" effect. In the example below, the glissando will last for the duration of the first quarter note and stop when the pitch of the second quarter note is reached. This is called "one beat gliss".

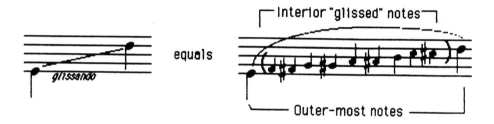

"Tuplets": Un-even sub-divisions

Similar to duplets and triplets, except larger, these "tuplets" are rhythmic surges within structured metric patterns, involving anywhere from four to fifty compressed notes. They can last from as little as one beat, to several measures. Notationally, a horizontal bracket is placed over the note heads/rests in a tuplet, with a number specifying the size (number of notes/rests) within. Generally, there are two approaches to their performance: **measured** and **non-measured**, or, **precise** and **casual**.

Measured (precise) implies that the tuplet is small enough (or the tempo slow enough) for each note to be articulated with precision and clarity. *Non-measured* implies that there are too many notes compressed within the tuplet (or the tempo is so fast) that the articulation of each note would be impossible (or academic). Instead, each note should become blurred and "run together" with the others.

Tempo clarification: Regardless of the size of a tuplet, a slower tempo will usually allow a large tuplet to be cleanly articulated because more time is available for execution. Fast tempi reduce the amount of time available, blurring the articulation of even a small quadruplet.

What follows is a demonstration of how measured tuplets sound. Speak each example several times in a moderate to slow tempo, using the suggested sentences. Then chant the rhythm without the words. The notes within the tuplet should be equally compressed within the allotted space of time (one beat; 2 beats; one measure; etc.) so that *no one note lasts longer than any of the others*.

Non-measured tuplets can be of any size upwards of 8, and are by nature rhythm's "true radicals". Always of a soloistic nature, they are to metered rhythm what a sports car is to a tricycle: bold, fast, and uncommonly exciting. Because of their great size, they can fill an entire measure or more, but can also compress into single beats; the tighter the space, the faster and more blurred the tuplet becomes. Found in the highly virtuostic piano music of Chopin and Lizst, their presence in a score is one of the most technically challenging aspects of musical performance.

Imagine each of the above examples performed in just one or two beats in a fast tempo!!!

8.5   The Canon

For both composers and choreographers, the canon is one of most widely used and dependable compositional devices. The glue that binds canons together is **Imitation**: one part copies another. The simplest type of canon is the children's "Round", such as *Row, Row, Row your boat*. Once all have learned the melody, voices enter at *different* times, singing the *same* melody.

A Visual 3-part Canon (Round)

Begin

1st voice ● ○ ◉ ◉ ✪ ◉ ⊗ ⊗

2nd voice ● ○ ◉ ◉ ✪ ◉ ⊗ ⊗

3rd voice ● ○ ◉ ◉ ✪ ◉ ⊗ ⊗

End

 Maxim #106: Canons (Rounds) employ a technique called *Imitative Counterpoint*: interwoven linear lines that reinforce each other through the *re-use* of material from part to part.

Canonic Length.   The primary difference between canons and rounds is length. Rounds are relatively short (4 to 8 measures), highly repetitive, and are sung over and over until the leading voice stops, thereby terminating the other voices which are "following the first voice". Canons are much longer, usually non-repetitive, and can sometimes serve as the basis for an entire composition (Pachelbel's *Canon* for example). The trick in canon composition is the establishment of the interval of time that elapses between the entrance of the first voice to the entrance of the second "canonic" voice. This "**canonic interval**" can be of any length, from half-a-beat to several measures. Once established, the canonic interval is seldom changed, regardless of how many voices are yet to enter. Canons take their names from the canonic interval: a "canon at one beat"; a "canon at 2 measures"; etc.

Composing canons.   Instead of writing one part all the way through and then rewriting it in the second voice at the determined interval, canons are written in a zig-zag fashion to maximize the contrast between the voices. Below is a "2-part canon at one measure", i.e., two voices at the canonic interval of one measure:

(1) Establish the first measure by selecting a meter and rhythm:

(2) Then make a 2-part score, transferring the contents of the first measure to the second measure of the 2nd "canonic" voice:

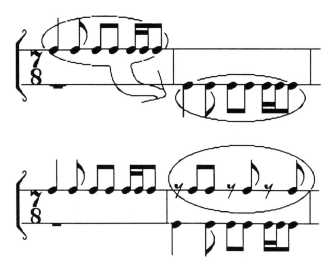

(3) Now go back to the top voice and write a contrasting second measure, one which uses a different rhythmic scheme than the one in the 2nd voice:

Note how the addition of the 8th rests in the top voice allows the second voice to "peek through", making the top voice seem like an accompaniment to the lower voice.

(4) Now transfer measure #2 to the canonic voice's measure #3:

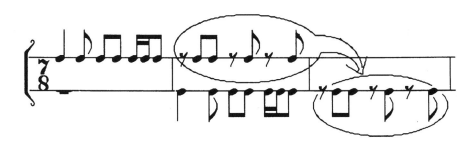

(5) Now, as in step #3, write a new third measure in the top voice which contrasts with the lower voice:

(6) This procedure is continued, measure-by-measure, until the first voice is terminated. But the canon will not come to an end until the canonic voice finishes its imitation:

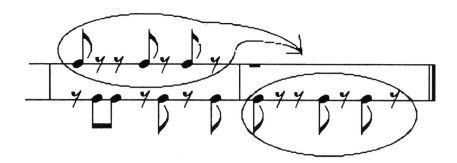

Optional False Ending.   It is sometimes desirable to create a non-imitative "false ending" to allow both voices to conclude together. The leading voice is extended until the second voice ends in the last measure. Rounds do not end this way but many canons do, as all voices ending together is less "anti-climatic":

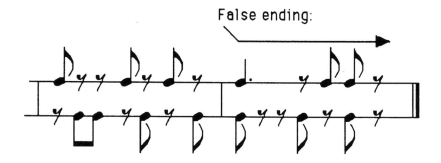

In canons of more than two voices, each voice other than the last voice can be given a false ending as well, until the last voice finally finishes the imitation:

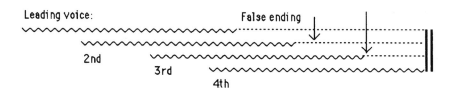

Here, a schematic of a 4-part canon with an imitative ending:

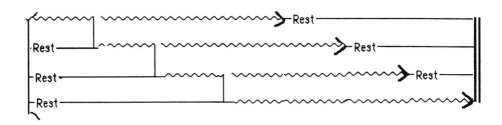

 MOVEMENT CONCEPTS

8.6 Danced Canons

Canons in dance follow the same rules as those in music. In a danced canon, a group of dancers perform the same choreographic phrase, but since different dancers begin the phrase at different times, viewers see different parts of the phrase simultaneously. This can be a very pleasing viewing experience, as dancers "pass" choreography to each other. Viewers recognize what they have seen before, but also appreciate how different parts of the same phrase interact when they are in performance at the same time.

The illustrations on the previous page, demonstrating false endings and imitative endings, apply to dance as well as rhythmic canons.

Using these illustrations, notice when several parts in a canon are active simultaneously. These passages provide the most complex viewing – or listening – to the audience.

8.7 More Palm Facings

When the arm is carried differently than the normal or standard way, the direction the palm faces can be placed next to the arm gesture to modify it. The symbol for the palm (followed by the required direction) is written outside the arm gesture columns and is the same for both right and left palm; specific identification is rarely needed.

They are members of a group of symbols called "BODY PRE-SIGNS", which call attention to parts of the body that do not have their own particular, private column in the LN staff. Body pre-signs are ALWAYS followed by a direction symbol or other movement indication. The timing of the action described by the pre-sign and direction symbol begins at the beginning of the pre-sign, and extends through the end of the direction symbol. Below are some examples of arm gestures modified by particular palm facings:

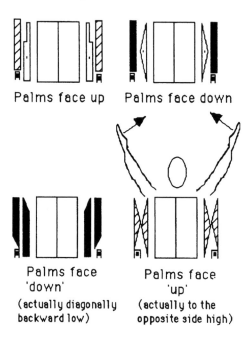

Palms face up   Palms face down

Palms face
'down'
(actually diagonally
backward low)

Palms face
'up'
(actually to the
opposite side high)

Palm facings last only for the duration of the arm gesture they modify, unless followed by a hold sign.

At right, because of the hold sign, the palm continues to face down (place low) until count 4, when it is cancelled by a return-to-normal sign. The 'away from' sign also cancels holds on palm facings.

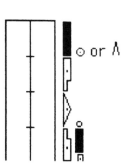

Thumb-edge of the hand

An alternative to describing arm positions via palm facings is to specify where the thumb-side of the hand is facing. Sometimes it is easier or clearer to describe an arm position in this way. The symbols for thumb-edge are:

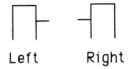

Left   Right

These symbols are pre-signs, just as palm signs are. By themselves, they are incomplete. They merely identify a part of the body for the reader, and must be followed by a direction symbol so that we know where that body part faces. Note that the thumb-side (thumb-edge of the hand) pre-sign will never make the thumb itself move. This symbol pinpoints one surface of the hand, the thumb-side surface. The subsequent direction symbol gives the spacial orientation or facing of that surface of the arm. The arm gestures on the preceding page can all be notated by describing the direction in which the thumb-side of the hand is facing.

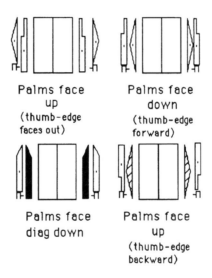

Palms face
up
(thumb-edge
faces out)

Palms face
down
(thumb-edge
forward)

Palms face
diag down

Palms face
up
(thumb-edge
backward)

 Maxim #107: Palm facings and thumb-side symbols are examples of "body pre-signs." Body pre-signs are always followed by a direction symbol or other movement indication, and are included in the timing of an action.

8.8 Six Degrees of Contraction

We have seen previously that **X** is the basic symbol for "shortening" or "contracting". In the support column, **X** shortens the distance of a step or a landing from a spring, or of the distance between the feet in an open position. In the gesture columns, **X** shortens the distance between the foot and the hip, or the hand and the shoulder, resulting in a contraction of the limb.

Since the arms and legs contract to varying degrees, depending on the choreography, it is important to be able to specify these different degrees of bend. LN can specify 6 degrees of contraction in the arm or leg. The symbol **X** changes to describe each degree.

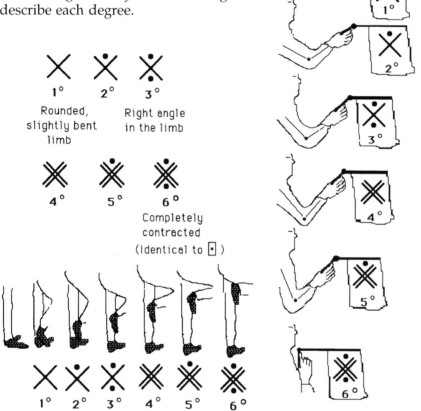

There is one major point of theory concerning contracting the limbs: *the relationship of the hand to the shoulder, or of the foot to the hip, must never change in either direction or level as the limb bends.*

There are two ways of bending the arm or leg: **folding** and **contracting**. In folding, the free end (hand or foot) moves in an arc toward the fixed end (shoulder or hip), moving out of its original position as it does so.

For the arms, folding occurs at the elbow; the lower arm moves on a curve, bringing the free end toward the base. When contracting, the spatial relationship between the free and fixed ends remains constant; the distance *between* them merely diminishes.

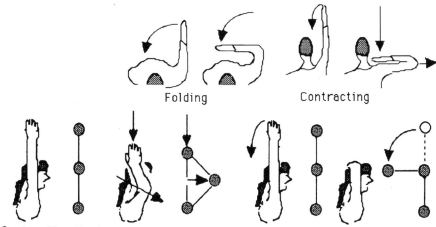

Folding   Contracting

Contracting the hand to the shoulder   Folding the arm from the elbow

Because the relationship of the free and fixed ends remains constant in contracted arm and leg gestures, it is a comparison of hand-to-shoulder or of foot-to-hip that will determine the direction and level of the arm or leg. *Once direction and level are clear, the degree of contraction can be added*:

Do **not** be concerned about the elbow or the knee when judging the direction of a bent gesture, only when judging *degree* of bend. Notice that since contraction is part of the information describing a movement, it needs to be part of the timing of that action. Direction symbols are shortened to allow **X** to enter their count.

The rotation of the arm or leg will affect where the elbow or knee moves in space as the limb contracts.

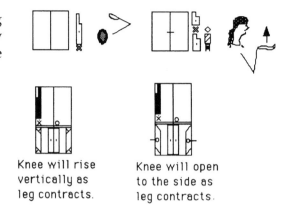

Knee will rise
vertically as
leg contracts.

Knee will open
to the side as
leg contracts.

 Maxim #108: LN can specify 6 degrees of contraction in the arm or leg. The relationship of the hand to the shoulder, or of the foot to the hip, does not change in direction or level as the limb contracts.

8.9 Contact and Touching

When parts of the body touch, or when movers contact a partner or object, a horizontal bow is used to join the parts. The horizontal bow is called a "contact" or "connecting" bow. Score readers need to notice the ends of the bow, since they extend to the two entities that touch. The middle of the bow is of no consequence; it can arc upward or downward as room and visibility permit on the staff:

Entrechat quatre
The legs contact
(beat) in the air.

Plie´ action in which
the gesturing &
supporting leg touch.

Contact bows by themselves indicate "touching". They can be modified with "X" if "grasping" is involved. The logic here is that "x" is the symbol for "shortening" or "contracting," and grasping is an action that involves contracting the hand:

Grasp

The left grasps
the right

The right grasps
the left.

CLARIFICATION. Notice that bows are of 2 main types: vertical and horizontal. Vertical bows extend through time as it unfolds through the counts and measures of a staff. Therefore, *vertical bows link things in time.* Horizontal bows extend across the columns of the staff and link parts of the body, and across the staffs for individual dancers. Therefore, *horizontal bows link things in space.*

8.10   Table of Bows

LINKING ACTIONS IN TIME AND SPACE

Caret $\rangle$ Links a transition from 2 feet to 1 to produce a shift of weight.

$\gtrless$ Zed Carets link a leg gesture to a support or vice versa to show that one leads directly into the next.

Tie $)$ Links 2 actions in time, creating a blending in performance (also called <u>Simultaneous Action Bow</u>).

Bracket $\rfloor$ Links 2 or more actions with the same modifier (such as a series of arms gestures all modified by "X").

Contact $\smile$ Links actions, parts of the body, or physical objects in space (also called a <u>Connecting Bow</u>).

QUALITATIVE

Phrasing Bow   Groups actions as belonging to one movement idea. Adds temporal shaping (beginning & end) to a sequence.

Initiation Bow   Describes an impulse of energy as an action begins.

Impact Bow   Describes an increase of energy as an action concludes

Maxim #109: In LN, vertical bows link things in time. Horizontal bows link things in space.

NOTATION

 ### 8.11   Repeats: large and sectional

The *1st and 2nd ending* is used when a section or melody of moderate length repeats with two distinctly different "endings". For example, a section or melody (normally from 8 to 16 measures) is performed once, then immediately repeated. At the end of the repeat, the first ending is replaced by the second, allowing for a change of material in the last measure(s) the second time around. This technique is frequently used in popular song writing; the first verse is almost always repeated (usually with new words), with a new melodic/harmonic transition into the next section:

Moderate length - 1st & 2nd endings

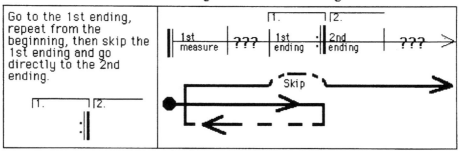

Large repeats (usually 16+ measures) tend to be a factor in the "form" of musical composition, i.e. the total length of musical sections, movements, and complete compositions. The "big repeats" described below may each occur once in a composition, or all may appear within the framework of one really large work, butting up against each other in a series of repeated sections that make up the whole. One example of a common use of a large sectional repeat is the traditional 1st movement of a classical symphony, which repeats the statement of the theme completely before going on with the rest of the movement. Rather than reprint the music, the players simply "turn back" to the top of their music and start again.

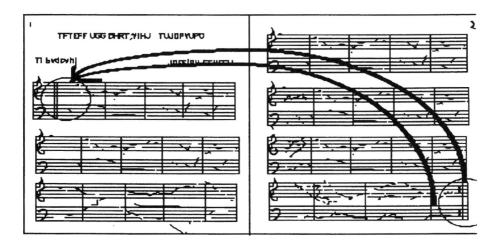

In the above example, the players will repeat back to the beginning, going on to page 3 only after replaying pages one and two completely.

Big Repeats – encompassing large sections

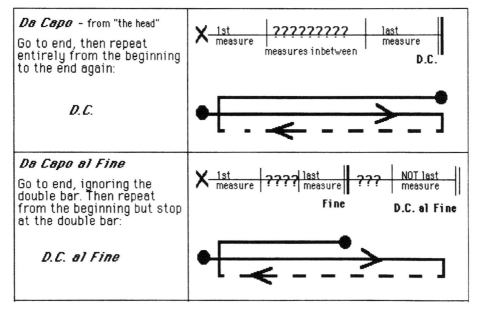

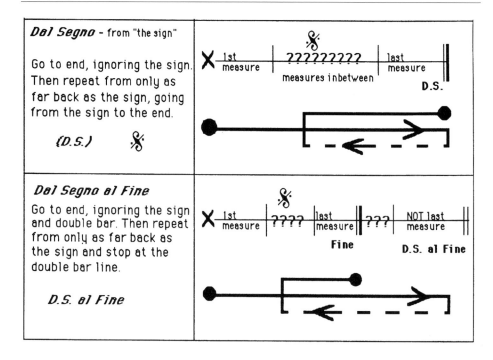

The coda is an extended, dramatic ending which sometimes occurs at the end of a large sectional repeat or movement.

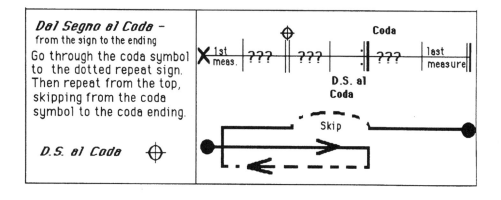

8.12   Scoring for Percussion/Creating New Symbols

Notation for the RN composer and the dance notator has one major difference in that while dance scores are written usually for combinations of men and women only, percussion scores can stipulate hundreds of combinations of instruments from a triangle to a bull whip. The selection of which instruments to choose depends largely on their sound, timbre (tone), physical characteristics, and personal taste.

Standard Percussion instruments (of the orchestra)
These instruments are divided into two major categories:
(1) tonal (marimba, xylophone, tympani, etc.), and
(2) non-tonal (snare drum, cymbals, woodblock, etc.).

A second categorization details the physical properties by which these instruments produce sound:

(1) stretched skin (snare drum, tympani, bass drum, etc.),
(2) metalic (cymbals, tubular bells, chimes, etc.), and
(3) wood (temple blocks, xylophone, marimba, etc.).

A third categorization details the method by which sound is produced. Since all must be struck by something (which is why they are called 'percussion' instruments), the striker can be either:

(1) hard sticks/ hammers (wood or metal),
(2) soft sticks/ hammers (cloth, rubber, etc.),
(3) human hands (finger tips, full palm, gloved, non-gloved, scratched, etc.), and
(4) anything else you can imagine (such as items normally found in a hardware store).

Scoring for percussion can therefore involve a high degree of detail. For example, since every one knows how the snare drum and bass drum sound, one can successfully write for them in a simple, straight-forward style:

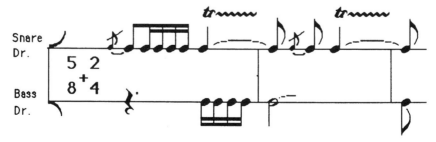

But, as is more usually the case, the above score will further stipulate tempo, dynamics, and expression, as well as the types of sticks to use (soft or hard) and where on the drum heads the sticks should hit (center, side, or rim). These added details can drastically change the sound of the instruments and enhance the overall musicality of the score:

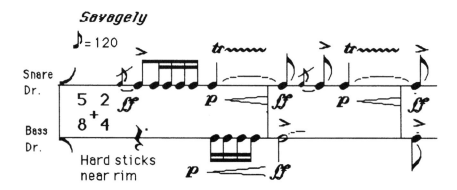

One of the most fascinating aspects of writing for percussion is the constant need to invent solutions to notational problems. Suppose the above piece also included a part for 5 different-pitched chinese temple blocks and a suspended cymbal *all played by one player*. The notation for this would have to involve 5 lines (one for each of the blocks) and a separate line for the cymbal, with an indication that these be played by the same person. There are numerous solutions to this problem, one of which is presented below:

Notice that the **number** of players have been defined, their **parts** separated, and the bar lines have been **disconnected** between players 1 and 2. The blocks and cymbal have been enclosed by a bracket on the left margin which tells player #3 to play both instruments. When scoring for multiple instruments and players, any notation which clarifies 'who plays what when' is permissible and advisable.

Creating new symbols
During the process of notating RN scores, it is sometimes useful (and fun) to invent symbols which represent sounds, instruments, etc. that do not belong to the 'standard' orchestral instruments described above. Because of this, the actual symbols used on paper can vary widely from score to score and composer to composer. Suppose you are writing a piece for stamping feet and 3 vocal sound effects. One sound is a rising "Whoosh" from low to high; one is to loudly shout "pow" as a sound effect, not as a word; and the 3rd is to shout the word "Go". Since 'whoosh' is semi-musical, pow is a sound effect, and "Go" is a word, the notation should try to visually reflect the specific differences between these sound qualities. For example, a conventional notation for the 'Whoosh' and Pow would not be as effective as one created for it because they are sounds, not words: the invented notation conveys this more effectively:

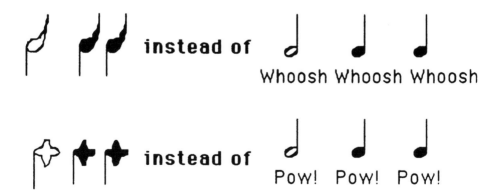

By placing a set of instructions (Key) at the start of the score, performers are informed as to the meaning of the symbols and the way in which the sounds are to be performed:

KEY

 = "Whoosh" A semi-sung whooshing sound from low to high. Adjust the rise to fill the duration of the note's value.

 = "Pow". A Batman-like sound-effect which sounds more like <u>being</u> "Powed" than saying Pow.

Go = Say "Go" as you would say "Sit" to a dog.

▲ = Stamp one foot.   ◆ = Stamp both feet.

 = Alternate stamping both feet, left to right or right to left.

Note: To read the full score to *Go PowWhoosh* see Chapter Wrap 8.15.

8.13   Repeats: large and sectional

We have already seen how repeat signs can be used outside the staff to encompass major sections of a score. When this technique is used, the measure numbers of the initial performance will appear as usual, and the numbers of the measures in the repeat performance(s) will appear in parentheses where needed as shown:

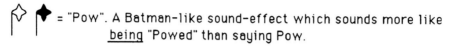

In some dances, repeats occur within repeats. To make this easy to read and understand, large slanted repeats are placed further outside the staff, bracketing the smaller repeats within them.

In this example, the 1st 2 measures are performed a total of 3 times. The next 3 measures then unfold sequentially, leading into a repeat of the entire 9-measure section, to the other side.

Repeat signs then, can take 3 basic forms:

%   Slanted inside the staff

÷   Horizontal outside the staff

✕   Slanted outside the staff
    to bracket horizontal repeats

Small differences between the original and the repeat of a sequence do not necessarily mean that repeat signs can not be used. Rather, the difference is noted within the space left for the repeated measures.

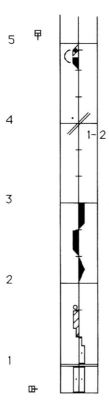

Repeat measures 1-2 to the other side, with a slight variation in how they conclude.

Table of Repeat Signs

INSIDE STAFF: these signs are centered in the amount of counts or measures to be repeated.

OUTSIDE STAFF: these signs appear in pairs, the upper one to the right of the staff; the lower to the left.

%   Repeat a measure (or part of a meas., or more than 1 meas. exactly)

//.   Repeat a measure (or part of a meas., or more than 1 meas.) to the opposite side

%₃   Repeat meas. #3

//₃   Repeat meas. #3 to the opposite side

ᴬ%   Do the same as dancer A

ᴹ//₃   Do what dancer M did in meas. #3, but to the other side.

÷   Exact repeat

≑   Repeat to the other side

$\frac{\div}{3}$ Do a total of 3 times on the same side

$\frac{≑}{3}$ Do a total of 3 times, alternating sides

⊼   Large sectional repeat, as written

⊼   Large sectional repeat, to the other side

    Repeat ad lib (as many times as desired) to the same or alternating side

 as in

Maxim #110: In repeat signs inside the staff, numbers refer to measures of the score, and tell which measure(s) of movement to repeat. Outside the staff, numbers in repeat signs indicate the total number of times to do a movement sequence.

1st and 2nd "endings"

In the same way as music notation, a dance score can direct the reader to 1st and 2nd endings within repeated sections. The different endings are bracketed, to the left of the staff, with numbers indicating their order of performance. Measure numbers help move readers through the score.

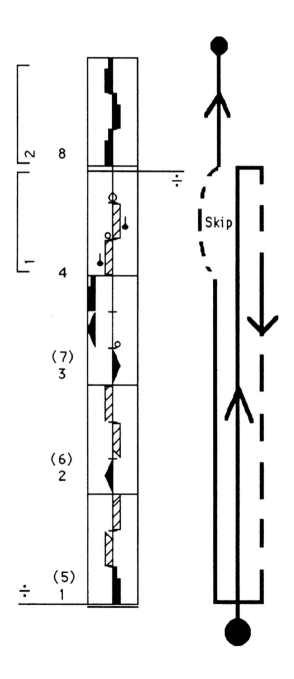

1st and 2nd "beginnings"

For choreography that repeats with altered beginnings, the same bracketing technique is used.

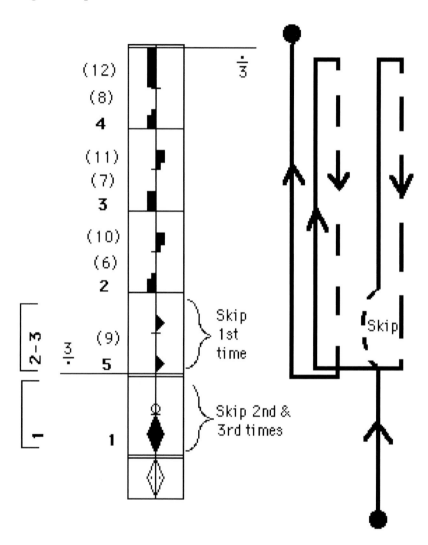

RHYTHMIC APPLICATIONS

8.14   Beyond "2 against 3"

Musicians and dancers share a unique similarity as performers, in that they are frequently called upon to be simultaneously polyrhythmic in different body parts. The hands of the pianist are seldom performing the same rhythms, which is also true for the upper and lower body of the dancer. In chapter V we had our first encounter with the polymeters called 2 *against* 3 and 3 *against* 2. Below are listed several other polymeters that can be practiced in each hand, and later moved to different body parts.

3 against 4 and 4 against 3.   Since the numbers 3 and 4 meet at 12, this pattern divides twelve pulses into 4 groups of 3 against 3 groups of 4. Metrically, this would be the equivalent of putting 12/8 against 3/2:

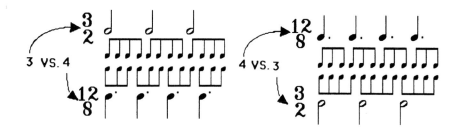

In terms of arithmetic, *3 against 4* and *4 against 3* are equal. But as a design they are different. Think about the way they are described: a "3" is placed against a "4" or a "4" is placed against a "3". These are perfect illustrations of superimposition, since each assumes a 'base' meter against which another metric pattern is set: 12/8 against 3/2 or 3/2 against 12/8.

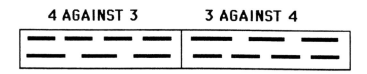

To practice *3 against 4*, try saying the following sentence in the indicated rhythm in 12/8:

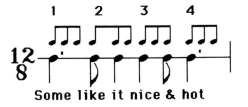

Some like it nice & hot

To clarify that we are in a "4", let's remove all syllables that don't fall on the beat:

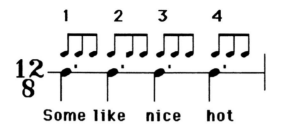

- Now try tapping the rhythm with both hands, allowing one hand to touch the '4' (Some like nice hot); the other hand, the '3' (Some it and).

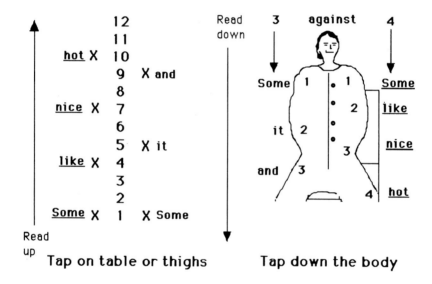

- Practice the left hand alone with the words, then the right hand.
- Practice with both hands together.

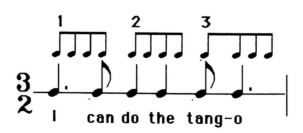

- The, practice switching hands so the right hand takes the "4" and the left, the, "3" and vice versa.
- To practice *4 against 3*, try saying the following sentence in 3/2:

By stressing the syllables that fall on the three principal beats in 3/2, we arrive at:

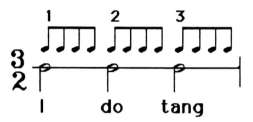

- Now try tapping this rhythm with both hands, allowing one hand to do the three principal beats of 3/2 while the other falls as shown below left.

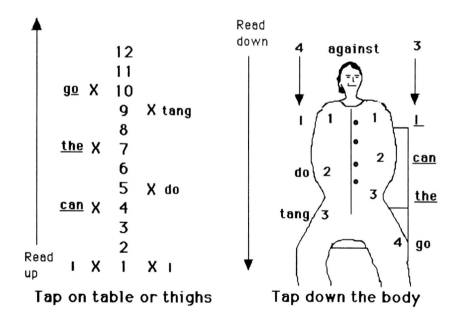

- Practice the left hand alone with the words, then the right hand.
- Practice with both hands together.
- The, practice switching hands so the right hand takes the "4" and the left, the "3" and vice versa.

2 Against 5 **and** *5 against 2.*   Since the numbers 2 and 5 meet at 10, this polyrhythm divides 10 pulses into 5 groups of 2 against 2 groups of 5. Metrically, this is the difference between 5/4 and 10/8:

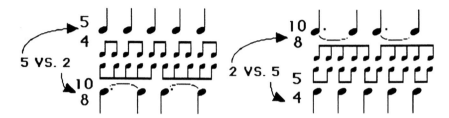

To practice both *5 against 2* and *2 against 5*, try saying the following sentence in the indicated rhythm:

I can't do the rhum-ba

To stress the syllables that fall on the five principal beats in 5/4, read the notes with stems down; for the superimposed 2, read stems up:

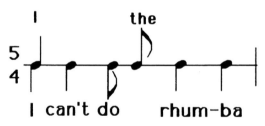

- Now try tapping this pattern with both hands, allowing one to express the natural stress of 5/4, while the other falls between the 3rd & 4th beats.
- Practice the left hand alone with the words, then the right hand.
- Practice with both hands together.
- The, practice switching hands so the right hand takes the "5" and the left, the "2" and vice versa.

```
                              10
                               9   X ba
                               8
                               7   X rhum
                   the X       6
                               5   X do
                               4
                               3   X can't
                               2
                    I  X       1    X I
```

5 against 3 and 3 against 5. Since the numbers 5 and 3 meet at 15, this polyrhythm divides 15 pulses into 5 groups of 3 against 3 groups of 5. Metrically, this can take place only in a time signature based on 15, such as 15/8.

To practice both *5 against 3* and *3 against 5*, speak the following sentence in the indicated rhythm in 15/8:

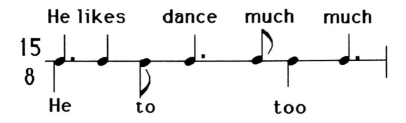

- By stressing the syllables that describe the basic 5 beats, we see:

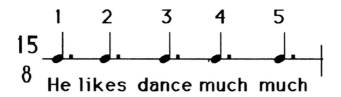

- Now try it in both hands, allowing the right to create the natural stress of 15/8, while the left falls between the beats.

- Move the left hand alone with the words, then the right hand alone.

- Try switching hands so the left hand takes the "5" and the right, the "3", and vice versa.

			15		
			14		
			13	X	much.
			12		
too	X		11		
			10	X	much
			9		
			8		
			7	X	dance
to	X		6		
			5		
			4	X	likes
			3		
			2		
He	X		1	X	He

MOVEMENT APPLICATIONS

8.15   Clusters: polymetric

Arms in 3/Walks in 2   Arms in 2/Walks in 3

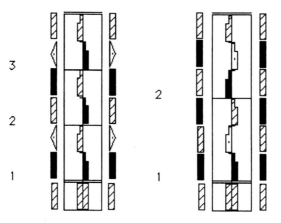

Arms in 3/Walks in 4   Arms in 4/Walks in 3

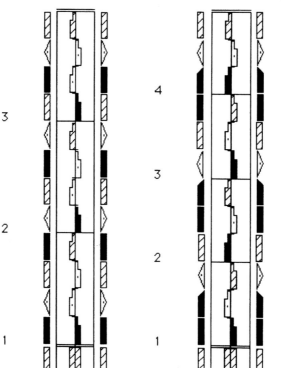

Clusters (continued)

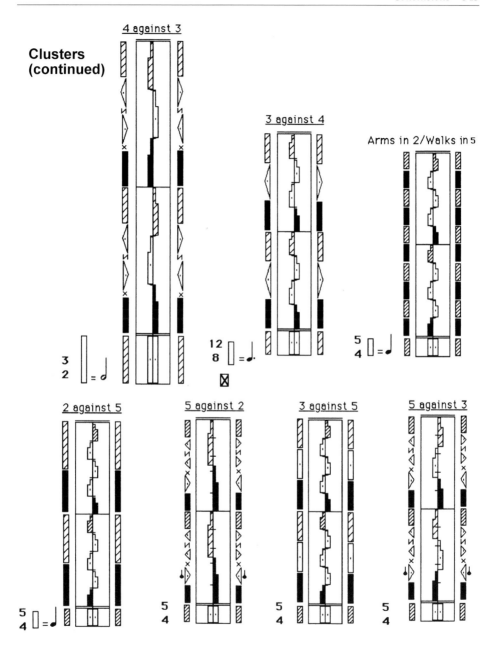

CHAPTER WRAP

8.16   RN Etudes

SUMMER IS ACUMIN IN
An 'Invention' using variable meter
and polymetric superimposition

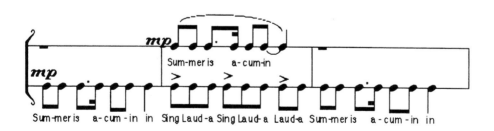

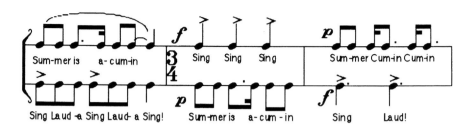

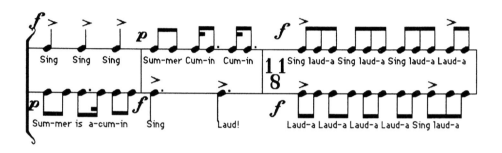

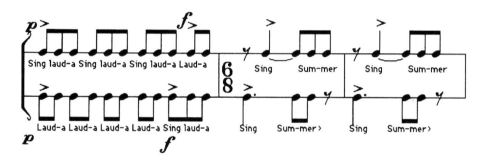

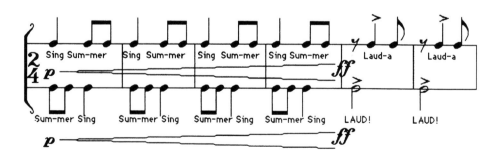

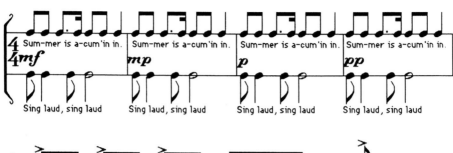

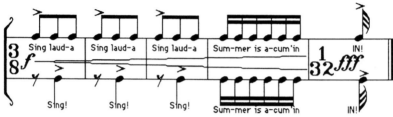

Quarduplets

Quintuplets

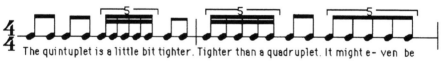

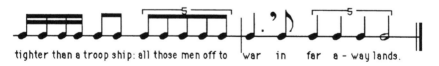

Sextuplets

The poor sex-tuplet! Every-body Thinks its just a cou-ple-a-tri- pl- ets in a row!

Septuplets

I will now sing for you a sep-tu-plet! I'm hopeful you'll really want to hear it a - gain.

#5 - Non-measured tuplet

O K! Let's do the alphabet! A B C D E F G H I J K L M N O P Q R S T U V W X Y Z

Now let's do it double-time. A B C D E F G H I J K L M N O P Q R S T U V W X Y Z

Bricks!

by Caroline Soriano

Explanation:

The campus of SUNY Purchase is constructed from brown bricks, and while Caroline was a student there, the name of the firm that supplied the food in the cafeteria was Flick. Composed in 1986, this is a perfect example of a 2-part canon at 1 measure.

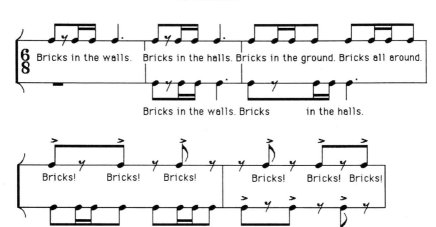

Bricks in the walls. Bricks in the halls. Bricks in the ground. Bricks all around.

Bricks in the walls. Bricks in the halls.

Bricks! Bricks! Bricks! Bricks! Bricks! Bricks!

Bricks in the ground. Bricks all around. Bricks! Bricks! Bricks!

GOPOWHOOSH

8.17   LN Etudes

Baiduska: **A Greek Folk Dance**

researched and notated by Eleni Ioannou

Cue #23

"Baiduska" is a Thracian Greek folk dance. Thrace is in the Northeastern part of Greece. "Baiduska" was originally danced in Thrace by Greek refugees from Eastern Romylia; however, it is also danced in Macedonia but with some differences in the steps and rhythm.

"Baiduska" is a lively dance with a continuous flowing movement. It is usually danced with the accompaniment of a gaida or a lyre. The former is a wind instrument mostly used in Thrace (bagpipe), while the latter is a string instrument. "Baiduska" can be danced to various musical meters: 5/8, 3/8, or 2/4, depending on the area of Greece where it is danced. However, it is mostly danced in 5/8, 7/8 and 9/8 which are meters commonly found in ancient Greek tragedies. Therefore the dance follows a poetic meter consisting of long and short beats.

Traditionally, the formation of the dance had a certain significance. The dancers formed an open-circle in a certain order. First in the circle were the old men, then the unmarried men and then the married ones. All the married women followed the married men, then the unmarried women and at the end of the circle were the old women. By having this formation in the dance, the men never had the chance to hold hands with women. Only the last married man and the first married woman held hands. However, this middle couple had to be close relatives, meaning either a husband and wife or a brother and sister.

STYLISTIC NOTES

"Baiduska" is danced in a phrase of 10 measures of 5/8, felt (2 + 3). The dance is also divided in three parts in terms of its circling. It goes counter-clockwise, clockwise, and then there are steps in "place". It also has three changes in terms of facing the focal point.

The dance starts with hop-steps that go counter-clockwise. The focal point is to the dancers' left. The arms in these steps do not turn with the body. As a result, the dancers retain a position in profile, reminiscent of ancient Greek friezes. In these hops, the dancers are not supposed to jump high.

All the transitions are smooth and nothing should interrupt the continuity of the dance. The body is held upright throughout, with a sense of pride. In the 5th measure the arms push quite forcibly to the back, and the steps have a similar accent, which has been described as "walking with a limp". However, this characterization is questionable.

The legs are neither rotated in nor out and the knees are relaxed. The dance in general is not earthy, but rather has a springing quality. As with most of the Greek folk dances, "Baiduska" uses non-swivel turns to change the dancers' relationship to the circle center.

Baiduska: A Greek folk dance
 (A simplified version)

Notated by Eleni Ioannou
(1992)

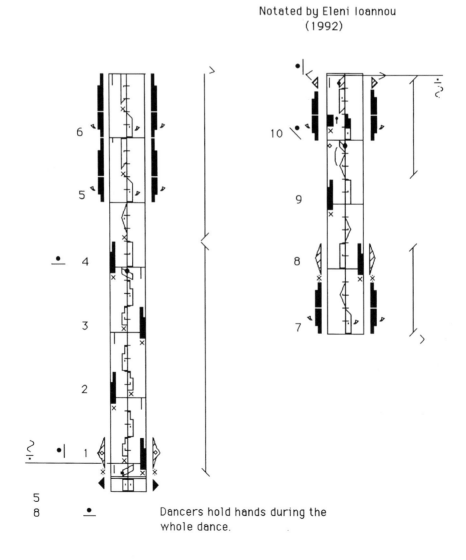

Dancers hold hands during the whole dance.

8.18 Last Tricky Rhythms

Cue # 24A

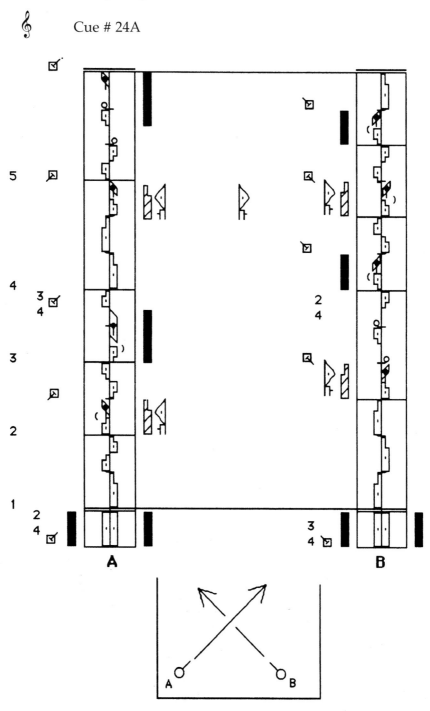

Cue # 25

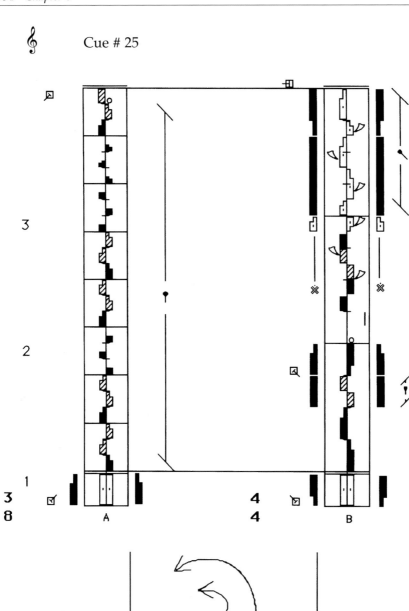

8.19 Suggested Assignments

 Compose a short score for 2 percussionists, each playing at least 2 instruments. If you have trouble finding appropriate percussion instruments, invent your own.

* Write a duet for 2–4 speaking parts, using a poem or some nonsense words. Explore the "special effects" detailed in this chapter (i.e., trills, glissandos, etc.).
* Write a 2-part polymetric piece for one voice in 7/8, the other in 4/4. Conclude when both voices reach the 56th eighth-note. Choreograph movement for these parts.
* Write a short canon with words at 1-measure, in any time signature.

 Try a false ending and then a real ending. Which do you prefer? Why?

 Develop other walking/arm polymetric patterns as those in 8.17. Try putting 6/8 against against 5/8 (meeting at 30), or putting 7/8 against 3/8, meeting at 21.

Choreograph a movement canon of moderate length, in any meter of your choice, for 4 parts. Alternate measures of movement that have contrasting uses of space, level, and time/energy. This will ensure a visually striking canon, one with good use of opposition between the parts.

APPENDIX A

Table of Maxims

The following lists all the maxims with page reference numbers for easy access.

Chapter 1

Maxim #1: Speed equals Time. Add more time between beats and you go slower. Reduce the time between beats and you go faster. This is called TEMPO. (page 1)

Maxim #2: There are only two subdivisions of a beat: duple and triple. (page 2)

Maxim #3: Beats are steady. Rhythm is flexible and comes in three categories: thru, full, and sub-beat. (page 3)

Maxim #4: The basic order of values (BOV) is based on the binary numerical progression of 1 2 4 8 16 32. (page 4)

Maxim #5: Tempo (or speed of beat) will in most cases determine the size of the note value assigned to the beat. (page 6)

Maxim #6: There are three ranges of tempo: slow, medium and fast. Within these categories lies a wide range of gradations from extremely slow to extremely fast. (page 8)

Maxim #7: The shape of direction symbols indicates the direction of movement. (page 9)

Maxim #8: Always read LN from the bottom to the top. The center line of the LN staff divides left from right. The support columns are found on either side of the center line. (page 10)

Maxim #9: The shading of a direction symbol will indicate the level of movement: low, middle, or high. (page 11)

Maxim #10: For general indications, RN symbols are placed on the staff line while LN symbols are placed alongside the staff line, in columns. Different columns "belong" to different parts of the body. (page 13)

Maxim #11: Pins indicate the relationship of the feet to each other. (page 14)

Maxim #12: Hold signs must be used to keep one or both feet on the floor. They also maintain the level of the previous support. (page 15)

Maxim #13: To determine the number of feet you are on at any given moment, read each count in the support column INDEPENDENTLY. (page 16)

Maxim #14: Taking a step involves moving the center of weight to a new place, transferring the weight into the direction specified by the symbol in the support column. Close attention should be paid to timing. (page 18)

Maxim #15: Calligraphy is the penmanship of RN. Accurate notation leads to a higher understanding of the components of rhythm. (page 20)

Maxim #16: Autography is the penmanship of LN. Accurate notation leads to a better understanding of the components of movement notation. (page 23)

Maxim #17: All rhythm is assumed to be connected, continuous, and flowing, unless the insertion of a rest (or some other instruction) is introduced. (page 25)

Maxim #18: Sub-division is a highly effective internal process in the battle against "rushing the beat." It is especially helpful when working with slow, lyrical passages. (page 27)

Maxim #19: The timing of Laban movement symbols is determined by the size (length) of the symbol itself. Musical notes NEVER change size. The timing of musical notes is determined by the color of the note head and/or the presence of a stem, flag, or beam. (page 30)

Maxim #20: Two pins are used when (1) notating starting positions, and (2) when the same position of the feet is repeated with a change of level. One pin is used to show an active foot closing into a new position. (page 32)

Maxim #21: Closed positions of the feet are those with the supports directly below the center of weight; open positions are those with the center of weight *between* the supports. (page 33)

Maxim #22: *Stepping into* open positions involves one active foot and one foot staying in place, holding or changing level. *Staying* in an open position involves keeping the feet where they were in their relation to the center of weight. (page 34)

Chapter 2

Maxim #23: Meter is the organization of numbers of beats into "measures" of time. In short, *meter measures musical time.* (page 41)

Maxim #24: The note assigned to the beat and the number of beats that are to occur in each measure will determine which time signature is in use. (page 42)

Maxim #25: Simple Time refers to any time signature where the beating note is divisible by two without a fraction. (page 43)

Maxim #26: Meter applies different plastic qualities (energies) to beats depending upon their position within a measure. These energies are referred to as Crusic, Metacrusic, and Anacrusic. (page 44)

Maxim #27: The characteristics of each time signature are based upon a specific pattern of crusic and non-crusic qualities. (page 46)

Maxim #28: When rhythm is applied to meter, it will tend to modify the basic metric characteristics (crusic, metacrusic, anacrusic), depending upon which rhythmic patterns occur on which beats. (page 51)

Maxim #29: Pickups are used when a preparation is required. They amplify the downbeat since they occupy a weaker division of a previous measure. (page 52)

Maxim #30: External pickups occur prior to the first beat of a composition, adding weight and amplification to the crucis. (page 55)

Maxim #31: Movement that begins on the first count of a measure is always called "1". Movement occurring in a preparation space is called "&, & a, e & a", etc. (page 55)

Maxim #32: The pre-signs X and backward N can be used to modify the sizes of steps and open positions of the feet. (page 57)

Maxim #33: Double X and double backwards N can be used in the support columns to indicate a more extreme change of scale for steps and open positions. (page 57)

Maxim #34: The presence of a caret in the ancillary column means a shift of weight from 2 feet to 1 WITHOUT taking a step. (page 59)

Maxim #35: When reading steps within which there are changes of level, emphasize fluidity in the transition between levels and keep the center of weight moving in the direction indicated. These steps will produce *undercurves* and *overcurves*. (page 61)

Maxim #36: Beams serve many purposes in RN, two of which are: (1) the reduction of time it takes to write out individual flags; and (2) the visual grouping of complex rhythms. (page 62)

Maxim #37: Alignment is the notational process that graphically permits the writing of more than one part at a time. (page 66)

Maxim #38: Regardless of the repeat sign and its instructions, all repeat signs in RN and LN refer back *to the last written notation* and NEVER to a previous repeat sign. (page 69)

Maxim #39: Repeat signs inside the staff are always centered in the amount of material (beats or measures) to be repeated. (page 70)

Chapter 3

Maxim #40: Dots are added to notes and rests to create ternary values (divisible by 3 without a fraction). A dot indicates the addition of the next smaller value in the BOV to the dotted symbol. (page 85)

Maxim #41: Phrases gather together into larger thoughts the individual elements of rhythm, beat and meter. Cadences help phrases "breathe" by introducing pauses (mid-cadences) or conclusions (closing cadences). (page 87)

Maxim #42: Internal pickups can occur as echoes of an external pickup. They help to shape phrasing and create a rhythmic 'familiarity'. (page 89)

Maxim #43: Articulation and accent alter the way in which a sound is attacked, and how long and with how much energy it is sustained. (page 93)

Maxim #44: Accents heighten the attributes of specific actions, stressing them and rendering them of special importance in a movement sequence. Strong accents are shaded. (page 94)

Maxim #45: A gesture is an action that does not bear weight. (page 95)

Maxim #46: The direction and level of leg gestures are determined by the relationship of the foot to the hip. The terms "free end" and "extremity" apply to the foot; "fixed end" and "point of attachment" apply to the hip. (page 95)

Maxim #47: Hold signs are not necessary for leg gestures because they do not take weight. (page 97)

Maxim #48: Steps and leg gestures can not happen at the same time. Leg gestures can begin halfway through a step. (page 98)

Maxim #49: Arm gestures are written outside the staff, with one column left blank between the staff and arm gestures. (page 99)

Maxim #50: Judge the direction and level of arm gestures by comparing the free end (hand) to the fixed end (shoulder). (page 100)

Maxim #51: Movements for the arms are smooth and continuous (legato) when there is no separation (i.e., time) between direction symbols. (page 102)

Maxim #52: Hold signs are not needed in the arm columns. *No new symbols* mean *no new movement*. (page 102)

Maxim #53: Movements for the arms are separate and distinct (staccato) when there is empty space (i.e., time) between direction symbols. (page 102)

Maxim #54: Relationship pins can add detail as to how the arms relate to each other or to the body. (page 104)

Maxim #55: In RN, ties combine any two notes into one new longer duration. Similar to dots, ties *connect* two note values while dots *enlarge* a single note. (page 106)

Maxim #56: Bows are linking tools that connect notes or actions in time or intent. (page 107)

Maxim #57: Always write rhythm in one notational symbol whenever possible. If this is not possible, use the fewest number of symbols. Dotted notes are always preferable to ties under this rule. (page 117)

within measures of Irregular meter. Depending on tempo, each subgroup is usually felt as one beat. (page 184)

Maxim #73: All Irregular Time signatures can be felt generically, or can be subgrouped in a variety of configurations. (page 186)

Maxim #74: Triplets may be thought of as curves within a straight landscape and duplets as straight lines within a curved landscape. (page 188)

Maxim #75: "2 against 3" and "3 against 2" are terms for the simultaneous juxtaposition of duple and triple metric patterns WITHIN THE SAME MEASURE. (page 190)

Maxim #76: The shape of a turn sign indicates which way to turn, and its placement on the staff indicates whether a turn is on 1 or 2 feet. (page 191)

Maxim #77: The *length* of the turn sign indicates timing, and pins within turn signs indicate the *degree* of turn. (page 192)

Maxim #78: No level in a turn sign means to stay in the level of the previous step or preparation. Partial shading within a turn sign indicates a change of level DURING the turn. (page 193)

Maxim #79: Front signs after every turn give the dancer's new stage facing direction. (page 194)

Maxim #80: Ties are used to blend steps and turns. *Where* the tie starts and ends tells how far transference of weight extends *through the turn.* (page 196)

Maxim #81: Turns in the air are notated with a turn sign over both support columns, plus a release from the floor indicated with air lines or leg gestures. (page 196)

Maxim #82: Turns that begin in the air and continue on the floor use ties to connect the landing with the continuation of the turn. The landing and 2nd turn sign are joined. (page 197)

Maxim #83: Space holds keep a part of the body in the previously stated spatial direction while the rest of the body turns. (page 199)

Maxim #84: Transitional turns are unemphasized actions that change a dancer's facing in preparation for a more major action. These often take the form of non-swivel turns that use space holds on the standing leg to prevent the foot swiveling. (page 200)

Maxim #85: Turn signs in the leg gesture columns describe parallel, turned-out, or turned-in rotations of the legs. (page 203)

Maxim #86: White or "open" pins are used to specify the degree of turn-out or turn-in for the legs. Leg rotations that appear in starting positions last until cancelled, as do all turn signs in the leg gesture columns. (page 204)

Chapter 6

Maxim #87: Syncopation is a violent distortion of a normal accentual (metric) pattern. Any rhythm that heavily accents those divisions of a measure (or beat) which are metrically weaker is syncopated. (page 221)

Maxim #88: Syncopated rhythms which do not show accent marks may not be performed with enough force to make the syncopation effective. Remember – **accent your syncopations, ON paper as well as IN performance.** (page 229)

Maxim #89: Dynamics are notational markings within a score that indicate to the performer the relative "volume" and intensity of sound to be produced at a given moment or beat in time. (page 232)

Maxim #90: The crescendo (increase) & dimenuendo (decrease) symbols can be used in combination with a variety of other symbols to change the dynamics of a movement or phrase. (page 235)

Maxim #91: Numbers under floorplans correspond to measures and/or counts within the LN score. (page 239)

Maxim #92: Pins, often in combination with letters, identify dancers on floorplans and show facings on stage. Lines and arrows show the path and extent of travel; wedges, the final facing. (page 241)

Maxim #93: Floorplans must follow one another with clarity and exactness as to dancers' placements on stage. Modifications to lines and arrows describe travel for more than one person. (page 241)

Chapter 7

Maxim #94: Metric Registration is a process in which the common denominator between time signatures of differing beat assignments is displayed above the bar line between the change. (page 264)

Maxim #95: Variable Meter refers to the changing of time signature at places where the natural crusic weight of the downbeat is desired. Any time signature may be placed adjacent to any other. (page 264)

Maxim #96: Alternating Meter refers to two (or more) time signatures that switch back and forth in a pre-arranged alternating pattern. (page 266)

Maxim #97: Monometer (single-beat measures) refers to the dividing of a steady pulse-base into measures, *each of which acts as if it contains only one beat, regardless of the number of pulses in the measure.* (page 268)

Maxim #98: Additive measures refer to standard time signatures that are divided in unorthodox ways. (page 268)

Maxim #99: Straight path signs appear outside the staff, to the right.

They describe linear travel by incorporating direction symbols or stage area signs. (page 271)

Maxim #100: Circular paths describe curving travel. The direction of *travel* is given in the support columns. The direction and amount of circling is shown by the path sign. (page 275)

Maxim #101: Focal point orientation replaces Front Signs in circle dances. (page 276)

Maxim #102: Focal points can replace pins in turn signs. When they do, the new orientation to the focal point will also appear outside the staff in place of Front Signs, to reinforce the end result of the turn. (page 278)

Chapter 8

Maxim #103: Superimposition refers to the over-laying of one metric pattern on another within the *same* time signature. (page 308)

Maxim #104: Mixed Polymeter refers to the simultaneous mixing together of *different* metric patterns in *different* time signatures. (page 308)

Maxim #105: Mixed polymeter refers to the simultaneous occurrence of different time signatures, in different parts, which may independently change meter at any time. (page 310)

Maxim #106: Canons (Rounds) employ a technique called **Imitative Counterpoint**: interwoven linear lines that reinforce each other through the *re-use* of material from part to part. (page 316)

Maxim #107: Palm facings and thumb-side symbols are examples of "body pre-signs." Body pre-signs are always followed by a direction symbol or other movement indication, and are included in the timing of an action. (page 321)

Maxim #108: LN can specify 6 degrees of contraction in the arm or leg. The relationship of the hand to the shoulder, or of the foot to the hip, does not change in direction or level as the limb contracts. (page 324)

Maxim #109: In LN, vertical bows link things in time. Horizontal bows link things in space. (page 325)

Maxim #110: In repeat signs inside the staff, numbers refer to measures of the score, and tell which measure(s) of movement to repeat. Outside the staff, numbers in repeat signs indicate the total number of times to do a movement sequence. (page 334)

APPENDIX B

Music Cues

*Unless otherwise indicated, all music by Joseph Reiser

The first six cues correspond to Chapter 1, pg. 3

Cue #1: Thru-beat 1. J. S. Bach: *Air on a G String (Reduced).*
This melody's phrasing alternates a two measure thru-beat followed by 2 measures of sub-beats. Notice how the melody stretches, floats, 'lingers' over the top of the beats in the "walking bass line".

Cue #2: Thru-beat 2. Chopin: *Prelude in E minor (Reduced).*
Here, although written 200 years after Cue #1, the same technique is used. The melody is composed almost entirely of thru-beats, which again adds to the music's quality of longing and sadness.

Cue #3: Full-beat 1*. The melody and harmony in this piece 'march' together in the same full-beat rhythms (except for the tuba).

Cue #4: Full-beat 2*. Similar to cue #3, all notes (melody and harmony) move together in the same, slow, full-beat rhythms.

Cue #5: Sub-beat 1. Carl Czerny: *The Art of Finger Dexterity (Reduced).*
Here, the sub-beat melody in the (lower) left hand moves four-times as fast as the beat in the (higher) right hand. Half way through, the hands switch.

Cue #6: Sub-beat 2*. In this rendition of *Yankee Doodle*, the trumpets sometimes move four-times as fast as the drummer, who maintains the full-beats.

Cue #7: Phrase-shifting*. Chapter 2, pg. 74
The accompaniments for these three metric variations (in 2/4, 3/4, and 4/4), are each performed 4 times in succession. Each repeat of the music equals 2 repeats of the movement notation. Each musical repeat is preceded by a 2-measure introduction in the appropriate meter.

Cue #8: Phrase-shifting*. Chapter 2, pg. 79
The accompaniments for these three metric variations (in 2/4, 3/4, and 4/4), are each performed 2 times in succession. Each repeat of the music equals 2 repeats of the movement notation. Each musical repeat is preceded by a 2-measure

introduction in the appropriate meter.

Cue #9: Staccato, legato, and tenuto. J. S. Bach: *Bourree No. 1 (Reduced)*. Chapter 3, pg. 90
Bach's Bourree is performed three times in succession, each time with a different 'touch'. When listening, pretend to play along with your fingers, experimenting with the beat qualities: *flick* for staccato, *glide* for legato, and *dab* or *press* for tenuto.

Cue #10 A: Arm and leg gestures*. Chapter 3.22.1
The accompaniment for this etude in 4/4 is preceded by a 2-bar introduction. The music encompasses 4 complete repeats of the movement notation.

Cue #10 B: Arm and leg gestures*. Chapter 3.22.1
The accompaniment for this etude in 3/4 is preceded by a 2-bar introduction. The music encompasses 2 complete repeats of the movement notation.

Cue #11: Phrase-shifting*. Chapter 3.22.2
The accompaniments for these three metric variations (in 2/4, 3/4, and 4/4), are each performed 2 times in succession. Each repeat of the music equals 1 repeat of the movement notation. Each musical repeat is preceded by a 2-measure introduction in the appropriate meter.

Cue #12: Accents*. Chapter 3.22.3
The accompaniment for the accent etude in 3/4 is preceded by a 2-bar

introduction. The four repeats of the music encompass 4 repeats of the movement notation.

Cue #13: Phrasing assignment. J. S. Bach: *Passacaglia in C Minor*. Chapter 3, pg. 129
The first three phrases of the passacaglia are played here as an accompaniment for the Doris Humphrey-based excerpt.

Cue #14: Polka*. Chapter 4.26.1
Accompaniment is provided for this etude, played 4 times in succession. The music encompasses 4 complete repeats of the movement notation.

Cue #15A: Circle dance – Slow tempo*. Chapter 4.26.3
A slow rehearsal tempo is performed in this cue. The music is played just one time for one complete performance of the dance.

Cue #15B: Circle dance – Fast tempo*. Chapter 4.26.3
This faster version is played twice, for two complete performances of the dance.

Cue #16: Taiwanese Tribal Dance*. Chapter 4.28
Accompaniment for this Taiwanese dance is provided here, played one time for one complete performance of the dance.

Cue #17: Selyanchitsa. Anonymous. Chapter 4.28
The music for this dance is performed three times, each repeat taken faster and faster. Each repeat

of the music equals one complete performance of the dance.

Cue #18: Polonaise. Jess Meeker. Chapter 5.25
Accompaniment for this Ted Shawn dance is provided here, played one time with a one-measure introduction.

Cue #19: 7.15 Triplets with leg circles*.
After a 2-measure introduction, accompaniment for this etude encompasses 8 complete repeats of the movement notation.

Cue #20: 7.15 Gallop, skip, leap*.
After a one-measure introduction, the accompaniment for this etude is repeated 4 times for 8 complete repetitions of the movement notation. Each musical repeat is again preceded by a one-bar intro.

Cue #21: 7.17 Alta Regina. Anonymous.
Accompaniment for this renaissance dance is provided here, played six times. There is no introduction.

Cue #22: 7.19 Alta Regina assignment. Anonymous.
Accompaniment for the variations on the renaissance dance is provided here, played six times. There is no introduction. Watch out for tempo changes, meter changes, and syncopation.

Cue #23 A: 8.16 Baiduska – Slow*.
After a 2-bar introduction, accompaniment for this Thracian Greek folk dance is provided here, played four times for 8 complete repetitions of the movement notation.

Cue #23 B: 8.16 Baiduska – Fast*.
The same musical accompaniment in a faster tempo.

Cue #24: 8.17 Last Tricky Rhythms*.
Accompaniment for this duet in mixed variable meter is played as follows:
• Four beats for preparation;
• Part A twice (2/4 then 3/4) for 2 complete repetitions of the A notation;
• With no introduction, part B twice (3/4 then 2/4) for 2 complete repetitions of the B notation;
• A & B together twice with no introduction.

Cue #25: 8.17 Last Tricky Rhythms*.
Accompaniment for this duet in mixed meter is played as follows:
• Three beats for preparation;
• Part A twice (3/8) for 2 complete repetitions of the A notation;
• With no introduction, part B twice (4/4) for 2 complete repetitions of the B notation;
• A & B together twice with no introduction.

INDEX